WHACKED!

Death by Coincidence

By Ed Kugler

Cover Design

The cover for this book and all my books is done by Steve Alexander at Swassworks. He is incredible, creative and talented. For *Death Rattle of the Republic* his son Preston Alexander, a recent college graduate in graphic arts contributed as well. They're not cheap but worth it. If you would like to contact them just email me and I will connect you.

Table of Contents

WHACKED!

According to the Oxford English Dictionary ...

In England the term Whacked means you're tired, bushed or exhausted.

In middle America the term Whacked means to hit someone, probably over the head.

In urban America the term means to kill someone, probably for hire.

This book is all about number 3.

Introduction

In my last book, *Death Rattle of the Republic - 100 Years of Diabolical Deceit and Unthinkable Acts*, I outlined the long, difficult road that has led to America's destruction. It's depressing but true. In *Whacked! - Death By Coincidence*, we'll take a scary trip along the road of coincidence where so many have perished on the battlefield of chance, guilty of nothing but trying to do right.

A coincidence is when two or more events happen simultaneously or unexpectedly. Coincidences might be surprising, remarkable, spooky, or, as you'll see, at times, deadly. The CIA has this to say to their operatives headed to Moscow. They were taught, "Twice is a coincidence, but three times is enemy action." A high percentage of the folks you're about to meet are indeed victims of coincidence. In fact ... they were Whacked.

Here is a quick example to whet your appetite for our journey of coincidence. *In Hit List: An In-Depth Investigation into the Mysterious Deaths of Witnesses to the JFK Assassination*, Author Richard Belzer notes,

"One needn't wonder whether thirty deaths reach the threshold of "too coincidental" mathematically or whether three hundred unnatural deaths do so. One simply needs to verify the correct math. Over seventy unnatural deaths out of approximately 1,400 witnesses occurred during a fourteen-year period. Note that the correct odds of that occurring are 1-in-715 million trillion trillion."

Death by coincidence is not new. It began when Cain slew Able, and it's been a tool of the adversary ever since. Whether they call themselves the Left, Socialists, or Communists, in the end, they're tools of Satan. Historically, we know them as Mao, Lenin, Stalin, Castro, Pol Pot, Chavez, and many lesser-known madmen. Even less known are the killers by coincidence.

As a nation, we've gone from George Washington's words, *"If the freedom of speech is taken away, then dumb and silent we may be led, like sheep to the slaughter,"* to the words of the infamous Ugandan Dictator Idi Amin, who said, *"There is freedom of speech, but I cannot guarantee freedom after speech."*

In *Whacked!* You'll see firsthand the many coincidences tied to icons of American life. They often relate to epic events in our history. Are those icons responsible for the trail of death that followed their rise to power? They say not, but you decide as you read the stories chronicled in the following pages.

As you read on, give yourself permission to consider that our politicians and their minions are, in fact, as evil as they appear. For many, that is hard to believe.

"Expedience is the first law of nature.

The wolf knows nothing about morality.

It tears out the throats of sheep and then eats them.

That does not make it evil.

Animals can always be trusted to do what's expedient.

With man, you have to assume the worst."

Craig Dilouie

The Early Years

Getting *Whacked* has proven to be an effective way to silence your critics. In communist nations, it's done openly; in free countries, a coincidence or two will do.

One's coincidence of getting Hacked is often triggered by the person with the guts and integrity to do what's right. Doing what's right and speaking out against wrongs is usually known as "whistleblowing". At our country's beginning, we find the origin of current-day 'Whistleblower Laws'.

It began with Third Lieutenant Richard Marven and Midshipman Shaw. During the Revolutionary War, these two naval officers 'blew the whistle' on the British for torturing POWs by the Continental Navy. Their actions and subsequent trials resulted in the Continental Congress enacting the 'Whistleblower Protection Law.' It was made law on July 30, 1778, unanimously.

In more modern times, in the early 1800s, William Morgan was born in Virginia in the 1770s. He married in 1819, and they moved to Canada. They had two children, and Morgan started a brewery. After some success, a fire destroyed the brewery, and he and his family returned to the United States.

The family took up residence in Batavia, New York, where Morgan started a newspaper business. While in Canada, Morgan became involved with the Freemason Society. He attempted to associate with the local Freemason society in New York but was rejected. He redoubled his efforts, visiting several lodges of Freemasons, all to no avail. Purely by coincidence, I'm sure, things went from bad to worse.

Angered by the rejection, William Morgan announced his intention to publish a book exposing the Freemasons' secrets. He called the book Illustrations of Freemasonry. Morgan soon discovered that the secret society wished to remain hidden.

First, his newspaper was hit in an arson attack. In September 1826, Morgan was arrested on theft charges everyone knew to be fabricated. He was thrown in jail, never to be seen again.

The most reliable rumors at the time said Morgan was kidnapped by local Masons, placed in a boat and taken to the middle of the Niagara River, drowned, and left to float away. The public outcry that followed inspired the formation of the Anti-Masonic Party in opposition to President Andrew Jackson's Democrats.

President Andrew Jackson was only one of two Presidents to achieve the highest Masonic rank and become Grand Master of their State. The other was President Harry Truman.

In 1864, Army Captain Silas Soule commanded Company D, 1st Colorado Cavalry, which was present at Sand Creek on November 29, 1864. He courageously refused an order to join the massacre that slaughtered Indian women, children, and older men.

Captain Soule quickly reported the facts of the massacre to another officer, who alerted the federal government. A Congressional inquiry followed with Soule testifying against the massacre's commanding officer, John Chivington.

In a stunning coincidence, Captain Soule was soon murdered. He was 26, and his murder was viewed as possibly in retaliation. Dying at 26, Soule is remembered for his moral courage regardless of risk.

Speaking of Presidents, on April 14, 1865, President Abraham Lincoln met his fate when he was shot and killed by John Wilkes Booth. Nothing to see here; the case is closed. In fact, Booth came from one of the most distinguished acting families in the country and was known by many. He was often described in such a way you'd think he was the Brad Pitt of his day. Even then, the media immediately labeled him a 'crazed sympathizer of the South.'

Heading to Ford Theater that fateful night, President Lincoln was set to attend with General Ulysses S. Grant, his victorious Commander, and his wife. A Washington Times article promoting the event even listed the good General first before the President.

In a strange twist of coincidence, General Grant canceled the afternoon of the play. Undaunted, Lincoln asked Speaker of the House Schuyler Colfax and his wife to attend. He declined. He then asked Secretary of War Edwin Stanton if his chief aide, Major Thomas T. Eckert, might participate with him as an escort. Secretary Stanton declined. Lincoln then asked Major Eckert directly, and he refused when declining the President of the United States was a severe breach of protocol.

If all that isn't a clue, Metropolitan Police Officer John F. Parker was the sole officer assigned to protect the President that fateful night. Parker was not a top-notch officer, having been before the performance board multiple times and often found sleeping on the job. When the President was shot, Parker was nowhere to be seen. The guard's absence and activities were never mentioned publicly or investigated.

Parker was later fired from the police force. Mrs. Lincoln reportedly told him she would always hold him accountable for the murder of her husband. Perhaps fittingly, Parker was buried in an obscure cemetery with no markings or known images of him surviving.

In yet another coincidence, Simon O. Hanscom, editor of the Washington National Republican, publicly stated that he had gone to Ford's Theatre on the night of the assassination to deliver a message to the President at the White House's request. He also stated that no one was in or around the President except his wife and their two guests when he delivered the message. Hanscom was never officially questioned about his night visit by the Congressional inquiry or his fellow journalists.

After shooting Lincoln, Booth made his way to Maryland to a friend's farm, where on April 26, a mere 12 days after the assassination, a soldier shot and killed John Wilkes Booth. Booth left a diary that was hidden from the public for two years. One line in it alluded to him returning to Washington and clearing his name. There was an official inquiry in DC, and like the JFK assassination decades later, nothing came of it.

The early years also saw the assassination of President Garfield by a man the media branded a 'religious fanatic.' You'll learn that 'labeling' is a common practice.

In the late 1800's Europe had a wave of assassinations. Anarchists murdered M. F. Sadi Carnot, President of France; Elizabeth, Empress of Austria; and Humbert I, King of Italy. Ushering in the 1900s was the death of President McKinley on September 19, 1901. While attending the Pan-American Exposition at Buffalo, New York, on September 6, 1901, President William McKinley was shot. He died 8 days later.

The assassin, Leon F. Czolgosz, was a factory worker dubbed by the press' an anarchist'. In a twist of irony, 5 days before the assassination, a known anarchist group published a warning about Czolgosz being a threat to the President. Czolgosz maintained he had acted alone; many believed otherwise.

As you read on, eerie coincidences follow very prominent people.

The Masters

As mentioned earlier, in my last book, *Death Rattle of the Republic—100 Years of Diabolical Deceit and Unthinkable Acts,* I detailed the long road of communism that brought America to its deathbed. Year after year, the diabolical tumor of communism grew larger, permeating more and more of American society and embedding itself into our politics, leading to our destruction.

And if there is one trait that stands out amongst communists, it is silencing their enemies. Sometimes, they whack individuals, some quietly, others publicly with no shame. Other times, they eliminate the dead wood en masse; some are sent to the gulags while others are lined up and shot.

In 1913, Ismail Enver Pasha became the Minister of War for the Ottoman Empire. Ismail became part of what was to be a triumvirate leadership following the coup d'etat. Three were to rule, but Ismail ruled without the other two. He alone orchestrated the Armenian Genocide, the complete destruction of Greek nationals.

As a result, 1.2 million Armenians, 500,000 Assyrians, 480,000 Anatolian Greeks, and 350,000 Greek Pontians died at the direction of one man. In fact, overseeing the murder of 2.5 million people was the first time the word 'genocide' was born.

Between 1917 and 1924, Vladimir Lenin ruled Russia. He took over following the Bolshevik Revolution. Under his leadership,

1,000,000 political and religious leaders were murdered. He had 500,000 Cossacks, 50,000 white prisoners of war, and 240,000 striking workers executed. All because they got in the way of the ruler.

In the mid-1930s, one of the most infamous killers emerged, Adolph Hitler. While not a communist, his Fascist actions were similar and rendered the same result. Instead of political enemies, Hitler preferred a racial, anti-Semitic, and imperialist ideologies rather than totalitarian communists. Hitler oversaw the killing of 25,000,000 people, the majority systematically executed.

Herbert von Bose was the Press Chief of Adolf Hitler's conservative Vice-Chancellor, Franz von Papen. Von Bose used his position inside the government apparatus to pass on information about secret atrocities and wrongdoings committed by the Nazi Government. He passed the information to the foreign press.

Claud Cockburn, editor of the London-based muckraking journal *The Week*, ran with it. Von Bose's goal was to make the world aware of the atrocities. On June 30, 1934, he was murdered by a squad of SS men dispatched to his office by Heinrich Himmler, who shot him in the back of the head.

Upon the death of Vladimir Lenin in 1924, Joseph Stalin became the leader of Russia until he died in 1953. During that time, Stalin's iron fist accounted for, by best historians' estimates, 20,000,000 deaths of his fellow citizens. He instituted the infamous Gulags and used forced famines and outright executions to keep his people in line.

1948 was a big year for communist murderers. Kim Il Sung ruled North Korea's communist regime from 1948 to 1994. North Korea remains the world's most secretive government that is now governed by his son, Kim Jong Un. Under Kim Il Sung, 1,600,000 of his countrymen were murdered. Under Sonny Boy, the death toll continues to climb as dissent of any kind is not tolerated.

Also, in 1948, another tyrant took charge of a communist regime, Mao Zedong. Mao was and hopefully will remain the winner of the communist killing contest. Mao reigned until he died in 1976.

During his leadership, over 70,000,000 of his fellow citizens were murdered. That is the size of Great Britain today.

As we moved into the 50s, 60s, and beyond, the world became more civilized, and death counts decreased. In 1979, Ethiopia's President Mengistu Haile Mariam was responsible for 1.5 million deaths from his involvement in a campaign known as the Ethiopian Red Terror. Then there was Ho Chi Mihn from my war. While Hanoi Jane loved him, the 3,800,000 Vietnamese who lost their lives from political violence during his reign probably not so much.

Then came Pol Pot, Cambodia's communist ruler, who arbitrarily directed the killing of over 1.7 million Cambodians between 1975 and 1979. In his words, he 'cleansed' 20% of the country's population, resulting in 20,000 mass graves in what became known as the Killing Fields.

The likes of Castro, Idi Amin, and Chavez are minor players in mass murder compared to the evil doers outlined above. While from different cultures, places, and ethnicities, these leaders had one thing in common ... communism. As was detailed in Death Rattle of the Republic, Communism is Satan's operations on Earth. It is evil personified.

World War II brought communism to America courtesy of President Franklin Delano Roosevelt. As documented in *Death Rattle of the Republic,* his administration was filled from top to bottom with traitors and malcontents, all communists, who did not have our nation's best interests at heart. FDR referred to Joseph Stalin as 'Uncle Joe.'

From the end of the war to the present day, the communist ideology has been metastasizing throughout the fabric of America until we've been surrounded with evil as we're being swept into our totalitarian one-world government future. And with it came the age-old communist tactic of silencing your enemies one way or the other. Welcome to our future.

Coincidence Goes Prime Time

Whacked! is a compilation of people who spoke up or knew something and, unbeknownst to them, met the ultimate fate of death under questionable circumstances we think of as 'coincidence.' It's a sad and telling tale of tears and heartache for the families of the Whacked! And a hard dose of reality for the rest of us. Evil does exist in this world and in the United States.

Interspersed throughout our journey are short stories for context and history to provide a proper perspective on what happened during our victim's coincidence. Did all these people die by dark coincidence? Well, let's read on, and you decide.

We'll begin with ...

A LITTLE CONTEXT ...

World War II brought to the world the covert use of exploding cigars, poison needle umbrellas, radioactive coffee, and spy cats for the Kremlin. These weapons of war, to be used on individuals, were the work of the KGB and the OSS, the forerunner of today's CIA. These gruesome methods of death, the early version of biochemical warfare, were used by both sides.

Emerging with the introduction of the Cold War, the Russians operated a Special Bureau of the KGB that had a lab to develop undetectable means of exterminating human beings. One such early method used by Soviet agents was an atomizer containing a bio-poison. It left no wound or evidence of the cause of death. And it didn't stop there.

Other 'natural killers' were created that could induce heart attack, cerebral apoplexy, and other medical disorders, leaving little or no trace. These were and are developed by both the KGB and the CIA. Yet, are they the most effective way to remove one's opponent? A study now available from the CIA found that the most effective technique is a contrived accident because, if done properly, it causes little excitement and is only casually investigated.

Studies found that an easy and rare method is the use of drugs. They are practical, especially if the subject is under medical care and the assassin is trained as a doctor or nurse. One source noted that an overdose of morphine delivered as a sedative will cause death silently and is challenging to detect." One agent told the publication Spotlight in 1945 that certain forms of refined cyanide would cause or appear to cause embolism.

It is essential to see things in the proper context because, as Americans living the good life, it is nearly impossible for the average citizen to comprehend this level of evil. In my research for Death Rattle of the Republic, I studied several books written by Russian dissidents. Independent of one another, every author described the same problem with Americans: Americans cannot accept the degree of evil in the world. That evil has come home in a wave of destruction we are witnessing.

As you read on, keep this in mind. In an era of whiz-bang technology and artificial intelligence, can you even imagine the ways these evil folks have designed to take care of us? We face a dark and dangerous future for ourselves, our children, and our grandchildren.

The Forties

What Did Your Government Do?

It was a significant decade for the world and our government. World War II, the most crucial armed conflict in history, ravaged Europe and destroyed Japan and gave us memories of the Holocaust, D-Day, Pearl Harbor, Hiroshima, and Nagasaki.

World War II, the war to end all wars, was fought to free us from those dreaded Nazis and the maniacal Japs, or so we were told. The end of the war birthed the United Nations, a feel-good organization meant to prevent future wars, but today is our model of a world government in waiting.

The end of the war also brought the Nuremberg Trials, where Nazi war criminals were tried for their evil deeds. Well, as you'll read below, many Nazis were tried while the chosen ones were spared by American politicians.

The Forties also saw the birth of the State of Israel, the division of the British Empire and the Chinese Civil War that brought Mao Tse Tung to power when the US withdrew support for Nationalist Chinese freedom leader Chaing Kai Czech.

But have you ever heard of Operation Paperclip? It was a secret US intelligence program run by the Office of Strategic Services (OSS) that quietly brought over 1,600 scientists, engineers, and technicians to the United States after World War II, all Nazi's.

That would be those dreaded Nazis. And yes, the majority of them were 'former Nazis'.

While the Germans were those nasty and dreaded people heading into the war, they weren't all that bad. They couldn't lend a helping hand and apparently be forgiven for their hand in murdering 6,000 Jewish people.

Our leaders quickly established the JIOA (Don't you love acronyms?) or Joint Intelligence Objectives Agency to target the exact scientists we wanted to come and work for us. This may be where the term 'all's fair in love and war came from.'

Most of the recruits were known members of the SS; that fact was casually dismissed with the help of the media. The media further helped the government cover up the entirety of Operation Paperclip for many years. One notable recruit was Wernher von Braun, a real-life rocket scientist and a member of both the Nazi Party and the SS.

The Forties were when the major communist seeds were planted in our government, and we began acting like it.

1945

December 20, 1945

Russian Allied Defectors: In the words of one American POW who escaped a trip to a Russian Gulag, "I was prepared to fight, to be wounded, to be captured, even to die, but I was not prepared to be abandoned."

That bitter US soldier was the victim of a momentous decision made by the head of our Joint Chiefs of Staff, Dwight D. Eisenhower, when he announced on December 20, 1945, the forcible repatriation of the remaining two to five million anti-Communists in Allied hands. They were sent back to their Soviet enslavers.

These were Russian soldiers and citizens who had given themselves up to either the Germans or the Allies during the fighting. They thought that when the war ended, they would stay with the Allies. But thanks to a written deal demanded by Stalin at Yalta, all those turncoats, in Stalin's mind, would be sent back. It is worth noting that our representative at Yalta for FDR was Alger Hiss, who would be found to be a communist spy.

While that deal was atrocious, that's not the worst. The Russians didn't want to return and had to be rounded up by American soldiers at bayonet point and herded into freight cars in what became known as Operation Keelhaul. Everyone knew, including the downtrodden refugees, that they would be killed or serve out their lives in the dreaded Russian Gulags, where most would die anyway.

And while that is hideous, it's still not the whole truth. What is mind-bending is that 20,000 American troops and 30,000 British troops were abandoned by Eisenhower and his British counterparts and left to their fate in Stalin's Russia. The atrocity has been handled in such secrecy by our government that Freedom of Information Act requests regarding it, to this day, are routinely denied on the grounds of 'national security.'

Included in the secrecy was the brutal massacre at Kaitlyn Forest in Poland. Kaitlyn Forest was perpetrated by Stalin and covered up with the full knowledge of FDR. Alexandr Solzhenitsyn called Operation Keelhaul "the last secret of World War II." But at least one General got sideways with Eisenhower over these atrocities; that would be General George S. Patton.

December 21, 1945

General George S. Patton was injured in an automobile accident in Kaeferthal, Germany. He received medical help quickly and was transferred to an army hospital in Heidelberg, Germany, where he died on December 21. Did he die from his injuries in the accident?

The official War Department death certificate lists "Pulmonary Edema & Congestive Heart Failure" as the cause of death. That means his heart failed to clear his lungs. Is that a complication caused by the car accident? We'll never know because there was no autopsy. Officials told Mrs. Patton that there were no qualified pathologists available. Case closed. The lack of an autopsy shows up in many coincidences you'll learn about in this book.

Those who served under Patton, many home from the war, were convinced he was murdered. Patton was no wallflower, and Eisenhower had relieved him of his duties for making disparaging statements towards the Soviet Union. He was also outspoken in his opposition to handing Poland to Russia and to the return of Russian defectors to Stalin.

General Patton had a nephew, Fred Ayer, Jr., an FBI official stationed in France. When he heard of the accident, he immediately responded, "Accident hell. It was murder. Those communist sons of bitches killed him." Intelligence operatives thought the same.

The accident itself was a trail of confusion. Three soldiers take a military Six-by from the motor pool for a joy ride but don't sign it out. It's on a Sunday, and they are far from where they are supposed to be. In a flat, open-road area, the Six-by approaches the vehicle General Patton is riding in. According to witnesses, the Six-by is driving straight and suddenly, without warning, turns sharply and hits the Patton vehicle head-on in broad daylight.

The perpetrator who stole the Six-by for the joy ride was never charged, and the accident was never investigated. One errant OSS investigator began to look at the situation and was promptly disciplined and sent home with the threat of demotion.

There have been the 'eyewitness' statements from first responders never able to provide statements. A Colonel Sitzinger, Patton's friend and a fellow commander said Patton told him he was going home to resign and "straighten this mess out." He said he heard the crash and ran to see the car and truck smashed" and Patton incapacitated. He claimed an ambulance took Patton not to the

130th but to the 115th Station Hospital, where he expired not two weeks later but that very day.

In addition, Niagara Falls, N.Y. policeman Kazmir L. Sawicki claimed that as an MP serving in Germany when Patton died, he had been the first person to the accident scene and had cradled the General until he was basically ordered to leave by higher-ups who arrived and stated they would take over. Patton, he said, was not injured inside his car, as all other witnesses claim, but was hit by a passing truck while he was urinating outside and beside his vehicle.

There were even more discrepancies among the 'witnesses' as well. But the last anomalies in this coincidental death were the goings at the army hospital in Heidelberg. There were even discrepancies as to what hospital he was taken to. On December 18, Patton amazed his doctors with his excellent health. Even under the enormous burden of his broken neck, his vital organs continued to function almost perfectly. Captain [Dr.] Kent said, "The heart tones were good, no murmurs were audible, and his blood pressure was 108 over 70'. Plans were made to bring him to the States, which was an arduous journey in those days.

In the days prior, General Patton told hospital authorities he'd overheard something troubling and requested a guard be placed in his room. Before that happened came the 'heart attack' that claimed his life. He died alone. It is a sad story that got sadder many years later when two OSS investigators who were around at the time of the accident told the public that they were involved in his death.

Without going into detail, and the specific info is available in several books about his death, many official records are mission. You'll see this phenomenon throughout our chronicle of the Whacked.

Question, did the outspoken war hero General Patton die in a simple highway accident? Or was he Whacked?

You decide.

1948

A LITTLE CONTEXT ...

Lyndon Baines Johnson, LBJ, emerged onto the national political stage in 1948, securing his first Senatorial seat from Texas. This marked the beginning of a significant chapter in American history, as he ascended to the role of Vice President following President JFK's untimely demise. His tenure was marked by the controversial Vietnam War, a conflict that mirrored the questionable origins of his initial election.

You'll meet many people in this book who coincidentally passed from this life early on the road to LBJ's rise to fame. It all started on election day 1948 in Duval and Jim Wells Counties in southwest Texas. Johnson had lost a previous bid for the Senate and was going up against former and popular Governor Coke Stevenson this time. But this time, LBJ, power-hungry and ruthless, had a plan.

One of the key figures in Johnson's political network was George Parr, a man with a unique understanding of how to manipulate the voting system. Parr and his associates were adept at 'voting the Mexicans,' a strategy that would play a pivotal role in the 1948 election.

In a dramatic turn of events, the election was swayed in Johnson's favor at the last minute by the 'Mexicans,' who were incentivized to cast their votes. Parr controlled the powerful Democratic machines in those two counties. He was known as the Duke of Duval for a reason.

The affair became known as the 'Box 13' scandal, allowing Lyndon Johnson to steal the 1948 US Senate race from former Texas governor Coke Stevenson by just under 150 votes.

Stevenson eventually found out about the cheating and, for various Texas political reasons, passed on challenging the election. As you read on, several coincidences occur as the skeletons in LBJ's closet begin to rattle.

1949

May 22, 1949

James Forrestal, the first US Secretary of Defense, they say, died at 1:50 AM, although there were no witnesses. All that is known with absolute certainty is that Forrestal's body was found on a third-floor canopy of the Bethesda Naval Hospital in Maryland. He had somehow fallen from his 16th-floor room.

In a bit of irony, perhaps by coincidence, Forrestal was found with his bathrobe belt tightly wound around his neck. Forestal's hospital room was never treated as a crime scene. His autopsy was never made public. Workers were never interviewed, and no one bothered to answer why the orderly assigned to his room was absent. Curious, wouldn't you say?

James Forestal was a devout Catholic and patriotic American who served as Secretary of the Navy during World War II. Before his government service, he was President of a financial institution on Wall Street. He had a difficult time during the war and as Secretary of Defense. At the time of his death, he was being treated for depression.

The Naval Investigative Service investigated the incident and could not determine why he fell from the window. The press quickly called it suicide. Led by notorious Wall Street Journal and syndicated columnists, Forrestal was mercilessly attacked in the media. President Truman relieved him of his duties, further impacting his mental state.

Did he commit suicide that fateful night? The government wants you to believe that. But there are quite a few anomalies. Officials say Forrestal was suicidal. If that were the case, why was he placed on the 16th-floor VIP area rather than monitored as one who is suicidal? Or, why was a high government official, who was suffering from severe depression not provided exceptional security. And then there is the issue of RW Harrison, a hospital apprentice assigned to Mr. Forrestal that night, who was nowhere to be found when he fell to his death.

The backstory you need to know is that Forrestal was very close to a young Senator named John F. Kennedy and another young Marine veteran turned Senator, a boy named Joseph McCarthy. They shared a common concern... the encroachment of communism into our federal government. They weren't shy about letting others know how they felt. Being anti-communist under FDR and later Truman was not a popular thing to be.

To further add to the mystery, JFK's diaries and close friends would later confirm that Forrestal was deeply troubled by events he learned about during the war. They were egregious events, but none more egregious than learning that FDR knew about the attack on Pearl Harbor four days before it happened. A decent and moral man, the truth took a toll, and he clearly struggled to know what he knew.

Did he know too much? Did he jump to his death, or was he helped out that window by others?

Question, did Secretary of Defense James Forrestal jump to his death at Bethesda? Or was he *Whacked?*

You decide.

The Fifties

What Did Your Government Do?

The decade of the Fifties brought America the Korean War courtesy of the newly minted No More War United Nations. It was a proxy fight between China and Russia on the one hand and the United States on the other. It was our first war to end in a stalemate, but it wouldn't be our last.

The Cold War had begun between the Soviet Union and the United States. Stalin gave way to Khrushchev, and the arms race was on. We didn't know then that war and the arms race were about filling bankers' pockets.

Russia successfully launched Sputnik 1, the first satellite to orbit the earth. That sent the U.S. into a tizzy, and the Space Race was on, which brought about NASA as we know it today.

The Fifties were a decade of social change in America. The Supreme Court ruled public schools could not be racially segregated. It was unconstitutional, giving the Civil Rights Movement a needed boost.

The Civil Rights Movement brought significant events. When Rosa Parks refused to give up her seat on a public bus it spawned the Montgomery Bus Boycott. It made Dr. Martin Luther King a household name and laid the groundwork for more change in the Sixties.

Fidel Castro led a Cuban Revolution that ousted Batista and his Casino empire, which was run by the American mob. Dr. Jonas Salk introduced his polio vaccine, rock and roll music hit the scene, and President Eisenhower began building what is now the U.S. Interstate Highway System.

Did you know that was when the OSS of World War II gave way to what is now the Central Intelligence Agency (CIA)? And notably, during this time, they began, against the sage advice of George Washington to stay free of foreign entanglements, intervening in other countries' businesses.

Faced with strife in the Philippines, the CIA researched which myths and superstitions the Philippine people had that could be used to disrupt agitators.

They discovered that they were afraid of vampires. Armed with this knowledge, they once disrupted a group by snatching a local man, murdering him, and putting teeth marks on his neck. They then hung him upside down for his friends to find, which terrified the village.

In documents since released, we learn it was all to elect Ramon Magsaysay as President. Through the CIA, he was a puppet for the U.S. for several years. And it was only the beginning.

1951

October 22, 1951

John Douglas Kinser was a World War II veteran and amateur actor who worked as an attendant at an Austin, Texas, golf course. He died from a gunshot to the chest. The killer was a 30-year-old student who casually walked up to John Kinser, ordered a pack of cigarettes, and then shot him.

It turns out John Kinser was having an affair with the shooter's wife. And as it turned out, an affair with LBJs sister, Josefa.

It could have been a simple case of a wronged husband killing his wife's lover. Or he could have crossed the wrong politician. We'll never know.

Question, was Kinser a victim of a simple murder? Or was he *Whacked?*

You decide.

1952

April 17, 1952

Sam Smithwick, former Deputy to Sheriff George Parr, the Duke of Duval, involved in the Box 13 affair and LBJ stealing votes, showed up dead, hanging in his cell at Huntsville State Prison, Huntsville, Texas. Smithwick was serving a life sentence for the murder of a news reporter investigating the questionable LBJ election.

Shortly before his death, Smithwick had written to former Governor Coke Stevenson, LBJ's opponent in the contested election, telling him he would come clean and testify to the truth of the stolen election in court. On the day Stevenson traveled to Huntsville to interview Smithwick, he stopped and called prison officials to notify them of his arrival time. He was told his subject was dead. Stevenson would never get to the bottom of Box 13.

When former Texas Governor Dan Moody, who served as governor of Texas from 1927 to 1931, heard of his 'suicide' he said, *"If the district attorney here had done his duty, Lyndon Johnson would now be in the penitentiary instead of the United States Senate."*

Question ... did Smithwick write to Governor Stevenson offering his support and then decide to kill himself? Or was he *Whacked?*

You decide.

1953

January 8, 1953

Harold Blauer a professional tennis player who competed against the famous Bill Tilden, widely considered one of the greatest tennis players ever. Blauer suffered a bout with depression partially caused by his recent divorce. He checked himself into the New York State Psychiatric Institute, where he died after being given a series of injections being tested by the US government.

Shortly after check-in, he was diagnosed as a pseudo-neurotic schizophrenic. He spent a short time as an inpatient and was said to be improving with a scheduled release date. That's when doctors began 'treating' Blauer with a series of injections. These injections were administered through doctors who had no idea what they were injecting,

Dr. James Cattell told investigators, *"We didn't know whether it was dog piss or what it was we were giving him."* Dr. Cattell and others, were acting on a classified agreement between the their employer and the Army Chemical Corps. They were testing various chemicals for potential use in warfare. The shots killed Harold Blauer.

There was an extensive cover-up, and not until 1975 did the government admit to Blauer's family that he had been injected with a mescaline derivative that caused his death.

Blauer was tested as part of a deal made with the Army Chemical Corps. The principal researcher at the New York State Psychiatric Institute was Dr. Paul Hoch. It turned out that Hoch was a CIA consultant on the MK-Ultra project and a driving force behind it.

Question ... was Harold Blauer Whacked by the CIA during their testing?

You decide.

November 28, 1953

Frank Olson, described as a brilliant chemist, fell to his death on the 10th floor of the Statler Hotel in Manhattan. Olson worked for the US Army's Special Operation Division. He was at the forefront of researching mind-altering technology. The technology was part of the CIAs controversial MKUltra program.

As mentioned, exotic tools to eliminate enemies emerged from World War II. An interesting quote from a principal at the time is intriguing. Dr. George Estabrooks, PhD, Chairman of the Department of Psychology at Colgate University, said in 1942, *"I can hypnotize a man, without his knowledge or consent, into committing treason against the United States."*

The infamous MKUltra program grew out of the work of people like Dr. Estabrooks. The program was so secret that from its start at the beginning of the fifties, its existence was unknown outside of the intelligence world until 1975, when the Church Committee started to make their own investigations of the CIA's mind-control-related activities.

When the covers were lifted on all the CIAs' studies,' they uncovered operations with elaborate names delving into manipulating the minds of foe and friend alike. In the 60s, they even gave LSD to unsuspecting Americans to document their reactions. And you think our government would never poison us with a fancy new vaccine? But then I digress.

So what does all that have to do with Frank Olson's untimely death? It's the CIA who knows? The government's final report was ruled a suicide.

Question ... did Frank Olson commit suicide? Or was he *Whacked?*

You decide.

1957

May 3, 1957

Senator Joe McCarthy died at 6:02 p.m. at Bethesda Naval Hospital. In a page 1 story, the *New York Times* reported: *"Washington was shocked by the Senator's sudden death. A hospital spokesman said McCarthy 'had taken a turn for the worse between 4 p.m. and 5 p.m.'* You'll note some commonalities in these coincidences, namely, no autopsy was performed.

Joe McCarthy is the man McCarthyism was named after. McCarthy was convicted by the Senate, made a scapegoat by the media, and a target of all the embedded communists in our government whom he was after. If you read *Death Rattle of the Republic,* you'll know that long after his death, when the *Venona Papers* were released in the early 90s, McCarthy's accusations was proven beyond a shadow of a doubt.

But at the time of his death, he was embattled. Depressed over the death of his good friend Jim Forestal, suffering from a knee problem, he was admitted to Bethesda Naval Hospital. A mere 5 days later, he was dead.

Here is a chronology of events ...

Sunday, April 28: According to his wife, McCarthy was admitted to Bethesda Naval Hospital with a knee injury at 5:00 p.m. The knee problem was related to an injury sustained during World War II when he served in the Marines. He was admitted to the neurology ward with a preliminary diagnosis of "peripheral neuritis," an inflammation of the nerves. According to official records, his diagnosis was changed later that night to 'acute hepatitis,' and he was placed in an oxygen tent.

Monday, April 29: The press was admitted to his room to photograph him. They report no sign of an oxygen tent. The *New*

York Times would later report on May 1 that the oxygen tent was removed on April 30.

Tuesday, April 30: The Associated Press reports that Senator McCarthy improved but remained in serious condition. The diagnosis of acute hepatitis remained. A hospital spokesman said, *"His condition is considered serious but not critical. He is slightly improved from this morning, however." McCarthy is "responding well" to treatment. No indication was given for how long the Senator might remain hospitalized."* In the same story, an aide in McCarthy's office noted his surprise as the Senator hadn't complained of being ill during the past week. Keep this in mind as you read on.

Wednesday, May 1: The *New York Times* runs a story with the headline: *McCARTHY IMPROVES; OUT OF OXYGEN TENT.* Remember that there was no sign of an oxygen tent on Monday, yet it was reportedly removed on Tuesday. His condition was reported to the public as 'improved.'

Friday, May 3, at 6:02 p.m., Joseph R. McCarthy is pronounced dead. New York Times reported: *"Washington was shocked by the Senator's sudden death. A hospital spokesman said McCarthy 'had taken a turn for the worse between 4 p.m. and 5 p.m.'*

Here is where things get coincidental. Hepatitis is an internal ailment, but according to the hospital, he was being treated in the neurology ward." A hospital spokesman said, *"Senator McCarthy had not had the infectious type of hepatitis, but an acute form of the disease."* So much for his knee injury.

In a CYA exercise, the hospital tried to cover its tracks with the following official statement: *"Senator Joseph R. McCarthy was admitted to the US Naval Hospital April 28 1957 with acute hepatitis following several weeks' illness at his home. He was considered seriously ill at the time of admission, and his condition progressively failed and he expired at 18:02 May 2 1,957."*

Not so fast, Bethesda. The good Senator was admitted to the hospital with a preliminary diagnosis of peripheral neuritis, not acute hepatitis. And secondly, both his family and office staff consistently stated he had not been ill at home before his trip to Bethesda on April 28.

Umm? On Saturday, May 4, the *New York Times* reported, *"The origin of the ailment was not known and no autopsy was planned."* Of course not. The paper also reported a hospital spokesman told them, *"When Senator McCarthy was admitted to the hospital last Sunday, he was sent to a neurology ward because of a preliminary diagnosis indicated he has peripheral neuritis, an inflammation of the nerve."* The spokesman further noted McCarthy was moved to a medical ward when the diagnosis was changed to acute hepatitis.

Shortly after his death, infamous columnist Drew Pearson began a smear campaign feigning inside information that McCarthy died of alcoholism. Drank himself to death. Pearson was also one of the media who pursued Jim Forrestal to his death. Years later, when the truth of the CIA Operation Mockingbird surfaced, Drew Pearson was found to be a shill for the Agency.

Question ... did the beleaguered Senator from Wisconsin die from acute hepatitis? Or was he *Whacked?*

You decide.

The Sixties

What Did Your Government Do?

The 1960s were wild, upside down and began changes to our nation we're still feeling today. It started with the first American advisors sent to Vietnam; President John F. Kennedy was elected with the help of the Chicago mob and apparently wasn't supposed to win. We now know the CIA aided and abetted his assassination shortly after that.

Dr. Martin Luther King delivered his 'I Have a Dream' speech and a few short years later met the fate of JFK when he was assassinated. He was followed by Robert F. Kennedy, the President's brother, who delivered a message when he, too, was assassinated. Lots of coincidences began around this time.

John Glenn became the first American to orbit Earth, and Yuri Gagarin became the first human in spaceflight for the Soviet Union. The Sixties saw the Civil Rights Act and the Voting Rights Act passed, and social upheaval became the order of the day, as did drugs, which blanketed the nation on college campuses coast to coast.

LBJ continued his path of destruction with the Gulf of Tonkin and our jump into the Vietnam War with both feet. Operation Rolling Thunder began, and as the jets rolled across Hanoi and Haiphong Harbor, the number of American POWs started piling up in North Vietnamese prisons.

The decade's close saw the Summer of Love in San Francisco; hippies entered the culture, and Woodstock mainstreamed the whole affair. College campuses were on fire, and a path of destruction became history across America as the body count in Vietnam reached epic proportions.

The Sixties also brought the Cuban Missile Crisis, Khrushchev banging his shoe on the UN podium, and a maniacal push by many to take out Fidel Castro. The CIA was obsessed with assassinating Castro, and JFK didn't support the efforts that were ongoing when he took office. With JFK now history, the CIAs quest to rid Cuba of Castro gained speed. According to Fabian Escalante, who worked for Cuban counterintelligence, they planned or tried 638 times.

They tried to poison his cigars, and they asked the Chicago Mob for help. They tried poison pills. The Mobsters hired a local assassin, who gave the pills to an ice cream parlor employee who was supposed to slip them into Castro's ice cream. When he went to retrieve the poison pills from the freezer, they were frozen solid in the coils of the freezer. It sounds like an episode of Hogan's Heroes.

But they didn't give up. They knew Castro loved scuba diving, so they planned to put explosives under a painted sea shell in the hope that he'd pick up their sea shell while scuba diving. Which he loved. The plan was eventually tossed and deemed impractical.

They even tried to enlist an American lawyer, who was negotiating the release of Bay of Pigs hostages, to contaminate Castro's scuba diving suit with a fungus that would give him a deadly disease. The lawyer couldn't make it happen. Then they trained his lover to poison him, but she got cold feet and backed out.

Despite their efforts, Castro lived to a ripe old age, but what they learned was put to good use elsewhere, as you'll see by the coincidences described in these pages.

1960

A LITTLE CONTEXT ...

In the late 1950s and early 1960s, Billy Sol Estes became a household name. He was a con man extraordinaire from Texas, a friend of LBJ, and a contributor to his campaign. Billy Sol bilked anyone he could with various schemes for land, cattle, and other commodities.

In 1962, at President Kennedy's behest, a congressional investigation ensued. The investigation raised questions of how deeply LBJ, then Vice President, might be connected to Billy Sol. There were many twists and turns, but in the end, Billy Sol Estes was found guilty of fraud and tax evasion and sentenced to federal prison.

There were many Estes investigations, trials, and revealing scandals. JFK knew the truth and wanted LBJ off the ticket for the upcoming election. In a twist of irony, Billy Sol was represented by LBJ attorney Douglas Caddy. And, of course, we know JFK bought the proverbial farm, and LBJ and his quest for power continued.

1961

June 3, 1961

Henry Marshall died on his farm near Bryan, Robertson County, Texas. He was shot five times with his own rifle. A Robertson County official declared the death a suicide.

Marshall, 51, was a senior clerk with the Robertson County (Texas) office of the Agricultural Adjustment Agency (AAA). In 1960, he investigated the activities of Billie Sol Estes, a wealthy benefactor of Lyndon B. Johnson. His investigation revealed Billie Sol Estes was involved in an illegal scheme to buy cotton allotments.

Marshall's investigation confirmed the rumors of Billy Sol Estes' evil deeds on behalf of LBJ.

His murder came before the case went to trial. Billy Sol Estes would be convicted of fraud and tax evasion multiple times. At the end of his second parole in 1983, he testified before a Robertson County Grand Jury that Lyndon Johnson ordered the murder of Marshall. Estes said Mac Wallace killed Marshall because he feared Marshall would link LBJ to the cotton allotment scam.

Before a Grand Jury, the Texas Rangers were able to get the death of Marshall changed from suicide to homicide.

Question ... was poor Henry Marshall the unfortunate victim of a murder? Or was he *Whacked?*

You decide.

October 13, 1961

Prince Louis Rwagasore, Burundi's first Prime Minister, was assassinated by a Greek mercenary while dining at the Hotel Tanganyika in Bujumbura, the capital of Burundi. He was only 29 years old at the time of his death.

He had been elected Prime Minister 16 days earlier, in a landslide that shocked everyone by his winning 80% of the vote. At the time, Burundi was a colony of Belgium. The Belgians supported the Christian Democratic Party. A suspect was identified and confessed to the murder. He was a Christian Democrat and, at trial, implicated the Belgian Governor, but his testimony was ignored.

Question ... was newly elected reformer Prince Louis Rwagasore murdered by a disgruntled loser? Or was he *Whacked?*

You decide.

December 25, 1961

Josefa Johnson, the sister of then Vice President Lyndon Baines Johnson, returned to her home in Fredericksburg, Texas, after being at a Christmas Eve party at the LBJ Ranch on Christmas Day 1961. Upon return, she reportedly died of a cerebral hemorrhage. She was 49. Despite Texas state law, no autopsy was performed.

Like her Brother, LBJ, she was known to be a wild child with a lust for power. The twice-married and divorced Josefa is said to have worked for Hattie Valdez's private club (wink/wink). She was involved in helping LBJ in his successful 1948 senatorial campaign.

Josefa had at least two infamous affairs. One with John Kinser and the other with Mac Wallace, the man Billy Sol Estes fingered for killing Henry Marshall. She knew LBJ's dealings from the inside, and it worried him because she had loose lips. Later in life, she was known to be an alcoholic.

Douglas Caddy, LBJs attorney, some thirty years after Josefa's death, wrote the Department of Justice claiming that she, along with several others, were the victims of murder in a collaboration between Billy Sol Estes, Mac Wallace, Cliff Carter, and LBJ.

Question ... did Josefa die a natural death? Or was she *Whacked!*

You decide.

1962

April 4, 1962

George Krutilek, 49, an accountant for Billy Sol Estes, was discovered dead in his pickup parked in the sand hills near Clint, Texas. His pickup exhaust reportedly had a hose connected to the passenger compartment. His death was ruled a suicide despite an

El Paso pathologist concluding that carbon monoxide was not the cause of death but rather a severe bruise on Krutilek's head.

His body was found 2 days before he was to be questioned by the FBI in the Billy Sol Estes fraud case and a day before Estes was indicted.

Question ... did George Krutilek suck fumes and die. Or was he *Whacked?*

You decide.

Marilyn Monroe, a famous Hollywood actress, was found dead in her apartment. The Coroner ruled her death an accidental drug overdose.

Marilyn Monroe was and remains a Hollywood icon. Books have been written about her life, and movies have been made about her life and death. She was known for her many affairs, none more so than the rumored affair with President John Kennedy. There were rumors at the time; today, there is evidence she did have an affair with President Kennedy and his Brother Bobby, then U.S. Attorney General.

Bobby's tryst began when his Brother, the President, asked him to pay her a visit and persuade her that things were over. The President was said to be concerned that Ms. Monroe might be upset if he broke off the affair and said something damaging to the media.

This is one of the rare cases where an autopsy was performed as required by law. The autopsy revealed, as we now know, she had no drugs in her system. She died on a Friday, and close friends maintain she was planning to go public about the affairs on the following Monday.

Did Ms. Monroe overdose as reported? Or was she *Whacked?*

You decide.

1963

November 22, 1963

President John F Kennedy died of gunshot wounds in Dallas, Texas, for all to see and remember forever. Countless books, movies, and documentaries have been produced covering the assassination of America's beloved President.

A suspect was quickly apprehended and subsequently shot. As you progress through this book, you will see that this event sets off a series of coincidences that are hard to comprehend. In this case, you'll learn that over 70 witnesses and figures met a coincidental end to their lives.

The coincidences began immediately after the Presidents death when the Dallas Police Officer who arrested alleged shooter Lee Harvey Oswald was shot and killed. Then, the supposed shooter, Lee Harvey Oswald, was shot days after being arrested.

The long trail of deadly coincidences continues to this day. The truth is that JFK ruffled many Deep State feathers. Here are the three that stand out.

When he returned from Dallas, he told those closest to him he was taking action to abolish the Federal Reserve. That is a no. It was set up by the global financial gurus in 1911, and everyone knows it will remain.

Secondly, he had made it known he would, in his words, 'break the CIA into a thousand pieces. He hated the myopic focus on killing Castro and believed there were better ways.

Third, he told his closest advisors he intended to reduce troop levels in Vietnam and get the U.S. out.

You see how that worked out for him.

Question ... do you believe JFK was assassinated by a lone, crazed gunman? Case closed? Or was Camelot *Whacked?*

You decide.

November 22, 1963 (later in the day)

Dallas Police Officer JD Tippit was shot and killed on duty, reportedly while trying to apprehend Lee Harvey Oswald. That is the official story. You might be interested in a few non-truths and strange coincidences in Officer Tippets's story.

His story begins as he leaves his house that fateful morning. According to his wife, Officer Tippit hugged his oldest son Allen, saying, *'No matter what happens today, I want you to know I love you.'* His wife later said Tippit's overt affection toward his son was uncharacteristic. This was the last time young Allen Tippit saw his father alive.

A couple anomalies to share ...

Witnesses confirmed that minutes after the assassination of the President, a Dallas Police car pulled up outside of Oswald's apartment. The officer, not identified, honked twice, and Oswald came out and got into the car.

Witnesses elsewhere observed what turned out to be Officer Tippit on 10th Street in Dallas, stopping to talk to a man walking nearby. They observed the person walk over and casually chat with the officer. At no time was the encounter confrontational.

Officer Tibbit then exited his vehicle and began to walk towards the individual when the assailant pulled a gun, shot him 3 times in the chest, walked a couple steps, turned, and shot him once more in the head. Then casually walked away in broad daylight. A wallet with Oswald's driver's license in it was found at the scene. The wallet would be Oswald's 'second wallet' to be seen. The other was at the Book Depository building.

Despite the above facts, the official narrative of the shooting is that Officer Tibbit received the radio bulletin looking for Lee Harvey Oswald and stopped someone who fit the description. The problem with that narrative is the witnesses of the shooting unanimously described someone who did not fit Oswald's description.

The other problem with this narrative is that the timeline of Oswald's supposed shooting of JFK and subsequent sitings does not put him at the location of Officer Tippets's murder. An odd coincidence, wouldn't you say?

The Warren Commission did not hear or consider any of the witnesses to the Tippit murder. It was Lee Harvey Oswald who shot Tippit and no one else.

The Commission inaccurately claimed that Tippit was on his routine patrol when killed. In fact, he was nowhere near his assigned route for the day, which was in Oak Park. It's also interesting that Officer Tippit was never transferred to the Presidential detail that fateful day.

Question ... did Officer Tippit meet his demise at the hands of Lee Harvey Oswald? Or was he *Whacked?*

You decide.

November 23, 1963

Jack Zangetti, a mobster with links to the Chicago Mob who managed a high-end casino in Oklahoma, was found dead in a swimming pool with gunshots to his body. He was found in late November but believed to have been dead for up to 10 days.

The significance of the date of his death, November 23, is the day Zangetti told friends, *"A man named Ruby will kill Oswald tomorrow, and in a few days, a member of Frank Sinatra's family will be kidnapped just to take some of the attention away from the assassination."* He also said, *"Three other men—not Oswald—killed the President."*

In a coincidence, I'm sure, the next day, Jack Ruby took out Oswald, and indeed, Frank Sinatra Jr. was kidnapped on December 8.

Question ... did Mr. Zangetti slip and fall in the pool? Or was he *Whacked?*

You decide.

November 24, 1963

Lee Harvey Oswald was shot and killed on live T.V. while in the custody of the Dallas Police. And just as Jack Zangetti told his dinner companions, the shooter was an unknown nightclub owner by the name of Jack Ruby.

The irony in Oswald being shot is that he was perhaps the most famous criminal of the century; he purportedly killed the President of the United States and was being walked through the Dallas Police Headquarters surrounded by a bevy of police officers and T.V. cameras and was shot for all America to see.

Jack Ruby walked unchallenged into Police Headquarters, walked amongst a group of cops charged with protecting the man who shot the President, pulled out a gun, and made the hit on Oswald. Now, that is a coincidence.

Question ... was Jack Ruby a super sleuth who slithered amongst Dallas' finest and killed the now infamous Lee Harvey Oswald? Or was he *Whacked?*

You decide.

November 28, 1963

Karyn Kupcinet, an aspiring actress in Hollywood, was discovered dead on November 30, 1963. The Coroner ruled she had been deceased for two days. The crime scene was strange, with clothes strewn about and Ms. Kupcinet lying on the floor, naked, her head on a pillow. Karyn's death is surrounded by speculation. There were no signs of robbery, and her neck was broken. Two foreign, unknown fingerprints were found at the scene.

It was big news nationwide. Ms. Kupcinet was the daughter of Irv Kupcinet, one of the nation's most respected and popular newspaper columnists and perhaps the biggest newsman. Irv

Kucinet was also socially friends with the leaders of the Chicago mob, and his best friend was the infamous mob lawyer Sidney Korschak.

Karyn had once met Jack Ruby, who her father knew. Following JFKs assassination, in shock, Karyn fled with some friends to Palm Springs to get away. While in Palm Springs, she met with Paul Dorfman, a known Chicago mobster known as Red. While together, Karyn's father, Irv, called Dorfman to get some info on Jack Ruby, who had just shot Oswald. Coincidence?

Birds of a feather flock together, but why whack a friend's daughter? Speculation abounds, but the best thinking at the time was that it could be a message to Irv, their friend, and nationally recognized newsman, not to do his regular diligence in going after Ruby, who also had ties to the Chicago mob. Many thought the theory was too 'out there.'

Whatever the case, Ms. Karyn returned from Palm Springs and ended up dead. Her murder has never been solved.

Question ... was Karyn Kupcinet the victim of a random murder with no motive since nothing was stolen and she wasn't raped? Or was she *Whacked?*

You decide.

December 2, 1963

Grant Stockdale, a wheeler-dealer in the highest echelons of the Democratic Party, former Ambassador to Ireland, and close friend of the recently assassinated President Kennedy, fell to his death from the 13th floor of the DuPont Building in mid-town Manhattan. His death was ruled a suicide.

As with many coincidences you'll read in these pages, the story doesn't end there. Stockdale was so close to JFK that on November 26, days after the assassination, he flew to D.C. to be with the President's brothers. When he returned, he told some close friends that *'his world was closing in.'*

On December 1, he met with his lawyer, William Frates. Frates said that Stockade was upset, scared, and didn't make much sense. He said that people were out to get him as he was involved in severe political issues that were about to come front and center. He also appeared to have ties to the Bobby Baker scandal.

He was also involved in the brewing caldron of corruption in Texas, which involved a seven-billion-dollar F-111 contract with General Dynamics Corporation. What did the Baker and General Dynamic scandals have in common? They both had genuine potential to destroy Lyndon Johnson's political career.

Question ... did high flyer Grant Stockade, well-connected and successful, leap to his death over his despair from the death of his friend Jack Kennedy? That was the official narrative. Or was Grant Stockade *Whacked?*

You decide.

December 3, 1963

Captain Michael D. Groves, Commander of the Honor Guard for JFKs funeral, died suddenly at the dinner table. The cause of death was undetermined; one suspicion was food poisoning.

In an odd coincidence, the Honor Guard Captain Graves commanded began practicing for a presidential funeral three days before the assassination.

Question ... did Captain Groves die of natural causes? Or was he *Whacked?*

You decide.

1964

January 23, 1964

A DEFINITE MAYBE ...

On this date, one Wayne Reynolds of Dallas, Texas, was working in his office, in the basement of his home, when he was shot in the head through a small window. Miraculously, Mr. Reynolds was hospitalized but did recover from his wounds.

The back story of Mr. Reynolds is that he was a witness to the shooting of Officer Tippit in Dallas. He was watering his lawn when the Tippits shooting occurred. He chased the subject after the shooting and, at one point, came face to face. He described the individual to the police. They said it was Oswald. He told the police it was not Oswald. That did not sit well, with the police becoming upset, and he says they asked him to recant his story. He would not.

On January 21, two days after Reynolds was shot, the FBI conducted an extensive interview with him. He did not change his story. The shooting at his home occurred 48 hours after his interview.

In February, after his return home, an attempt was made to kidnap his ten-year-old daughter. Then, he and his family began receiving death threats. Then Reynolds recanted his story and I.D.'d Oswald as demanded.

Note: This case is tied to the next one, Betty McDonald, aka Nancy Jane Mooney She was the alibi for the guy apprehended for shooting Reynolds. Read on and see her fate.

February 13, 1964

Betty McDonald (a.k.a. Nancy Jane Mooney), a stripper at Jack Ruby's Carousel Club in Dallas, hung herself in her jail cell hours after being arrested for disorderly conduct.

Ms. McDonald was an alibi witness for the suspect arrested for the Wayne Reynolds shooting. Her alibi was challenged. Later, she was arrested for disorderly conduct for arguing with her roommate in public. The roommate was not charged.

Ms. McDonald was found hanging by a noose made from her pants. Her death was ruled a suicide.

Question ... was the stripper so embarrassed by her incarceration for being disorderly that she killed herself? Or was she *Whacked?*

You decide.

February 17, 1964

Eddy Benavides, Brother of Domingo Benavides, was shot in the back of the head by a random bullet during an unrelated altercation. The murder has gone unsolved.

Domingo was another witness in the Officer Tippit shooting and identified the shooter as someone other than Lee Harvey Oswald. He testified that he was told by police to change his story. He received death threats. His Brother, Eddy, is known by all as his twin, although they were just brothers.

After the death of his Brother, Domingo told friends he felt guilty because he was sure his Brother's death was a case of mistaken identity. He changed his testimony and never received another death threat.

Question ... did Eddy die from a stray bullet? Or was he *Whacked?*

You decide.

February 28, 1964

Harold Orr, President of the Superior Manufacturing Company in Amarillo, Texas, was found dead in his garage. His death was ruled a suicide; he died of carbon monoxide poisoning.

Orr was a business associate of Billy Sol Estes. Harold Orr was arrested with Estes and received a ten-year prison sentence. He was allowed to go home prior to his incarceration. Insiders were told he was about to turn state evidence against Estes.

Did Harold Orr die of carbon monoxide poisoning? Or. was he *Whacked?*

You decide.

March 1964

Howard Pratt, the Chicago office manager of Commercial Solvents, a supplier of farm products for Billie Sol Estes, was found dead in his garage. His death was ruled a suicide as a result of carbon monoxide poisoning.

His death occurred just weeks after Harold Eugene Orr, the President of the Superior Manufacturing Company, was found dead of carbon monoxide poisoning. Both were embroiled in the Billy Sol Estes troubles of the day.

Question ... did Howard Pratt, like his boss Harold Orr, kill himself? Or was he *Whacked?*

You decide.

March 17, 1964

Hank Killam, a house painter from Dallas who had moved to Pensacola, Florida, was found dead on the street, his throat cut wide open, lying 50 feet from a broken department store window at 4:30 a.m. The police ruled it a suicide, while the Coroner ruled it an accident. The police believed Killam had thrown himself into the window in an attempt to commit suicide.

Killam's story is a twisted tale with all roads tying back to the JFK assassination. His wife was a dancer in Jack Ruby's Dallas club. He was known to associate with Lee Harvey Oswald. An unfortunate soul by the name of Bill Waters, whom you'll meet later, told investigators that Oswald and Killam visited him at his Mother's house before the assassination and talked about what might happen.

Following the assassination, Killam's wife told investigators he was obsessed with it, collected articles, and became afraid for his life. She said local and federal investigators hounded her husband until he decided to move to Florida to escape the harassment.

Killam moved to Pensacola and started working as a car salesman, but the investigators showed up there, too. He moved to Tampa, where they found him, and back to Pensacola, where he moved in with his Mother. He told her and his Brother he was done running and what would be.

On the night of his death, his Mother said he got a phone all around 4 a.m., dressed, and went outside. She heard a car pick him up. He didn't own a car. The officer who found him dead in the street was Officer Reeves.

An independent investigation revealed that Officer Reeves had reported responding to a call earlier to Killam's Mother's address, where he found Killam waiting in front of the house. The officer noted, *"There was fear showing in Killam's eyes and he claimed that he was going to be killed."*

There is much written about this case, even in the Congressional Record. The bottom line is, who would commit suicide by jumping into a plate glass window that broke and only cut his jugular vein, and then walk 50 feet and die when he bled out? Enquiring minds want to know.

Did Hank Killam throw himself into a plate glass window in an attempt to kill himself? Or was he *Whacked?*

You decide.

March 31, 1964

Bill Chesher, a Dallas auto mechanic, died of a heart attack. Mr. Chesher was the mechanic who worked on Jack Ruby's car. One researcher linked Chesher to information connecting Ruby and Oswald. Another mechanic at the dealership where they worked reported they had seen Oswald in Ruby's car.

Question ... did Bill Chesher die of natural causes?

Or was he *Whacked?*

You decide.

April 23, 1964

Bill Hunter, a reporter for the Long Beach Independent Telegram, was shot to death while sitting at his news desk at the Long Beach Police Department. The shooting was ruled accidental.

Bill Hunter's story is tied to that of Jim Koethe, a Dallas reporter, and Tom Howard, a Dallas attorney. Hunter and Koethe were longtime friends. Hunter had flown to Dallas to cover the assassination story. All three mentioned above had obtained permission to visit Jack Ruby's apartment the night Ruby took out Oswald.

Jim Koethe was putting together information for a book on the assassination, and Hunter helped as much as he could. On the night of his death, at approximately 2 a.m., Hunter was in his news office reading a novel when two detectives he knew walked in with him. Then, the story turns tragic.

Hunter was shot through the heart and died instantly when one of the officer's weapons discharged accidentally. In the first report, one of the detectives said he dropped his loaded weapon, and it went off, shooting Hunter

The Editor of the Long Beach Independent Telegram strongly protested that finding, and the official story that came out from the Police Chief was that the detectives were fooling around playing quick draw and accidentally shot Mr. Hunter. The two officers were trialed; neither was convicted, and both were put on three years of probation.

Question ... did Bill Hunter die as a result of a foolish accident by two police detectives? Or was he *Whacked?*

You decide.

May 8, 1964

Gary Underhill, a CIA contractor/agent, was found dead in his Washington, DC, home of a single gunshot behind his left ear. A shot behind the left ear is interesting since Underhill was right-handed. His death was ruled a suicide.

Immediately upon hearing of JFKs assassination, Underhill left his D.C. home and fled to a longtime friend's house on Long Island. Charlene Fitzsimmons recounted what he said hours after the assassination. Here is the first part of what she would write in a letter to New Orleans Attorney Jim Garrison after he began his investigation.

"This country is too dangerous for me. I've got to get on a boat. Oswald is a patsy. They set him up. It's too much. The bastards have done something outrageous. They've killed the President! I've been listening and hearing things. I couldn't believe they'd get away with it, but they did. They've gone mad! They're a bunch of drug runners and gun runners—a real violence group. I know who they are. That's the problem. They know I know. That's why I'm here."

Underhill lived in fear for his life. His friend sent a detailed letter to Jim Garrison, who planned to interview Underhill at his home in D.C. Before he could conduct the interview, Underhill was found dead in his bed.

Question ... did Gary Underhill off himself? Or was he *Whacked?*

You decide.

May 22, 1964

Hugh Ward and Deslesseps Morrison both died in a plane crash on this date. Hugh Ward was a private investigator and an accomplished plane pilot. Deslesseps Morrison was the Mayor of New Orleans, Louisiana.

Bless his soul, Morrison may very well have been a victim of circumstance. Hugh Ward, on the other hand, was known to be close to two people who were critical of the investigation into the JFK assassination. Those two were Guy Banister and David Ferrie, both known to be in the New Orleans mob.

New Orleans has turned out be the hub of planning for the JFK assassination. That eventually brought NO District Attorney Jim Garrison into the forefront as he began his investigation after Ruby shot Oswald. Garrison hired retired FBI agent William Turner to lead the investigation.

Turner would later write Rearview Mirror, in which he recounted his number one problem investigating was his potential witnesses were all murdered before he could talk with them. Private Investigator Hugh Ward was one of them.

Ward was piloting the plane that fateful day. Weather set in, and he had to change his flight plan en route. On the farm where the plane crashed, witnesses reported hearing the plane above, and both engines began sputtering simultaneously. When the aircraft broke through the clouds, it was too low and crashed, killing all occupants.

The ruling was a pilot error accident. But the plane's fuel tank was three-quarters full after the crash.

Question ... did Hugh Ward crash the plane by accident? Or was he *Whacked?*

You decide.

June 6, 1964

Guy Banister, Private Investigator and former head of the FBI's Chicago office died of a heart attack. Banister was described as a rabid anti-communist and anti-Castroist who had a well-developed file on people involved in those activities.

Banister and David Ferrie began working for the lawyer G. Wray Gill and his client, mob boss Carlos Marcello. On August 9, 1963, Lee Harvey Oswald distributed leaflets that supported Fidel Castro and his government in Cuba. On those leaflets was the address 544

Camp Street, New Orleans. This was also the office of Carlos Bringuier, an anti-Castro exile.

The leaflets Oswald delivered were found in Banister's office. And two witnesses tied Banister and Oswald as being seen together on more than one occasion. A detective who worked for Banister, Jack Martin, told the FBI after the assassination he believed Banister was involved in it.

Banister was set to be interviewed by Garrison's investigator, William Turner, but died before that happened. And all his papers and files on communists came up missing.

Question ... did Guy Banister die of a heart attack? Or was he *Whacked?*

You decide.

June 21, 1964

A DEFINITE MAYBE ...

On this date, Andrew Goodman, a civil rights activist, alongside two other activists, James Chaney and Michael Schwernewas, were murdered. They were involved in the Freedom Summer project to register voters. Several people were apprehended, supposed members of the Mississippi Ku Klux Klan. Case closed.

And the case has been closed. People went to jail, and justice was served. The actions of these three activists eventually resulted in the Voter Rights Act. But there are those, well connected, who have claimed these deaths trace back to Lyndon Baines Johnson. Rumors. Probably.

But there is the biographer who quoted LBJ in 1963 as saying, "These Negroes, they're getting pretty uppity these days, and that's a problem for us since they've got something now they never had before, the political pull to back up their uppityness. Now, we've got to do something about this; we've got to give them a little something, just enough to quiet them down, not enough to make a difference. I'll have them niggers voting Democratic for the next two hundred years."

That is an often-quoted line from LBJ, and he was pretty arrogant. Power was always LBJ's quest. You can see it increasingly as time progresses on the American political front.

July 21, 1964

Dr. Mary Sherman, known as a gifted physician and recently selected for a bio-weapons cancer research project, was found murdered in her home. She had multiple stab wounds in the heart, liver, stomach, labia minora, left arm, and right leg. Also, she suffered extreme burns on the right side of her body.

But that is where routine ends. Her right upper extremity and the right side thorax and abdomen were burned. Her vital organs were exposed. Her house was set on fire; fortunately, it turned out to be a minor fire. The reports from the crime scene were mixed. First, there was forced entry and a burglary. That was changed when her jewelry was in full view and not stolen.

There are books written on Dr. Mary's case, and it is a long, twisted tale; she was involved in developing a super-cancer to be used as a biological weapon. She was also known to be tied to anti-Castro groups and knew both Lee Harvey Oswald and Davie Ferrie.

Speculation abounds, but it doesn't bring Dr. Mary back.

Question ... was Dr. Mary Sherman simply murdered for who knows why? Or was she *Whacked?*

You decide.

July 31, 1964

Jim Reeves, an international country music star, died in the crash of the plane he was piloting. The official ruling is pilot error. Reeves performed in Dallas the night before JFKs assassination.

Reeves stayed behind that night, and his band moved on to Amarillo.

Reeves was widely known for his photographic memory. He would sometimes wow people at his shows with memory tricks. Friends who were with him shortly after the assassination said that when they saw Oswald's face on the TV, Reeves said, *"I know that guy. I've seen him at the club many times."*

It was later determined that he knew Oswald from performing in clubs in Dallas over the years. There is no known sinister part to the story other than guilt by association. What is odd is that when the plane went down and the call went out to first responders, the tower at the airport gave the coordinates of the crash in woods near the runway.

In a twist never explained, authorities directed the search to another area away from the crash site. The Nashville Tennessean reported in its Sunday edition that more than 2,000 persons were involved in the search effort, which was still unsuccessful.

The search included:

Civil Defense units.

Metropolitan police.

Williamson County sheriff's officers.

Members of the Donelson Citizens Band Radio Service.

Forty National Guardsmen.

Airmen from Stewart Air Force Base.

The three-day search prompted Mary Reeves to recall, *"This is ridiculous. They can't have just vanished."*

What becomes more interesting is that from the first call of the crash, authorities were searching for a briefcase that was said to be on the plane. Investigators confirmed that, in fact, Reeves got on the plane with a suitcase. When first responders reached the crash site on day four, when aviation people insisted they were wrong, the aircraft was found, but the briefcase was never located.

What was in the briefcase? We don't know. Why did they intentionally search the wrong area? We don't do that either. Is his death related to JFK? It's not apparent. But there are a high number of coincidences that imply things aren't as they seem. While the official ruling is pilot error, witnesses stated that one wing was coming off the plane on its final descent.

Did Jim Reeves make a fatal error resulting in his death? Or was he *Whacked?*

You decide.

September 1964

Gilberto Rodriguez Hernandez and Manuel Rodriguez Quesada were both heavily involved in gun-running and were high-level leaders in anti-Castro operations. Both died of gunshot wounds.

Many of the people you'll meet in this list of coincidences—such as Socarras, Rolando Masferrer, and Eladio del Valle—are linked to violent anti-Castro groups. Eladio del Valle was also an associate of David Ferrie and Guy Banister.

Both Manuel Rodriguez Quesada and Gilberto Rodriguez Hernandez were said to have inside information on who set up the JFK killing in Dallas.

In his book *First Hand Knowledge*, author Robert Morrow says a man by the name of John O'Hare, a 'CIA mercenary and assassin,' admitted to him that he killed both men. According to O'Hare, the men were eliminated because they might say too much.

Question ... were these two gunrunner anti-Castro dudes simply murdered? Or were they *Whacked?*

You decide.

September 18, 1964

C.D. Jackson, publisher of *Life Magazine* and purchaser of the infamous *Zapruder (JFK) film*, died of unknown causes.

Mr. Jackson bought the film to lock it away.

Question ... did Mr. Jackson die naturally? Or was he *Whacked?*

You decide.

September 21, 1964

Jim Koethe, a young reporter for the *Dallas Times Herald*, actively involved in the investigation of the JFK assassination, was found dead of a broken neck outside the shower in his apartment. As you read previously, Jim was friends with Bill Hunter, as both were working on the assassination story. Jim Koethe was also working on a book about what happened in Dallas.

Koethe stepped out of the shower and was felled by a karate chop to the neck, breaking his neck and killing him instantly. The event was ruled a homicide, and the result of the subject surprising a burglar. How you surprise someone when you step out of the shower is unclear. And, drum roll, please ... the only thing missing from the apartment was the manuscript and notes for the JFK assassination book Koethe was working on.

Question ... did Mr. Koethe surprise a burglar who happened to know karate and broke his neck? Or was he *Whacked?*

You decide.

October 12, 1964

Mary Pinchot Meyer, a D.C. socialite and former wife of Cord Meyer, was out for her morning jog in the park when she was shot once in the back of the head and once more in the heart. She died instantly. But this was no average D.C. homicide.

Cord Meyer worked for the CIA and was the head of Operation Mockingbird, the CIA's propaganda arm to control the media in America. Mary Pinchot Meyer divorced Cord a few years earlier and was a hot ticket in the D.C. social scene. Her sister, Toni, married Ben Bradlee, of Newsweek and Washington Post fame. The four of them hung out with James Angleton and his wife, with whom Mary attended Vasser. Angleton was the CIA head of counterintelligence. She partied with the elite, and one of those was President Kennedy.

Many people close to her believed that her affair with the President was more than met the eye. Some close to the President said Mary was his last great flame. Rumor had it that she and Kennedy had done LSD with Timothy Leary in the White House. Upon her death, Leary's associate, Van Wolfe, said, *"It's got to be one of the biggest coverups in Washington history."*

Cover up? Mary hobnobbed with the Washington political elite and intelligence community because of her husband. And Mary knew things. She was upset over the assassination and immediately went on a quest for details.

When the Warren Commission report came out, she was livid. She told friends she knew it was a whitewash and wouldn't stand for it. She would find her own truth. Days after publicly proclaiming her search for truth, she found it with two carefully placed bullets.

Mary was known to be a meticulous diary keeper. Upon hearing of her death, sister Toni and her husband, Ben Bradlee, immediately went to her apartment to find the diary for her kids. Upon arrival, they were greeted by counterintelligence guru James Angleton of the CIA. The diary was never found. (Wink-wink).

Question ... did Mary Pinchot Meyer meet her demise at the hands of a crazed murderer? Or was she *Whacked!*

You decide.

1965

A LITTLE CONTEXT ...

A half-truth or a lie will suffice with spooks and spies. The CIA had (and probably still has) a program known as Operation Mockingbird, which has been and will be referred to throughout this book. Some folks say it began as far back as 1948; others say it started in 1950; who knows?

The purpose of Operation Mockingbird was to gain influence in American media. To get them on the government's side and align their reporting with the CIA's narrative. In a 1973 document titled 'Family Jewels,' the CIA came clean to a reference to Operation Mockingbird in 1963, where they wiretapped two journalists who published stories based on classified information.

The bottom line is Congress got involved in what became known as the Church Committee. It was named after Idaho Senator Frank Church, who led the inquiry when information about the influence operation leaked. The operation engaged all the major newspapers, including the New York Times, the Washington Post, and others. Over 400 journalists were tied to Operation Mockingbird.

As with all Congressional hearings, nothing came of it, and we have what we have today: a very compliant press, mimicking the narrative of the day with a script provided from on high.

February 21, 1965

Malcolm X, a controversial black leader of his day and a former member of the Nation of Islam, was gunned down while speaking at the Audubon Ballroom in front of hundreds of attendees, including the NYPD. Five gunmen were identified by witnesses, two were captured by onlookers, and one was charged.

Malcolm X was indeed a controversial figure. He hated America and, by nearly all counts, hated white people. He joined the Nation of Islam and butted heads with its founder, Elijah Muhammad. He traveled internationally and sought to bring America to a world court for its atrocities. And he was no lover of Israel or the Jews.

There was a lot not to like about him, and it was the 60s, a time of social unrest, war protests, and a growing amount of violence. Malcolm was being watched by the FBI and the NYPD. He knew it, as did almost everyone else. There was no lack of detractors. J. Edgar Hoover, to put it mildly, was not a fan.

Malcolm X told his biographer, Alex Haley, *"It has always been my belief that I, too, will die by violence. I have done all that I can to be prepared. Each day I live as if I am already dead. I do not expect to live long enough to read this book in its finished form."*

It turns out X knew who was coming for him. At the scene of his murder, the names of five black Muslims were on a slip of paper found in his suit coat pocket. The investigation revealed Malcolm X's top bodyguard was an NYPD informant. The NYPD BOSSI unit, a highly secretive counter-intel unit, had members in attendance who made no effort to apprehend the shooters.

Much has been written about his assassination, and as with all events of its kind, there are many stories and lots of confusion. But what is known is that Malcolm's bodyguard, the informant, met with one of the shooters the night before the murder. That is in NYPD files.

Question ... was Malcolm X murdered by disgruntled Nation of Islam members, as the government narrative says? Or was he *Whacked!*

You decide.

March 27, 1965

Tom Howard died of a heart attack at the age of 48. Howard was with Jim Koethe and Bill Hunter, the last person at Ruby's apartment that night. He was not known to have heart problems.

Question ... was it simply Tom Howard's time? Or was he *Whacked!*

You decide.

May 28, 1965

Maurice B. Gatlin, a New Orleans attorney, fell from the ledge of a 6th-floor balcony and was pronounced dead. The Coroner ruled he had a heart attack and then fell over the edge. He was attending a meeting of the Inter-American Bar Association in San Juan, Puerto Rico.

Gatlin was a well-connected lawyer and fervent anti-Communist leader. He was also close to private investigator Guy Banister and associated with anti-Castro groups being investigated by New Orleans District Attorney Jim Garrison. He was also linked to exciting people, such as CIA agent E. Howard Hunt and mafia boss Carlos Marcello.

Hunt was the proverbial bad penny. He was said to have connections to a crime syndicate run by Seymour Weiss of Standard Fruit Company and to have sponsored the Guatemalan coup with Carlos Marcello. Hunt had once organized an anti-communist conference in Guatemala.

Gatlin was associated with the who's who of bad things happen to good people. Jim Garrison raided his office for information on the JFK assassination. He was reportedly a bag man for Guy Banister, carrying cash for the CIA in what turned out to be a group of the French foreign legion who wanted to assassinate Charles de Gaulle. Birds of a feather flock together is a tired old cliche ... but true.

Question ... did Mr. Gatlin die of a heart attack? Or was he *Whacked?*

You decide.

September 16, 1965

A DEFINITE MAYBE ...

An FBI source reported the KGB Residency in New York City received instructions on approximately September 16, 1965, from KGB headquarters in Moscow. They were ordered to develop all possible information concerning President Lyndon B. Johnson.

They wanted to know his character, background, personal friends, family, and from which quarters he derived his support in his position as President of the United States. Our source added that in the instructions from Moscow, it was indicated that 'now' the KGB had information indicating President Johnson was responsible for the assassination of the late President John F. Kennedy.

September 4, 1965

Melba Christine Marcades, a former stripper at Jack Ruby's nightclub and current drug mule, was killed when hit by a car and ran over. Her death was ruled accidental.

Ms. Marcades was an admitted mule for a heroine ring and would be a courier for the money. She was also known as one who had predicted precisely when and what would happen to JFK before his assassination. The guts of her story begin shortly before her demise.

It is told by Lieutenant Fruge of the Louisiana State Police. Lieutenant Fruge learned that Rose was a courier for the drug and prostitution ring that was known to be operating in the area. On November 20, 1963, during a pickup in Galveston and the ride back to Louisiana was tossed from the car by the traffickers. That is where Lieutenant Fruge and the deceased met.

While interviewing Marcades, Fruge was amazed to also find out the two men who tossed her from the car had discussed a conspiracy plan to assassinate President Kennedy in Dallas. Lieutenant Fruge would testify of this information to a Congressional committee in detail. Ms. Mercades, somehow, had prior knowledge of what happened in Dallas.

Question ... was Melba Christine Marcades a victim of a hit and run? Or was he *Whacked?*

You decide.

October 29, 1965

Lieutenant Commander William B. Pitzer, U.S. Navy, was found dead in his office, resting on his desk from a gunshot wound. His death was immediately ruled a suicide. Commander Pitzer died just a few days before retirement. He had spent that Saturday morning with his wife and went to the office with dinner plans that evening.

Lieutenant Commander William B. Pitzer was a crucial player in the autopsy of President Kennedy when his body was returned to Bethesda. As with so many of the unfortunate souls you've met here, this is a long story books have been written about. The bottom line is Pitzer knew the truth about the changes made before and during the autopsy to cover up the truth.

"When you have eliminated the impossible, whatever remains, *however improbable, must be the truth."* — Sherlock Holmes

A few things we know today ...

In 2010, Author/Researcher David Liston discovered an astonishing FBI report. It stated the President's body had been surgically altered (in addition to the tracheotomy) before the Bethesda autopsy.

The FBI report noted that the President's body, before the beginning of the autopsy, read as follows: it was ascertained that the President's clothing had been removed, and it was also apparent that a tracheotomy had been performed as well as surgery of the head area, namely, in the top of the skull. That means it was done in Dallas.

Another data point, FBI Special Agents James Sibert and Frank O'Neal testified under oath that President Kennedy's corpse was surgically altered before autopsy.

"FBI agents who were present at the NNMC when the body arrived noted in a field report that the "first incision" was made at 8:15 p.m. Based on comments made by one of the doctors present, they also noted that there had already been "surgery of the head area, namely, in the top of the skull." No such surgery had been performed in Dallas."

One investigator at the scene noted the evidence itself made it necessary to control the autopsy: The severe damage done to the President's head, including the massive exit wound at the rear, made it evident that he had been shot from the front. Many observed that the Secret Service 'kidnapped' the President's body from Texas authorities who actually had complete legal jurisdiction and who vehemently protested the seizure and ignored their legal authority in the case.

At Parkland, doctors reported seeing a neat and clearly delineated entry wound in the front throat, through which they made a standard emergency tracheotomy incision. By the time the body reached Bethesda, the incision in the throat was demonstrably larger.

The President's body was placed aboard Air Force One in a bronze ceremonial casket. It has been verified that the body arrived at the morgue in a plain shipping casket and that the bronze casket delivered separately was empty.

The anomalies in this case are too numerous to continue here. Commander Pitzer knew the truth about what was done to cover up the truth about how many shooters there were. The pattern you see here is repeated throughout this book.

Question ... did Lieutenant Commander William B. Pitzer die of a heart attack? Or was he *Whacked?*

You decide.

November 8, 1965

Dorothy Kilgallen ... a famous reporter and T.V. personality, a participant on *What's My Line*, was found dead in her posh 5-

story Manhattan apartment home, just off Park Avenue. The Medical Examiner determined that she died from acute ethanol and barbiturate intoxication and also noted circumstances undetermined.

Ms. Kilgallen was furious with what she saw as a coverup and let her opinion be known in her viral newspaper column. She said there was a whitewash of the JFK assassination. In fact, Kilgallen was the only reporter to have a jailhouse interview with Jack Ruby at his request. She was onto something.

Kilgallen told close friends she was saving all her info for her upcoming book, *Murder One*. Friends recall she was sure it would be a blockbuster and blow the lid off the case. The deeper in the case she dug, the more frightening it was. She told friends her life was in danger.

She made a mystery-filled trip to New Orleans. Her hairdresser, Marc Sinclaire, said, *"Her life had been threatened."* Her death was controversial and remains so. Since she knew people were after her, she gave backup copies of her material to her best friend, Florence Pritchett Smith, who died the next day. Her notes and manuscript for *Murder One* were never found. The backup notes which Dorothy had given her friend were never located either.

As with many of these coincidental cases, there is a lot written about the death of Dorothy Kilgallen.

Question ... did Ms. Kilgallen die of an accidental drug overdose? Or was she *Whacked?*

You decide.

November 9, 1965

Florence Pritchett Smith (also known as Mrs. Earl E. T. Smith), best friend of Dorothy Kilgallen and fellow columnist, died of a cerebral hemorrhage. She had been treated for leukemia, and officially, it was ruled as probably a result of that. And that could very well be true.

Except that Ms. Smith had been entrusted with the backup copy of Ms. Killgallen's book. That information was never found, meaning both copies of the information she discovered vanished.

Question ... did Ms. Smith die as a result of complications from her leukemia? Or was she *Whacked!*

You decide.

1966

January 9, 1966

Earlene Roberts, landlady of the rooming house where Lee Harvey Oswald lived, was found dead of a heart attack.

Mrs. Roberts was a nurse until she contracted diabetes and decided to rent rooms in her home in Oak Cliff, Dallas. On October 14, 1963, she rented a room to O. H. Lee, who turned out to be Lee Harvey Oswald. But the story doesn't end there.

When the Dallas Police called, Earleno didn't sing the tune they were playing. She should have been a key witness, but she testified that a Dallas Police car had sat outside and honked twice, and Oswald ran out and joined him. She also said Oswald came racing into the house at precisely 1 p.m. She knew that because a friend had called her at that exact time.

Mrs. Roberts stood her ground and told the police the car was number 106 at 1 p.m. This presented a problem for the narrative as 1 p.m. was the shooting time. Her relatives said that for the next 18 months, she was hounded by the Dallas police, day and night. She was leaned on to change her testimony.

Question ... did Earlene die from a heart attack? Or was she *Whacked?*

You decide.

February 16, 1966

Al "Guy" Bogard, a salesman at Dallas Lincoln Mercury and Lee Harvey Oswald witness, died of carbon monoxide poisoning. His death was ruled a suicide. He was found by his cousin.

Bogard, the car salesman who witnessed Lee Harvey Oswald—or an Oswald impersonator—test-driving a car at high speeds. That was significant because the honest Oswald reportedly could not drive. The person described as Oswald talked incessantly about Russia and said he could not afford the car but would be coming in for money soon.

People in the know thought it looked like, in intelligence parlance, creating a 'legend.' He also said he must return to Russia to get his car. Bogard also remembered he spoke loud so others could hear. The FBI challenged him and told him he had written the guy's name down on a business card but no longer had it.

The card was proof that someone impersonating Oswald had been at the car dealership. The FBI spent hours going through the dealership dumpsters looking for that card. The Bureau left no stone unturned to discredit Bogart. The cousin who found him, Jimmy Harper, said in a phone interview in 2001 that he *"knew that people were out to get him, and may have taken his own life for that reason."*

Question ... did Al Bogard die of suicide? Or was he *Whacked!*

You decide.

August 9, 1966

Lee Bowers, a tower man for the Union Terminal Company of Dallas, died as the result of an automobile accident. There was no autopsy, and the body was cremated shortly after the accident.

Bowers's testimony before the Warren Commission was considered explosive. He was one of 65 known witnesses to the JFK assassination who testified to shots being fired from the grassy knoll. Mr. Bowers was positioned behind and above the grassy knoll in his tower to be an eyewitness. He detailed several people's actions on and around the grassy knoll that directly opposed the official narrative. If he was correct, then the single shooter claims would be patently wrong.

Bowers did not die at the scene but from injuries sustained in the accident. Witnesses to the accident said a car ran him off the road and into the abutment. On the way to the hospital, he told first responders he thought he had been drugged at his stop at a cafe just before the accident.

Question ... was Bowers a simple victim of an auto accident and died of his injuries. Or was he *Whacked?*

You decide.

August 30, 1966

Marilyn Walle, also known as Delilah, Miranda, Marilyn Moon, Marilyn Magyar, and April Walle, exotic dancer and regular performer at Jack Ruby's Carousel Club in Dallas, died of multiple gunshot wounds. Her husband was arrested and convicted of her murder.

Marilyn Walle was a witness to the relationship between Lee Harvey Oswald and Jack Ruby, a fact the official narrative said was not valid.

Question ... did Ms. Walle die in a domestic situation at the hands of her husband. Or was she *Whacked?*

You decide.

1967

January 3, 1967

Jack Ruby, the infamous killer of Lee Harvey Oswald, died of an aggressive super cancer that surfaced after he won a judgment for a new trial.

Ruby consistently told those close to him he had been injected with cancer cells. That claim would probably be considered absurd today, but in the 60s, it was outlandish. What is known today, that wasn't known at the time, is that anti-Castro groups were working on a super cancer bioweapon to be deployed against Castro. And Jack Ruby had known ties to these groups.

There are more than a few oddities and coincidences in this case. Ruby was worried about his life, and many worried he would talk. Mafia boss Johnny Roselli told Washington Post reporter Jack Anderson that,

"When Oswald was picked up, the underworld conspirators feared he would crack and disclose information that might lead to them. This almost certainly would have brought a massive U.S. crackdown on the Mafia. So Jack Ruby was ordered to eliminate Oswald."

Ruby's fears were confirmed. He pleaded with Chief Justice Earl Warren to take him to Washington, D.C., where he would be safe and be able to explain what really happened. His request was denied. Another coincidence is that Ruby's rapid-onset cancer coincided with medical visits to him in jail from a well-known MKULTRA expert. MKULTRA was the top-secret CIA program, part of which was aimed at using drugs, hypnotism, and anything else available to control an individual's will.

As with so many of our subjects, books are written about Ruby and his demise.

Question ... did Ruby die from a random super cancer? Or was he *Whacked?*

You decide.

February 22, 1967

Eladio del Valle, Cuban Resistance leader and sought-after witness in Jim Garrison's investigation died of several gunshot wounds and machete blows.

In the exact same hour of del Valle's death, another Garrison witness set to testify, David Ferrie, committed suicide. Eladio del Valle worked simultaneously with the anti-Cuban underground, the CIA, and the underworld. It is believed he ordered the hit on Gilberto Rodriguez Hernandez and Manuel Rodriguez Quesada, who are listed elsewhere in this book.

Question ... was Eladio del Valle viciously murdered for no reason? Or was he *Whacked?*

You decide.

David Ferrie, anti-Castro operative and known associate of New Orleans Mob Boss Carlos Marcello, died of natural causes, according to authorities. Two typed suicide notes were found by his body.

Ferrie was recently indicted by DA Jim Garrison in the conspiracy to assassinate JFK. When served, Ferrie told Garrison, "You have just signed my death warrant."

Question ... did David Ferrie die of natural causes? Or was he *Whacked?*

You decide.

May 20, 1967

William (Bill) Waters, a sometime associate of Lee Harvey Oswald, was found dead. His cause of death was ruled a drug overdose from Demerol. No autopsy was performed.

According to Waters' Mother, Oswald and Hank Killam had visited her son, Bill, at her home before the assassination. She claimed her son attempted to talk the two out of their involvement in something he didn't believe would happen.

After that coincidence and the assassination, Waters called the FBI to report his encounter. He told his Mother that the FBI told him he knew too much and to keep his mouth shut. What's true and not is hard to understand in the world of coincidence.

Question ... did Waters die of a drug overdose? Or was he *Whacked?*

You decide.

July 23, 1967

Desmond Fitzgerald was in charge of all Clandestine Operations at the CIA and reportedly died of a heart attack. But it is well to note what Richard Case Nagell, a veteran Military Intelligence covert operative, had to say about Fitzgerald's death.

In *The Man Who Knew Too Much,* he says, *"Now there is a corpse that should be exhumed and examined by a qualified pathologist."*

Question ... did Fitzgerald die of a heart attack? Or was he *Whacked?*

You decide.

December 17, 1967

Harold Holt, 59, Prime Minister of Australia, went to a secluded beach with friends. He decided to swim in the surf and was never seen again. In just two days, the Australian government declared him dead by drowning. No sign of his body ever turned up. No sign of his clothes, nothing.

There are no signs of foul play. The oddity is how a Prime Minister can disappear. He was a strong swimmer, an active snorkeler, and comfortable in the water. There are differing stories regarding who was with him at the time. Official sources say one government official was with him. Other sources say he had a girlfriend whom he snuck away with some friends.

The Prime Minister supported the Vietnam War, which was becoming very unpopular in Australia. Those close to him said he was about to withdraw all Australian troops from Vietnam, which has led some to believe the CIA might have helped with this coincidence. His successor to the Prime Ministership was also a big supporter of the war.

We'll never know, but you must admit, going for a swim and never being seen again is quite a coincidence. Question ... was Prime Minister Holt a drowning victim? Or was he *Whacked?*

You decide.

1968

April 4, 1968

Martin Luther King, controversial civil rights leader, and Reverend, was killed by an assassin. A lowlife by the name of James Earl Ray was apprehended and charged with his murder.

As with so many of these high-profile, controversial coincidences, many books have been written on Martin Luther King's death. One particular book stands out as smoke and mirrors. On January 26, 1975, *Time Magazine* quoted from one such book, *The Making of an Assassin*. Author George McMillan portrays James Earl Ray as the proverbial racist.

McMillan claims that while Ray was imprisoned in 63 and 64, he would watch Martin Luther King on T.V. and exclaim, *"I'm gonna' kill that nigger King!"* And this is where the story begins.

McMillan is supporting the narrative of the race-hating James Earl Ray. But there's a problem with his story. The Jefferson City prison in 63 and 64 did not have T.V. in the cell blocks.

Why did McMillan put out an untruth? He was married to Priscilla Johnson, a CIA asset. To put Ms. Johnson in perspective, she traveled to Moscow in 1959 and just happened to interview, by coincidence, defector Lee Harvey Oswald. Her interview was set up by American consul John McVickar.

While there, Johnson shared a residence with Oswald's wife, Marina. A weirder coincidence occurred when Joseph Stalin's daughter, Svetlana, defected from the Soviet Union to the United States. She stayed with Johnson's parents. And when Svetlana Stalin wanted to write her biography, Priscilla Johnson wrote it. Isn't history fun?

Similar to Lee Harvey Oswald, James Earl Ray was loosely tied to the CIA and the mob. According to his Brother, their father was in the mob. Both Oswald and Ray were on federal authorities' radar for years. In Ray's case, he'd been on the books since 1948. Attorney William F. Pepper quotes a March 21, 1993 article by a reporter for The Memphis Commercial Appeal, Steve Tompkins: "Army intelligence had spied on Dr. King's family for three generations."

In William Pepper's book, *An Act of State*, he related that in December 1963, he found that FBI officials had met in Washington, D.C., to discuss the neutralization of King's leadership. He found they discussed things like hidden microphones, blackmail, wiretaps, burglaries, and tapes delivered to his wife proving his extramarital affair.

Infamous mobster Sam Giancana described the CIA and Mafia as 'two sides of the same coin.' The government is known to have used mobsters for covert operations to maintain plausible deniability.

That means it wouldn't be a big surprise to believe reports of a meeting in January 1968 in Appalachian, New York. The meeting was between representatives of the CIA, FBI, Sam Giancana, Carlo

Gambino, and Johnny Roselli. The government reportedly offered the three representatives of the dark side a $1 million contract to take out MLK. Giancana outright refused.

The unfortunate fact is that Martin Luther King Jr. was indeed murdered by someone. Was it a lone nut case by the name of James Earl Ray because he hated niggers? We don't know.

Question ... was Martin Luther King the victim of the lone gunman? Or was he *Whacked?*

You decide.

June 5, 1968:

Robert F. Kennedy, the Democratic nominee for President, was shot dead after a speech in Los Angeles.

After delivering his speech at the Embassy Ballroom of the Ambassador HotelKennedy received three bullet wounds, at least one well placed behind his right ear, resulting in his death, and another in his suit jacket. A young Arab man named Sirhan Sirhan was immediately tackled by bodyguards. Sirhan continued to pull the trigger of his .22 caliber pistol. He emptied his gun while being beaten by the bodyguards.

And that was the official line would be a lone crazy man, Sirhan Sirhan, somehow got into the kitchen, passed the bevy of bodyguards, and was close enough to shoot probably the next President of the United States while standing in front of him. Where did the entry wound behind his left ear originate? Like his Brother, JFK, RFK went down for the count.

A few oddities ...

Experts determined the bullets that killed RFK did not come from Sirhans Over Johnson.

At no point was Sirhan close enough to deliver the kill shot. Witnesses agreed on this point.

The Coroner determined the shots that killed him came from 1 to 3 inches away. Sirhan was never that close.

The primary shooter was at close range, behind the target to his right. Sirhan was confirmed to be at his front, and he left, approaching him.

Sirhan's weapon held only 8 bullets. 14 bullets were determined to be fired at the scene. Meaning there were at least two shooters.

Question ... was Robert F. Kennedy assassinated by Sirhan Bishara Sirhan? Or was he *Whacked?*

You   decide.

The Seventies

What Did Your Government Do?

The decade of the 1970s continued, and the madness began in the 1960s. Watergate brought down President Richard Nixon and gave us a slate grey President in Gerald Ford.

The Watergate break-in would go down in history as one of the dumbest moves by any President. Nixon had the Presidential race in the bag, but his hunger for power knew no bounds. His resignation was unprecedented in our nation's history and began the slide of confidence in government that continues to this day.

The ten-year Vietnam War ended unglamorously, with the world watching a futile evacuation of the US Embassy in Saigon as North Vietnamese troops stormed the streets. We also saw OPEC become a household name when the oil embargo sent gas prices soaring and hour-long waits for a gallon.

The Civil Rights movement continued its momentum, and the Women's Movement was now close behind in driving social change. The first African American candidate ran for President, and let's not forget ESPN sprang onto TV screens everywhere.

The Supreme Court gave us Roe vs. Wade, sentencing untold millions of unborn babies to their deaths. Elvis died, The Godfather and Star Wars won the Oscars, and the Cold War continued with Russia invading Afghanistan and stepping into its own Vietnam.

The 70s also brought to light a CIA project that began in the late 50s and ran through the '60s and later. The CIA operated what became known as Project MK-ULTRA. The project was a covert CIA mind control program. It was run by the CIA's Office of Scientific Intelligence. The program was driven by a perceived need to keep up with the Soviet Union, China, and North Korea.

The CIA recruited scientists, including chemist Sidney Gottlieb, who led the effort. They clandestinely performed a wide range of experiments, including the use of LSD and other drugs, hypnosis, and other psychological and physical torture techniques on unwitting people, including many American citizens.

Experiments were conducted at universities, research centers, prisons, and detention centers, often without the knowledge or consent of the participants. Recently released documents show iconic figures like Timothy Leery were paid to have parties at CIA apartments in New York and San Francisco, where they would hand out free LSD so their reactions could be observed.

Details of the program came to light in the 70s, resulting in Congressional investigations of which, as always, nothing came of it. The program caused significant harm, with some subjects experiencing psychological damage or worse. The full impact of MK-ULTRA will never be known because the CIA destroyed records during the hearings in Congress.

Think about the COVID-19 vaccines in the context of the CIA's history. Still think they're safe?

1970

July 30, 1970

Lewis Lomax, a well-known T.V. personality, black activist, and writer, died when the brakes on his car failed and he crashed.

Lomax was well known in the black community. In 1958, he became the first African-American television journalist to join WNTA-TV in New York. One of his notable contributions was collaborating with Mike Wallace on a groundbreaking five-part documentary called *'The Hate That Hate Produced.'*

In the late '60s, he started looking into the assassination of Martin Luther King and that of Malcolm X. He also looked into the role Guy Bannister might have played in the JFK assassination. His findings led him to implicate the American intelligence community.

Here comes Mr. Coincidence again ... after inking a movie deal based on his findings, his brakes failed on his car, and he was killed in the subsequent crash.

Question ... did Mr. Lomax die of an unfortunate auto accident? Or was he *Whacked?*

You decide.

1971

January 7, 1971

Malcolm Everett 'Mac' Wallace, economist for the United States Department of Agriculture, died in a one-vehicle accident south of Pittsburg, Texas. The circumstances of his death remain controversial.

Mac Wallace was a key player in LBJs rise to the top of the political ladder. He was convicted of the 1952 murder of John Douglas Kinser in the clubhouse of the Austin golf course he owned. Rumors persist it was done on the orders of LBJ.

In 1952, Wallace was viewed as LBJ's personal hitman. After Wallace's conviction for murder with malice aforethought, the jury recommended the death penalty. The judge handed down a baffling sentence of five years probation with no time in jail. He never served a day. His sentence was later overturned.

LBJ's longtime attorney, Lee Cofer, rewarded Mac Wallace with a new job at a Texas manufacturing company.

Question ... did Mac Wallace die from injuries incurred in his mysterious car accident? Or was he *Whacked!*

You decide.

April 26, 1971

Win Scott, CIA Station Chief in Mexico City during the time Lee Harvey Oswald was known to frequent intelligence circle in Mexico, died of a heart attack two years after his retirement.

During those two years, Scott wrote a manuscript about his career adventures. Upon his death, the CIA's Counterintelligence Chief, James Angleton, quickly confiscated many sensitive materials. Angleton took a manuscript and three cartons of files containing tape recordings of Lee Harvey Oswald.

Scott's son fought to get the materials back from the CIA. He got some things back, but everything regarding his father's life after 1947 was removed for 'National Security.' Which is an all too common ploy by our government.

Did Win Scott, a lifetime CIA agent, die of a heart attack? Or was he *Whacked?*

You decide.

May 17, 1971

Ed Voebel, a friend of Lee Harvey Oswald at Beauregard Junior High School in New Orleans, passed away at the age of 31 in New Orleans, Louisiana. The specific cause of Edward Sidney Voebel's death was not disclosed, but he died at the Ochsner Clinic in New Orleans.

His testimony was taken on April 7, 1964, at the Old Civil Courts Building in New Orleans regarding the Kennedy Assassination. Voebel was a witness whose testimony actually proved that there had to be an intelligence 'double' for Lee Harvey Oswald.

Author John Armstrong, decades after the fact, substantiated that at least two 'Oswalds' had to have been used in the spy games of the U.S. intelligence community before, during, and after his staged defection to the Soviet Union. It is believed that 'defection' was a brilliant maneuver.

Question ... did Ed Voebel die a natural death? Or was he *Whacked?*

You decide.

September 21, 1971

Cliff Carter, 58, Lyndon B. Johnson's administration member, died at 58 from pneumonia. Carter was a significant player in the transition of LBJ to the White House following JFKs death.

Penn Jones's January 1984 article in *Rebel Magazine* covers Carter's death. The article, titled Disappearing Witnesses, quotes the infamous Billie Sol Estes, who claims that Carter's death was urged by the Johnson clan, which was paranoid about Johnson's legacy.

Question ... did Cliff Carter die of pneumonia? Or was he *Whacked?*

You decide.

1972

January 1972

James Morton, President Gerald Ford's campaign treasurer, died suddenly. Little information is available on his death.

The *New York Times* reported on November 2, 1973, that Ford was questioned by a senate committee before he was appointed vice president. He was asked about the $38,000 used in his campaign for the House of Representatives, which was kept a secret.

The *New York Times* said, "*Ford confirmed under questioning that a committee organized in Washington raised $38,216 for his reelection in 1972, but he did not know the names of the donors. When queried why, he said the committee treasurer, James G. Morton, is now dead.*"

Watergate money had a way of being anonymous and disappearing.

Question ... did James Morton die a natural death? Or was he *Whacked?*

You decide.

February, 1972

James Webster and James Glover, were critical men in Congressman Maryland Congressman William Mills's campaign for reelection, were both killed in a car accident.

At the time, there was no connection to future events. After Watergate, the *Washington Post* reported on May 23, 1973, that Campaign Manager James Webster received an illegal $25,000 contribution delivered personally to him.

Question ... did these gentlemen die in a legitimate auto accident? Or were they *Whacked?*

You decide.

Robert McClean Wilson, an up-and-coming design engineer and technical writer at Marconi Defense Systems in Essex and Chelmsford, England, shot himself in the chest while cleaning his pistol.

The oddities are just beginning. Wilson was cleaning a loaded .45 pistol with the barrel aimed at himself. A strange thing to do for a man entirely involved in a local gun club.

What led up to this fateful day? Wilson decided to clean up his attack. He found boxes of sensitive and classified files from Marconi, where he worked. Shocked, knowing it wasn't his work, how did they get there? He didn't even regularly handle classified files.

Wilson was worried and wasted no time in contacting Marconi. A major internal investigation was quickly launched. After grilling Wilson for days, Marconi's security staff decided he had misplaced the files and dropped the matter.

Amazingly, Wilson survived the ordeal as the bullet missed his heart by half an inch. He returned to work at Marconi ... but that's not where the story ends.

Note: This story will be reconnected in May of 1983.

March 1972

Dr. and Mrs. Gary Morris died when their boat disappeared off the Caribbean Island of St. Lucia. Their bodies were never found, and the event remains a mystery.

Their deaths would not be in this book of coincidences but for a couple of later facts that surfaced. When Dorothy Hunt, wife of E. Howard Hunt went down in the United Airlines crash on December 8, 1972; Morris' name was in her wallet.

On October 3, 1975, the *Washington Post* published a story that read,

"The plane crash that killed Mrs. Hunt in Chicago has now been officially ruled an accident. But there's one bizarre coincidence that may never be explained. Her red wallet at the time of her death had a slip of paper with the name of a Washington psychiatrist, Dr. Gary Morris, on it."

A check on Dr. Morris's patients revealed that neither of the Hunts was his patient. And Dr. Gary Morris was dead at the time of the plane crash. Another coincidence is that Dr. Morris was an expert in hypnosis and was known as CIA operative E. Howard Hunt was said to use mind control in his espionage work. Fascinating.

Question ... did the Doctor and his excellent wife disappear, or was the boat never found? Or were they *Whacked?*

You decide.

April 6, 1972

Mrs. Andrew Topping, the wife of Andrew Topping, the man arrested for plotting to kill Nixon, died of gunshot wounds. Her death was declared a suicide.

Her death occurred two weeks after the Watergate break-in. Andrew Topping told police that *"he believed pro-right people beyond his control caused his wife's death."* There was no further investigation.

Question ... did Mrs. Topping commit suicide? Or was she *Whacked?*

You decide.

May 2, 1972

J. Edgar Hoover, longtime Director of the Federal Bureau of Investigation (FBI), died of a heart attack at the age of 77 ... or did he?

Hoover ruled with an iron fist for 48 years. Rumors persist that President Truman and Kennedy lived in fear of challenging him. One floating quote was this ... '*Hoover does not have to exert pressure, he is pressure.*' And that he did. He was a double-edged sword. For our nation of laws, he was the man. Under his leadership, the FBI enjoyed tremendous support and was viewed as a bastion of integrity.

But as with all of us, there were two sides to J. Edgar. While dying of a heart attack at age 77 is reasonable, there are those close to the situation who believed he may have had a little help along the way. At the time of JFKs assassination, it was speculated that a cover-up had to involve the FBI. Today, we know that it did. He was J. Edgar; he knew everything.

Today, the theory is that his death was not triggered by the JFK fiasco but rather by Watergate. Richard Nixon was President then, and in 1971, he established a White House Intelligence Unit, the first of its kind. Hoover vigorously objected, feeling it was taking power away from his FBI. Nixon may have been the first President to challenge J. Edgar's authority.

A short time later, Hoover's apartment was broken into into the first of two break-ins. These break-ins were later sworn to under oath by Filipe De Diego, an associate of the infamous E. Howard Hunt and G. Gordon Liddy, both of whom were later connected to the Watergate break-in.

Another twist in the Hoover plot is then-Attorney General John Mitchell.

Mitchell ordered the FBI to wiretap select organizations and critical people for him. Hoover agreed as long as the secret transcripts were kept in secret files in his office. Mitchell later reneged and asked a friend to secretly move the files to John Ehrlichman's office. Somehow, Senior FBI Agent William Sullivan, who later died in a strange hunting accident, was given the task of moving the files.

Admittedly, the White House was a den of thieves at the time, but Hoover died of a heart attack at age 77. Isn't that reasonable? Of course, it is. But consider this. The official cause of death was 'hyperactive cardiovascular disease.' But Hoover had no history of heart problems. As with many of our coincidences, no autopsy was performed on Hoover.

On December 12, 1973, the Harvard Crimson ran an article on the two burglaries of Hoover's apartment. They claimed that during the second burglary, Hoover's toilet articles were coated with a solution of the phosphate poison that, when touched, caused an immediate heart muscle seizure. Other sources mention the use of sodium-morphate, which accomplishes the same results. Stranger things have happened.

J. Edgar Hoover crossed Nixon, and he also publicly stated he believed that separate bullets, fired from different locations, struck Governor Connolly and President Kennedy. Did America's long-standing top cop outlive his usefulness?

Question ... did J. Edgar Hoover die a natural death from a heart attack? Or was his heart attack given a nudge, and he was *Whacked?*

You decide.

June 17, 1972

A LITTLE CONTEXT ...

On this date, one of the biggest scandals in American history began with a break-in of the Democratic National Committee headquarters at the Watergate Complex in Washington, D.C. It occurred during President Richard Nixon's administration and was leading up to the upcoming election.

When the truth came out, his administration was involved in a series of covert and illegal activities, such as bugging political opponents' offices, investigating activist groups, and using federal agencies for political purposes.

A chain of events followed, exposing a cover-up at the highest levels of the federal government. White House tapes were subpoenaed and, when received, had a mysterious 18 minutes missing. Many fatal coincidences followed this debacle, the least of which was President Nixon's resignation and the firing and jailing of some of his aides.

The entire affair was unprecedented in American politics.

October 16, 1972

Hale Boggs, Democratic Congressman and House Majority Leader from Louisiana, and two other men disappeared when the light aircraft they were in is believed to have crashed in Alaska. Neither the plane nor Boggs were ever found. He was officially declared dead on December 29, 1972.

Boggs was an influential Congressman and former member of the Warren Commission. His death came a couple months following the Watergate arrests. On November 22, 1973, the *Los Angeles Star* reported that "*Boggs had startling revelations on Watergate and the assassination of President Kennedy.*"

Richard Nixon was found to have made some unintelligible remarks about Congressman Boggs, which were found on the White House tapes, just seven days after the Watergate break-in.

Question ... was Congressman Boggs a victim of a plane crash? Or was he *Whacked?*

You decide.

December 2, 1972

Richard Lavoie, chief of security for International Telegraph and Telephone, died of a heart attack.

At the time of his death, Lavoie was away guarding Ditta Beard. Beard was an ITT secretary who claimed she had a memo that her company had contributed $400,000 to Nixon's campaign fund so that John Mitchell would not bust up some of ITT's holdings.

She went to columnist Jack Anderson, who broke the story. It was such a blow that ITT was concerned about Miss Beard's safety. She was moved from Washington to Denver, Colorado. Upon arrival, she was hospitalized for an apparent heart attack. After she was whisked away, Anderson claimed she could no longer testify.

Lavoie had a heart attack while in Denver.

Question ... did Richard Lavoie die of a heart attack? Or was he *Whacked?*

You decide.

December 8, 1972

Dorothy Hunt, the wife of convicted White House 'plumber' E. Howard Hunt was killed, along with 41 other people, when United Airlines Flight 553 crashed near Chicago's Midway Airport.

Both Dorothy and her husband, E. Howard Hunt worked for the CIA. While it has never been proven, there was a strong belief that Dorothy Hunt was carrying $100,000 in 'hush' money so her husband would not implicate White House officials in Watergate.

Admittedly, it seems far-fetched to take down a plane full of people to send a message to one man. But consider the odd coincidences that followed the plane's downing.

One day after the crash, White House aide Bud Krogh was appointed Undersecretary of Transportation, supervising the National Transportation Safety Board and the Federal Aviation Association - the two agencies investigating the airline crash.

One week after the crash, Nixon's deputy assistant, Alexander Butterfield, was made the new head of the FAA.

Five weeks after the crash, Dwight Chapin, the President's appointment secretary, became a top executive with United Airlines.

The NTSB and FAA ruled the crash was the result of equipment malfunctions.

Question ... was Dorothy Hunt and her 41 new best friends the victim of poor equipment at United Airlines? Or were they *Whacked?*

You decide.

Ralph Blodgett and James Krueger, attorneys for Northern Natural Gas Company, were killed in the same airplane as Mrs. Hunt and 39 others.

In yet another coincidence, the two attorneys reportedly were traveling with documents linking Attorney General John Mitchell to Watergate and documents of a secret transfer of El Paso Natural Gas Company stock made to Mitchell after the Justice Department dropped a $300 million anti-trust suit against the company.

Blodgett told friends the money may have been used for political espionage, and the last thing he said before boarding the plane was, *"I may never live to get to Chicago."*

Question ... were these two lawyers victims of circumstance? Or were they *Whacked?*

You decide.

1973

January 20, 1973

Lyndon Baines Johnson, the former President, died on January 20, 1973, in a helicopter ambulance en route to San Antonio, Texas. Johnson was old, depressed, and in ill health at the time he passed.

But just three months before his death, Johnson told the *San Francisco Chronicle, "We've been running a damn Murder Inc. in the Caribbean."* His revelation would come some two years before Senator Frank Church's committee revealed the plots to assassinate foreign leaders and long after he left the White House.

Probably means nothing except 'coincidentally' Johnson died in the arms of a secret service agent, Mike Howard, who in 1963 was assigned to protect Marina Oswald after her husband was killed.

Question ... did President Johnson die of natural causes? Or was he *Whacked?*

You decide.

May 1973

Robert McClean Wilson, the Marconi employee who 'shot himself' a year ago and lived, was found dead in his garage at home.

The verdict was accidental death by exposure to carbon monoxide poisoning. It seems he did this while he serviced his car, with the engine running and the garage door shut. Now, that's a coincidence.

Question ... did Mr. Wilson do two stupid things, and one killed him? Or was he *Whacked?*

You decide.

Gerald Jack Harlow, an apprentice working at Marconi in Chelmsford, England, was discovered dead in his flat with a knife protruding from his chest. After a quick investigation on the day of Harlow's death, crime was ruled out as a cause of death. A while later, his death was ruled a suicide.

Question ... did Gerald Jack Harlow stab himself in the chest and die? Or was he *Whacked?*

You decide.

May 26, 1973

J. Clifford Dieterich, a 28-year-old secret service agent assigned to Nixon, was killed when the President's helicopter crashed off the coast of the Bahamas in May of 1973.

Dieterich was one of seven men in the helicopter but the only one to die in the crash. This is purely speculation, but some believe that, after guarding Richard Nixon, he might have known too much.

Question ... was Special Agent Dieterich a victim of a freak accident? Or was he *Whacked?*

You decide.

May 24, 1973

William Mills, a Congressman from Maryland, was found shot to death, an apparent suicide. His death was another coincidence following Watergate.

The news came a day after it was disclosed that he failed to report a $25,000 campaign contribution given to him by President Nixon's reelection finance committee. It would later be revealed that the $25,000 came from the 1.7 million-dollar secret fund for 'dirty tricks' used by the Committee to Re-Elect the President.

Mills was discovered with a 12-gauge shotgun by his feet and an 'alleged suicide note' pinned to his body. The subsequent investigation revealed 7 other suicide notes.

Question ... did Congressman Mills die by his own hand? Or was he *Whacked?*

You decide.

June 30, 1973

George Bell, assistant to Charles Colson and special counsel to the White House, died of unreported causes.

Chuck Colson, of Watergate fame, was questioned about President Nixon's infamous' enemies list'. Colson told the House Subcommittee Investigating Watergate that the "late George Bell was responsible for the list of 200 celebrities and politicians whom the President considered dangerous."

Question ... did George Bell die of natural causes? Or was he *Whacked?*

You decide,

July 2, 1973

Nikos J. Vardinoyiannis, a Greek shipowner who contributed funds to Nixon's presidential campaign, died of a heart attack at the age of 42.

Watergate prosecutor Leon Jaworski investigated Vardinoyiannis for illegal campaign contributions to Nixon. Nixon's Justice Department declared the contribution was legal.

The Department reached this conclusion even though the contribution was made after one of Vardinoyiannis' companies was contracted to supply fuel for the U.S. 6th Fleet. Federal law bars foreign contractors from contributing to U.S. political campaigns, so the contribution is undoubtedly questionable.

Question ... did the Greek shipping magnate die an early death from a heart attack? Or was he *Whacked?*

You decide.

July 31, 1973

Lou Russell, an old friend of Nixon's, died of natural causes.

In testimony before the Senate Select Committee on Presidential Campaign Activities, Nixon's secretary, Rosemary Wood, stated: *"I met Lou Russell once when he came to the office. He said he worked on the old House Un-American Activity Committee and that he needed a job."*

Russell did indeed find a job that day with Cord Associates, a well-known CIA front run by James McCord of Watergate fame.

Question ... did Lou Russell die of natural causes? Or was he *Whacked?*

You decide.

September 11, 1973

A LITTLE PERSPECTIVE ...

On September 11, 1973, the Chilean military, led by General Augusto Pinochet, staged a coup and seized power, ending Salvador Allende's civilian rule. Allende died during the assault on the presidential palace under suspicious circumstances.

The coup was supported by the Chilean oligarchy, middle class, and some Christian Democratic forces, who believed it necessary to restore the status quo before Allende's election. The military junta led by Pinochet consolidated power and started a brutal campaign of political repression, torture, and human rights abuses against leftist and opposition groups in Chile.

It was soon discovered that U.S. military personnel were on the ground, and U.S. warships were off the coast standing by. Two U.S. journalists who were on the ground and exposed U.S. involvement were murdered. In one of the cases, the journalist was given a ride to his home by a supposed member of the U.S. Embassy, Captain Ray Davis. It was later learned that Davis was the leader of a covert U.S. military unit advising during the coup.

The coup marked the end of Chile's long democratic tradition and ushered in Pinochet's 17-year military dictatorship. Under President Richard Nixon and Secretary of State Henry Kissinger, the U.S. government was aware of and played a role in creating favorable conditions for the military coup.

Years later, in November 2011, a Chilean court indicted Captain Ray Davis. A year later, their Supreme Court approved a request to extradite Davis to Chile so he could be tried for his role in the deaths of the two American journalists.

Frank Teruggi, another American journalist in Chile, was also found dead. For the next 40 years, Horman's family fought to identify Horman's murderers and bring them to justice. In November 2011, a Chilean court indicted Ray Davis. A year later, their Supreme Court approved a request to extradite Davis to Chile so he could be tried for his role in the deaths of Horman and Teruggi.

September 17, 1973

Charles Horman, an American journalist, writer, filmmaker, and whistleblower regarding the 1973 Chilean coup d'état and America's involvement, ended up dead after being taken into custody after the coup.

Horman wrote about U.S. involvement in overthrowing the democratically-elected socialist President Salvador Allende. Shortly after the takeover, Horman was taken by Chilean soldiers to an ad hoc concentration camp in Santiago. His whereabouts were kept undisclosed for months until his body was discovered at a morgue.

The U.S. government maintained its innocence in Horman's death, but a 1976 State Department memo described the case as bothersome and involved negligence on our part, or worse, complicity.

The State Department memo read ...

"U.S. intelligence may have played an unfortunate part in Horman's death. At best, it was limited to providing or

confirming information that helped motivate his murder by the [government of Chile]. At worst, U.S. intelligence was aware the [government of Chile] saw Horman in a rather serious light, and U.S. officials did nothing to discourage the logical outcome of [Chilean] paranoia."

A Chilean spy charged as an accomplice in Horman's death claimed that a CIA agent was present during Horman's kidnapping and interrogation, and the same CIA agent was also present when Chilean authorities decided to execute Horman.

Question ... did Charles Horman die a natural death at the hands of Chilean armed forces? Or was he *Whacked?*

You decide.

September 20, 1973

Frank Teruggi, 24, an American student at the University of Chile and journalist, died after being abducted and murdered by the Chilean military during the coup.

Teruggi, a member of the Industrial Workers of the World (IWW), was kidnapped, tortured, and murdered for his articles on the coup.

Question ... did young Frank Teruggi meet his fate because of the coup? Or was he *Whacked* because of what he knew and where he was from?

You decide.

November, 1973

Jack Cleveland, a partner of the President's brother Donald Nixon, died in Canada.

Little information exists on Cleveland's death. At the time, he was wanted for questioning in connection with a possible government pay-off to Howard Hughes. Cleveland was suspected of being a go-between in a deal whereby Nixon's brother became interested in a large Nevada ranch.

The deal was allegedly in exchange for the President clearing the way for billionaire Hughes's takeover of Air West. Speculation? Maybe.

Question ... did Jack Cleveland pass away naturally while in Canada? Or was he *Whacked?*

You decide.

December, 1973

Beverly Kaye, 42, reportedly died of a 'massive stroke' in December while riding in the White House elevator.

Ms. Kaye was the secretary of Secret Service agent John Bull. Her job included storing and preserving the White House tapes. Kaye had told her friends and neighbors she knew the President (Nixon) and his aides were involved in the Watergate bugging and cover-up.

If you'll recall, there were 18 minutes of missing tape coincidentally erased before Congress got them. Since Beverly Kaye was in charge of the recordings, it is quite a coincidence that a 42-year-old healthy woman suffered a massive stroke.

Question ... did Beverly Kaye suffer a massive stroke? Or was she *Whacked?*

You decide.

December 20, 1973

Richard Cain, Chief Investigator for the Cook County (Chicago) Sheriff's Department, was murdered by a shotgun blast to his head at his side business, Rose's Sandwich Shop.

On the night of December 20, two masked intruders entered the sandwich shop and told all the employees, including Cain, to line up facing the wall. They then singled out Cain; he turned around and was shot in the face. It was a mob hit.

Richard Cain was a cop—and a dirty one at that. He was also on the payroll of Sam' the Man' Giancani and an FBI informant. In Mario Puzo's *The Godfather,* Cain is the model for the character of Frank Neri, a vicious Mafia contract killer with a police badge.

According to the Giancani's, Cain was one of the Dallas shooters in the JFK assassination. That has never been proven. But Cain was known by authorities to have inside information on what took place in Dallas.

Question ... did Richard Cain die because of his Mafia ties? Or was he *Whacked?*

You decide.

1974

1974

Jose Joaquin Sangenis Perdimo, a Cuban exile who worked with the CIA at the Bay of Pigs, died mysteriously in 1974.

Code-named "Felix," he is known to have worked with Watergate burglars Hunt and Barker. In 1972, he was awarded a secret merit medal by the CIA. The CIA stated he died of natural causes and did not notify his family until after the funeral.

Question ... did Jose, a CIA man, die of natural causes? Or was he *Whacked?*

You decide.

January 23, 1974

Murray Chotiner, a longtime close friend and aide of President Nixon's, was killed when a government truck ran into his car on January 23, 1974.

First reports of the accident said Chotiner suffered a broken leg; no other injuries were reported. However, he died a week later. To this day, his death is listed as killed in a car accident.

The *Los Angeles Times* reported on March 31, 1973, that Chotiner may have received the tape recordings from the Democratic campaign headquarters in the Watergate building.

Question ... did Murray Chotiner die as a result of a car accident? Or was he *Whacked?*

You decide.

July 3, 1974

Louise Boyer died from the 10th story of a New York apartment.

Mrs. Boyer was Nelson Rockefeller's personal assistant for 30 years. Her death was ruled a suicide. After Nixon's resignation as a result of Watergate, Rockefeller was considered to be Vice President.

Accusations were swirling, and an investigation was underway that gold had been illegally removed from Ft. Knox and that Rockefeller was involved. It is believed that Boyer was the source of that information.

Question ... did this very successful and steady woman jump to her death to commit suicide? Or was she *Whacked?*

You decide.

August 16, 1974

Clay Shaw, who years earlier had been acquitted of conspiracy to kill John F. Kennedy, died of a heart attack. Shaw was cremated immediately with no autopsy.

His death came a few weeks after Victor Marchetti, author of The Cult of Intelligence, revealed that Shaw had worked for the CIA. It was revealed Shaw had been on assignment in Mexico in 1963. That was the same time as CIA agent E. Howard Hunt and Lee Harvey Oswald.

Question ... did Clay Shaw die of a heart attack? Or was he *Whacked?*

You decide.

October 28, 1974

Lee Pennington, Jr., a CIA agent, died of an apparent heart attack.

Pennington worked at the CIA under Director Richard Helms. Helms assigned him the task of breaking into Watergate burglar James McCords's home, but the CIA Chief did not reveal this to investigators at the time.

Four months after Pennington's death, new CIA Director William Colby, on June 28, 1974, revealed to Senator Howard Baker that *"The results of our investigation clearly show that the CIA had in its possession, as early as June 1972, information that one of its paid operatives, Lee R. Pennington, Jr., had entered the James McCord residence shortly after the Watergate break-in and destroyed documents which might show a link between McCord and the CIA."*

What tangled webs we weave.

Question ... did CIA operative Lee Pennington Jr. die of a heart attack? Or was he *Whacked?*

You decide.

November 13, 1974:

Karen Silkwood, a chemical technician at an Oklahoma nuclear facility and the first female member of the union negotiating committee, died in a questionable auto accident. There was no follow-up investigation.

She made plutonium pellets at the Kerr-McGee Cimarron Fuel Fabrication Site in Oklahoma. She became a whistleblower to the Atomic Energy Commission regarding her concerns about the industry's inadequate health and safety standards.

After testifying to the Atomic Energy Commission about her concerns, she was found to have plutonium contamination on her body and in her home. While driving to meet with a *New York Times* journalist and an official of her union's national office, she died in a car crash, the circumstances of which were never explained entirely or investigated.

Question ... did Karen Silkwood die from a legitimate auto accident? Or was she *Whacked?*

You decide.

1975

April 1, 1975

George Parr, the Duke of Duval County and close friend and fixer for Lyndon Baines Johnson was found dead after a search by law enforcement officials.

The police helicopters spotted Parr's Chrysler in a fenced clearing on the southeast corner of his Los Horcones Ranch in Duval County, Texas. Parr had lots of problems; his latest was tax evasion. When the chopper landed, it found Parr slumped over the wheel of his car, a spent cartridge on the floor along with his dentures. Suicide?

Parr was the linchpin in the Box 13 scandal that put LBJ in Congress in 1948. In 1977, Parr's right-hand man in Alice, Texas, Jim Wells County, was Deputy Sheriff Luis Salas. After Parr's death and the deaths of LBJ and Coke, Stevenson Salas came clean.

Luis Salas admitted to lying under oath in the 'Box 13' scandal. He confirmed Parr orchestrated the scandal, and Johnson was present when Parr told Salas what needed to be done and that he. Salas certified the added names. A tangled web, yet no one to blame.

Question ... did George Parr die of a self-inflicted gunshot wound? Or was he *Whacked?*

You decide.

June 19, 1975

Sam Giancana, a nationally powerful mobster headquartered in Chicago with substantial business interests in Nevada, Miami Beach, Hollywood, and Latin America, was murdered in his home.

Giancana was known by all as "The Man". Everybody knew he was 'The Man,' including Chuck Nicoletti, the most notorious hitman in the country. The timing of 'The Mans' bloody murder was not just questionable to many; it was questioned by the United States Congress.

Giancana was the next man up for the Church Committee's investigation into the ties of organized crime and the CIA. His murder came days before he was to testify before the committee, prompting one committee member to say, *"One crucial witness has been murdered a few days before he could testify - Sam Giancana."* And this one couldn't be declared a suicide. It was gruesome.

Giancana was involved in the CIA plot to assassinate Castro. He was to testify on his involvement but flew to Houston for gallbladder surgery before his testimony. He flew home to Chicago and, two days later, was shot once in the back of the head and several more times up through his chin.

Giancana's daughter, Antoinette, believed her father's killer was the government and JFK's killer was the mob. Giancana was known to be a key player in delivering the votes for JFK to defeat Richard Nixon in the 1960 election. Chicago made the last-minute difference from the power of Joe Kennedy and Mayor Richard Daley.

Question ... was Giancana's murder a simple mob hit? Or was he *Whacked?*

You decide.

June 30, 1975

Merle D. Baumgart, an aide to Representative Peter Rodino of the House Judiciary Committee on Impeachment, was killed in a traffic accident. Washington police described his death as a routine traffic accident.

According to the Portland Oregonian, on June 30, 1975, police received an anonymous call to 'look into it.' (The accident.) The paper says U.S. agents joined the probe but kept it secret because of the stature of some individuals who might be involved. Nothing more was heard of it.

There is speculation that his work to impeach Nixon may have exposed him to information that was hazardous to his health.

Question ... did Merle Baumgart die in an auto accident? Or was he *Whacked?*

You decide.

July 14, 1975

Pat Price, a vital asset for the CIA/NSA for his observation skills, died of cardiac arrest at the Stardust Hotel in Las Vegas.

His death could be viewed as usual were it not for the fact that a few days earlier, he observed someone trying to put something in his coffee. Before his death, as he was checking into the *Stardust*, a man walked straight at him, bumped into him, and he felt a sharp pain in his arm. That was on July 13, and he became progressively sicker from then until his death early the following day.

Price was involved in top-secret dealings with U.S. intelligence and felt as though his life could be in danger. While awaiting paramedics, he had a friend pick up his top-secret files. His death is still discussed in hushed tones, and Russia is suspected of having a part.

Question ... did Pat Price die of cardiac arrest? Or was he *Whacked*?

You decide.

July 30, 1975

Jimmy Hoffa, the influential former head of the International Brotherhood of Teamsters, disappeared after lunching with friends. His disappearance has never been solved, nor has his body been found.

In the 1950s, 1960s, and 1970s, Jimmy Hoffa was considered the second most powerful man in the United States behind the President himself. He was a silent partner with Sam Giancana in seeing that JFK 'won' Chicago and beat Richard Nixon for the Presidency. The Mafia was a significant influence in JFK's 1960 election.

And it didn't sit well with Hoffa when JFK's brother, Robert F. Kennedy, then-Attorney General, went after the mob with a vengeance. He eventually convicted Hoffa on tax evasion charges and sent him to federal prison. Fast-forward, and President Richard Nixon pardoned Hoffa.

In a stunning coincidence, we delivered the first of several suitcases of cash to Attorney General John Mitchell. Of course, they were for the reelection campaign, appropriately named CREEP, for Committee to Re-Elect the President (no kidding).

Once out of jail, Hoffa had his eyes back on the prize, returning as head of the Teamsters Union. But a few of the big guys needed help with his plan. The name in this investigation was a who's who of organized crime.

Frank 'The Irishman' Sheehan Hoffa's hitman, Chuckie O'Brien, stepson of Jimmy Hoffa, Salvatore' Sally Bugs' Briguglio, Gabriel 'Gabe' Briguglio, Stephen' Stevie' Andretta, Thomas' Tommy'Andretta, Anthony 'Tony Pro' Provenzano, Anthony 'Tony Jack' Giacalone and Russell 'The Old Man' Bufalino.

Many books, articles, and documentaries about Hoffa's disappearance from The Red Fox restaurant outside Detroit. Geraldo, the FBI, or no one else ever found his body. But on his death bed, hitman Frank Sheehan called his lawyer in for a talk. Seems there were some things he wanted to get off his chest.

First, he said he was there when Hoffa asked mob leaders Carlos Marcello and Santo Trafficante to get rid of JFK. He said shortly after that request, Hoffa told him to deliver high-powered rifles to David Ferrie, Marcello's private pilot, to be used in Dallas. Revenge?

Secondly, hitman Sheehan said a message was delivered to Hoffa that he hadn't shown proper appreciation for what happened in Dallas. Truth? It's hard to say, but it is a deathbed confession that holds some sway in court.

Question: Was Jimmy Hoffa 'disappeared' because he got crosswise with some bad folks? Or was he *Whacked*?

You decide.

August 3, 1975

John Martino, a longtime mobster with ties to the Cuban Underground, died of natural causes.

Martino had a long association with Santo Traficante and Cuba. Before dying, he admitted his involvement in the JFK assassination to several people. Those around him claimed he clearly established his foreknowledge of the event.

Question ... did John Martino die of natural causes? Or was he *Whacked?*

You decide.

August 15, 1975

Joseph Tomassi, the 24-year-old head of the American Nazi Party in California, was shot to death on the front steps of his Los Angeles headquarters.

The *Los Angeles Times* reported two years earlier that *The Committee to Re-Elect the President* gave $10,000 in undisclosed funds to finance a covert campaign to remove George Wallace's *American Independent Party* from the 1972 California ballot. The *Times* went on to say that $1,200 of the fund found its way to Joe Tomassi, head of the *Nazi Party in California.*

Is there a connection to the madhouse of Richard Nixon? Who knows?

Question ... Did Joseph Tomassi die of a street murder? Or was he Whacked?

You decide.

October 5, 1975

Rolando Masferrer, also known as 'El Tigre,' a top Cuban resistance leader, was killed when he turned the key to his automobile, and it exploded. His murder remains unsolved.

El Tigre went back to the Batista days in Cuba. Known as a ruthless Army leader, he was known to have ties to the JFK assassination. He was an ex-Cuban Senator and newspaper publisher who is said to have fled Castro with as much as $10 million and didn't stop there.

Colonel William C. Bishop, a senior military liaison to the Executive Action Assassination Program, described El Tigre as the vital man for Alpha 66, an extremely violent anti-Castro movement that had strong ties to the Mafia via Trafficante's Mob in Florida. Of Rolando Masferrer, Colonel Bishop said, *"He's a guy who will cut your throat and smile while doing it."*

Masferrer has also worked with Watergate burglars Hunt, Sturgis, and Barker.

Question, was El Tigre murdered as revenge for a dirty deed? Or was he *Whacked?*

You decide.

1976

May 31, 1976

Martha Mitchell, estranged wife of former attorney general John Mitchell, died on Memorial Day. Sadly, she died of cancer in a hospital.

Martha Mitchell played a significant role in the Watergate scandal by being an outspoken figure who revealed critical details to the media. She learned about Watergate by eavesdropping on her husband's phone calls and meetings. John Mitchell was Nixon's trusted adviser and a former attorney general. He was also involved in authorizing the Watergate break-in.

As Martha Mitchell tried to disclose what she knew, she was immediately labeled unstable, unreliable, and a wicked witch. However, she kept talking and was right in her warnings about corruption within the Nixon administration. She was the first to call publicly for Nixon's resignation.

Question ... did Martha Mitchell die of cancer? Or was she *Whacked?*

You decide.

August 7, 1976

Johnny Roselli, the critical liaison between the CIA and the Mafia, was found dead when he washed ashore in an oil drum. He was found stabbed and shot, and his legs sawn off before being stuffed into the drum and sunk into the ocean. The official verdict was a Mafia retaliation killing.

Roselli was a big-time mobster who returned to Meyer Lansky, Jimmy Hoffa, and Al Capone. Capone sent him to Hollywood to develop their contacts there. He was later known as their man in Vegas. He was also friends with the reclusive Howard Hughes, who had CIA ties to his business ventures.

The coincidence in Roselli's death is perhaps the fact that when found, he was days before his scheduled testimony before Congress regarding the CIA plot to kill Castro.

Question ... was Roselli chopped up because of some mob feud? Or, was he *Whacked?*

You decide.

September 1976

A LITTLE CONTEXT ...

The House Select Committee on Assassinations (HSCA) was established in 1976 by the United States House of Representatives to investigate the assassinations of John F. Kennedy and Martin Luther King Jr.

As you'll read, the committee subpoenaed many key witnesses who suffered several coincidences that prevented their testimony.

The committee ran until 1978. They concluded, not surprisingly, that there 'might' have been conspiracies behind both assassinations but ruled out federal or foreign government involvement in either.

1977

February 15, 1977:

Susan Coleman, age 26, died of a gunshot wound to the back of the head. Ruled a suicide. No autopsy was allowed.

At the time of her death, Ms. Coleman was 7 months pregnant. She told friends it was Bill Clinton's child. At the time, Bill Clinton was Arkansas Attorney General.

Question ... was young Ms. Coleman a victim of suicide? Or was she *Whacked?*

You Decide.

March 19, 1977

Chuck Nicoletti, known to be a top hitman for the Chicago Mafia, died of three .38 shots to the back of his head. Officially called a Mafia killing.

Nicoletti let it be known he was unhappy with the recent hit on Sam Giancana, his benefactor. Nicoletti was also found to be in Dallas the day of JFKs assassination, and word on the street was he may have been one of the shooters.

Like Giancana before his murder, Nicoletti was scheduled to soon testify before the House Select Committee on Assassinations.

Question ... did Nicolleti meet his demise because the mob was unhappy? Or was he *Whacked?*

You decide.

March 29, 1977

George de Mohrenschildt, also known as Baron de Mohrenschildt and a descendent of Russian Royalty, died of a shotgun blast. Official verdict, suicide.

One coincidence in the case was de Mohrenschildt was the critical link between Lee Harvey Oswald and the CIA. He was also linked to several

extremely conservative Texas oil millionaires rumored to be involved in the JFK assassination. He, de Mohrenschildt, was a CIA asset used for various tasks. One of those tasks, according to attorney Mark Lane, was to babysit Lee Harvey Oswald for the CIA.

Question ... did the successful George de Mohrenschildt suicide himself? Or was he *Whacked?*

You decide.

April 5, 1977

President Carlos Prio Socarras, the last elected President of Cuba (1948 - 1952), was found dead of a gunshot wound outside of his home in Florida. Officially ruled a suicide.

President Socarras knew Jack Ruby and others in Ruby's circle. He also had ties to the Mafia and suffered the exact coincidence as several others in that he was days from testifying before the House Select Committee on Assassinations.

Question ... did President Carlos Prio Socarras commit suicide? Or was he *Whacked?*

You decide.

June 6, 1977

Louis Nichols, Assistant Director of the FBI, was found dead. Officially ruled a heart attack.

Louis Nichols was a special assistant to FBI director J. Edgar Hoover. Coincidentally, Nichols was Hoover's personal liaison to the Warren Commission. He was also one of six key FBI figures who mysteriously died within six months. That six-month period coincidentally was before their testimony before the House Select Committee on Assassinations.

Question ... was FBI Agent Nichols a victim of a heart attack? Or was he *Whacked?*

You decide.

August, 1977

Donald Kaylor, FBI Special Agent and FBI fingerprint expert who worked the JFK case died of a heart attack.

Kaylor was directly tied to the apparently falsely obtained palm print of Lee Harvey Oswald found on the rifle that was supposedly used to kill Kennedy. A funeral director would later testify to the fact the FBI went to the funeral home to obtain the prints from the now-dead Lee Harvey Oswald.

Question ... Did Agent Kaylor die of a heart attack? Or was he *Whacked?*

You decide.

August, 1977

James Cadigan, FBI forensic document examiner, died as the result of a fall at home. His death was deemed accidental. Cardigan was the document expert who examined evidence in the JFK assassination.

Question ... did Agent Cardigan die of an accidental fall at home? Or was he *Whacked?*

You decide.

August 1, 1977

Alan Belmont, FBI Special Agent working for Director J. Edgar Hoover, reportedly died, reportedly after a long illness. The fact is he died of pneumonia, supposedly contracted three days earlier at a horse show in Madison Square Garden.

Coincidence? Belmont was the primary officer in charge of FBI activities regarding the JFK assassination. That fact would put Belmont in the crosshairs of an FBI cover-up if there was one. Belmont was the second agent to buy the farm in those horrible six months. He died before his testimony.

Question ... did Agent Belmont die of pneumonia? Or was he *Whacked?*

You decide.

August 1, 1977

Gary Powers, an L.A. news helicopter pilot, died when the chopper crashed short of the airport. NTSB determined the cause of the crash was a pilot error.

Those of you old enough will remember Gary Powers as the pilot of the U-2 spy plane shot down over the Soviet Union in 1960. Powers was held in prison there for several years. Those years coincided at one point with Lee Harvey Oswald's time there.

Powers was known to be a meticulous pilot. The helicopter he was flying was reliable, he was experienced, and the weather was fine. Before the flight, he had reported problems with the fuel gauge. He became concerned and radioed that he would be returning to verify his fuel.

Witnesses said the helicopter dropped from the sky just outside the airport on his return. That particular helicopter was designed to counter the rotor to a soft landing should the power go out. Witnesses said the tail rotor fell off, causing the chopper to drop immediately. After the crash, they determined he had 3 hours of fuel onboard.

Question ... did Gary Powers, a very experienced and known to be meticulous pilot, die from his own error? Or was he *Whacked?*

You decide.

October, 1977

J.M. English, FBI Agent and head of the FBI Forensic Laboratory at the time of the JFK assassination. Cause of death, heart attack. Died before testimony.

Question ... was Agent English a victim of a heart attack? Or was he *Whacked?*

You decide.

November 9, 1977

William Sullivan, FBI Agent in charge of FBI Division Five, Domestic Intelligence, was killed in a hunting accident outside his home in New Hampshire.

Agent Sullivan's case is a doozy. Sullivan was the central figure the House Select Committee on Assassination wanted to talk with regarding his involvement in the Executive Action program that targeted Castro. He was also crucial to all the assassinations in the 60s.

As pressure mounted from all the investigations and the new Watergate scandal, Sullivan and FBI Director J. Edgar Hoover nearly came to blows. Hoover was forced to resign from the Bureau. Sullivan was scheduled to testify the following week before the United States Congress.

But in a stunning bit of coincidence, Sullivan was mistaken for a deer while hunting near his Spring Hill, New Hampshire home. A 22-year-old man claimed he mistook Sullivan for a deer and shot and killed him instantly. The young man, the son of a New Hampshire State Trooper, was charged and fined $500 for his 'mistake.'

But not so fast ... William Sullivan specifically predicted that he would be murdered. He also said it would be made to appear as an accident. Friends said his statement was not in passing but very serious. He had experience in the dark world and correctly predicted his fate.

Question ... was Agent Sullivan a victim of an accidental shooting? Or was he *Whacked?*

You decide.

November 18, 1977

Manuel Artime, exiled Cuban leader, died of cancer. But, Gaeton Fonzi, Special Investigator to the U.S. Congress' House Select Committee on Assassinations, was highly professional and respected. Fonzi concluded that Manuel Artime might have been a double agent working for Cuban Intelligence. And he believed Artime's death to be of a suspicious nature.

Question ... did Manuel Artime die of cancer? Or was he *Whacked?*

You decide.

1978

May 8, 1978

David Morales, a former CIA operative involved in the Bay of Pigs fiasco, died under questionable circumstances.

Morales made his last trip to Washington in early May to testify before the House Select Committee on Assassinations. Upon his return, a friend told him he wasn't looking well. Morales said, *"I don't know what's wrong with me. Ever since I left Washington, I haven't been feeling very comfortable."*

That night, he ended up in the hospital. His friend went to see him the following day and found him on life support in a room surrounded by sheriff's deputies. Later that day, he was taken off life support and died. There was no autopsy. The official ruling died of natural causes.

Before dying, Morales admitted to his wife and others his involvement in the JFK assassination and his foreknowledge of what would happen to him.

Question ... did David Morales die of natural causes? Or was he *Whacked?*

You decide.

August 29, 1978

Albino Luciani or the world knew him as Pope John Paul I had been ordained three days earlier, on August 26, 1978. The official cause was a heart attack. In fairness, Luciani was not in the best health, and a heart attack was possible.

There was some controversy regarding his installation as Pope. It came at a time of the Vatican Bank scandal for money laundering. The official story is that the case is closed. The unofficial story was that his death was tied to the Bank scandal. It was tied to a secret Masonic organization known as P2. It was founded by Lecio Gelli, a Fascist who was the only person who knew the members' names. He recruited well despite the Italian law that all Masonic members must register with the government.

P2 had high-ranking members of the Catholic church, military, government, politics, and the Mafia. It led to the Vatican Bank's involvement in money laundering. What did all that have to do with Pope John Paul I? He was not part of it; some think he was a liability and would blow the whistle. We'll never know.

Question ... was Pope John Paul I a victim of poor health and a heart attack? Or was he *Whacked?*

You decide.

September 11, 1978

Georgi Markov, a Bulgarian writer and dissident most known for his exposes of the Bulgarian communist government, died of ricin poisoning.

Markov was waiting for a bus in London headed for work at BBC. He jumped from a sudden pain in his right thigh that felt like a needle or pin entered his leg. Turning, he saw a figure in a long coat with an umbrella getting in a cab.

Still not understanding what happened, Markov continued to work at BBC World Service. As the day wore on, the pain was still bothering him. He noticed his leg had a red circular area. A few hours later, he began flulike symptoms, and his condition worsened.

He was taken to St James' Hospital, where his condition spiraled out of control until he died. Markov's autopsy revealed that he had been hit by a pellet filled with deadly ricin.

Metropolitan Police investigation concluded it was probably an assassin from the Bulgarian intelligence services. It remained a mystery for years until Soviet KGB defector Oleg Gordievsky confirmed it was a hit.

There is no question to ask here ... *it was a hit.* Nothing for you to decide.

September 24, 1978

John Paisley, CIA Officer and Director of the highly sensitive Office of Strategic Resources, was found dead when he washed ashore from the ocean. Paisley had been shot in the head execution-style and had diving weights affixed to his body. It is hard to even type this with a straight face; his death was ruled a suicide.

The CIA knew it had a mole at the top but didn't know who. The search for the mole was one of the highest in its history. James Angleton, the CIA's Chief of Counterintelligence, said the search became an obsession driving him crazy.

On the day of Paisley's demise, the people he talked with said he was in good spirits. The Coast Guard later found his boat but found no evidence of a shooting of any kind. A further coincidence is that Paisley was found to be eating at the time of his death, and there were no signs of food on his boat.

Veteran CIA officer Victor Marchetti testified that Paisley had extensive knowledge about the JFK assassination. He also pointed out he was murdered during the investigation of the House Select Committee on Assassinations. Marchetti's opinion was he was *"about to blow the whistle."*

A CIA memo later revealed the Coast Guard found some papers dealing with the Cuban crisis aboard his boat. Counterintelligence Operative Richard Case Nagell revealed that Paisley was the Soviet mole the CIA had been trying to identify for several years. What is not clear is if Paisley was assassinated by agents acting on behalf of the U.S. or Russia?

The official records to this day record Paisley's death as suicide. Once, when questioned, police officials said they believed he put on the ankle weights and shot himself as he jumped into the water. The gunshot was behind his left ear, and Paisley was right-handed.

Question ... did CIA leader John Paisley die of a self-inflicted gunshot wound? Or was he *Whacked*?

You decide.

1979

A DEFINITE MAYBE ...

1979 was a significant year in the history of coincidences. Bill Clinton was first elected Governor of Arkansas in 1979. That same year, he appointed Dr. Fahmy Malak as the state's chief medical examiner. Malak held that position from 1979 to 1991, and Clinton remained Governor until 1992.

In the pages ahead, you will read about many coincidences coming out of Arkansas. Many are connected to the Clintons and Dr. Malak, who made interesting, controversial autopsy rulings. Coincidence? Let's take a look.

Based on what you'll read on these pages, Dr. Malak needed to be removed, and Governor Clinton refused countless times. It could be a coincidence, or it could be that the ruling Malak made helped Clinton's mother, a nurse, avoid any scrutiny in a patient's death that the hospital knew should be investigated.

Who could find something wrong with the issues listed below?

Malak testified erroneously in criminal cases.

His rulings were regularly reversed by juries.

Outside pathologists routinely challenged his findings and won.

Once, he misread a medical chart and wrongly accused a deputy county coroner of killing someone.

He once testified in court on tissue samples that DNA tests later indicated had been mixed up with other tissue samples.

In 1985, Raymond P. Allbright, 50, of Mountain Home, was found in his yard dead of gunshot wounds after being arrested the night before on charges of theft. Malak ruled his death a suicide, although Allbright had been shot five times, and all five shots were to the chest.

In 1989, police said Andrew Smith, 59, shot himself and was declared brain-dead at University Hospital in Little Rock. Life support was withdrawn, and the patient died. The Deputy Coroner, Mark Malcolm, gave the order after consulting Malak. Later that week, Malak told officers he would have to rule that Malcolm murdered him. No one had consulted Smith's family. The investigation revealed Malak had misread the patient's chart and didn't think notification was necessary. A public outcry followed with calls for his resignation. Governor Clinton ordered him to apologize for his mistake.

In 1990, Gregory Stephens, 25, of Hot Springs, was fatally shot while sitting on the front porch of his home. The Prosecutor brought Ernest D. Lemons to trial on a murder charge. Eyewitnesses testified Stephens was fired from the street, 40 feet away. When Malak took the stand, he stunned the Prosecutor by testifying that Stephens had been shot point-blank. Knowing his case was doomed, the Prosecutor asked that the charges be dismissed. The killer walked free.

Perhaps the crowning achievement for Dr. Malak was his ruling in the deaths of teenagers Ives and Henry. You'll read their story elsewhere in this book, but the two young men were found dead on a railroad track near the Mena Airport. (Think drug operations). Dr. Malak ruled their deaths accidental. He concluded they had gotten high and fallen asleep and were run over by the train.

The problem with his ruling was the knife wounds in one and the bullets in the other. A Grand Jury overruled Malak's decision. Not happy with the verdict being overturned, Governor Clinton hired two out-of-state pathologists to review Malak's performance.

Just as the Doctor, or in this case, the Governor, ordered, they gave him high marks to Malak and said he should get a raise. A short two months later, Clinton sent a proposal to the Legislature to raise Malak's salary by 41.5% bringing it to $117,875.

It was later revealed that the visiting pathologists were paid $20,000 from Clinton's discretionary fund. They would later say *during staff meetings with state officials, that included Betsey Wright, Clinton's chief of staff, they agreed not to conduct a systematic review of Malak's cases.*

Malak had a controversial run with Clinton running cover for him. He is not only known for his utter incompetence but he is linked, as was the Governor, to the infamous Mena Airport drug smuggling operations with Barry Seal and the CIA, and Ollie North.

Three weeks before Bill Clinton announced his candidacy for president, he convinced Malak he should resign. Of course, he found another lucrative job in state government before doing so. In 1990, Malak accepted a position as a medical examiner in Florida.

In one of the most significant coincidences of all time, before Dr. Malak could take his new position in Florida ... he died by suicide.

The Eighties

What Did Your Government Do?

The decade of the 80s was spent recovering from the disastrous policies of Jimmy Carter and then the economic progress of Reaganomics' which saw reduced taxes, regulations, and expenditures to drive growth.

The Tax Reform Act of 1986 overhauled the income tax code. It also brought us the Immigration Reform and Control Act of 1986, which granted amnesty to a class of immigrants and fined employers for hiring undocumented workers.

President Reagan called Russia the 'evil empire' and ratcheted up the Cold War. He also introduced the 'Star War' program, officially named the Strategic Defense Initiative (SDI). It was to be a dome protecting the US against a nuclear attack.

Apparently, unable to stand our first decade without war in 50 years, we invaded Grenada supposedly to overthrow a pro-communist government. Reagan also silenced Libyan troublemaker Muammar Gaddafi when he sent a couple of jets streaking into his palace, claiming a couple of his wives. The bombing of Libya in 1986 in retaliation for terrorist attacks.

The 80s also brought us the Iran-Contra Affair. Our first big public display of our intelligence agencies is going rogue. Teacher Christie McAuliffe and 7 astronauts went to meet their maker when the Challenger Space Shuttle went poof on take off. And

Russia worked hard to cover up the Chornobyl nuclear meltdown that haunts them to this day.

Sandra Day O'Connor became America's first female Supreme Court Justice, and the AIDS epidemic swept the world. Justice Antonin Scalia was added to the Supreme Court, restoring some semblance of sanity to our left-leaning nation.

As the distance between World War II began to grow, revelations began to emerge about some of the goings-on during the Great One. One such revelation was the OSS, now CIA, instructions on how to sabotage the USSR. The Cold War produced lots of craziness, and the OSS field guide on sabotage was just one.

The guide was a sabotage field menu teaching its agents how to harass the Soviet Union. Here are a few tips ...

Demand written orders for everything.

Then, misunderstand orders.

Ask endless questions and engage in long correspondence about such orders.

Quibble over them when you can

Do everything possible to delay the delivery of orders.

Even though parts of an order may be ready beforehand, wait to deliver it until it is entirely prepared.

You can only order new working materials once your current stocks have been virtually exhausted, so the slightest delay in filling your order will result in a shutdown.

Order high-quality materials that are hard to get. If you don't get them, argue about it.

Warn that inferior materials will mean inferior work.

Based on my years managing truck fleets, this could have been from an old Jimmy Hoffa Teamsters manual. Or maybe it's the other way around.

1980

December 8, 1980

John Lennon, the iconic member of the famous Beatles, was shot to death in a hail of gunfire outside his home at the Dakota Apartments in New York City, with his son Yoko at his side. Later that day, news reports proclaimed a lone crazed assassin by the name of Mark David Chapman pulled the trigger.

But did you know there was no trial, courtroom testimony, or eyewitnesses? And like Sirhan Sirhan, Chapman testified he had no memory of shooting anyone. He later pled guilty to the shooting. A coincidence here is the 'lone nut gunman' reports that accompany so many of these folks who buy the farm.

First responder Lt. Arthur O'Connor, commanding officer of the NYPD's 2nd Precinct, noted Chapman's odd behavior. He said, "*If the assassin wanted to get away with it, he could have gotten away. A subway was right on the corner, and no one was around to stop him.*" NYPD Patrolman Peter Cullen, an officer in the first car at the scene, felt Chapman was not the shooter. He determined it may have been someone inside the Dakota.

You might be wondering, as I am, why the powers that be would care about a singer. The backdrop to Lennon and Yoko was the Vietnam War, protests, the Kent State shootings, and the anti-war movement. Lennon was viewed by the authorities as an agitator for the demonstrations taking place around the country.

Pushing the envelope as he became more radicalized after his association with Yoko Ono, In September 1971, the Lennons moved to New York City. In his own words, the first people who reached out to them were Jerry Rubin and Abbie Hoffman. A short time later, Lennon used the Mike Douglas and Dick Cavett to introduce his friends Jerry Rubin and Black Panther leader Bobby Seale.

Lennon began joining and speaking at street protests if that wasn't enough. At the University of Michigan campus on December 10,

1971, Lennon sang about 'The CIA selling dope.' In the Nixon era, it raised red flags.

An April 10, 1972, FBI memo from J. Edgar Hoover instructed, *"Initiate discreet efforts to locate subject [John Lennon] and remain aware of his activities and movements."* Further, more than a decade later, in March 1983, Yoko Ono's head of security, Dan Mahoney, located listening devices planted inside Lennon's Dakota apartment.

All of this apparently led the feds to hound him. Despite that, Lennon continued to poke them in the eye. On April 22, 1972, he spoke at a huge outdoor peace rally in New York City, then photographed himself standing beside a poster depicting 'USA surpasses all genocide records.'

The Immigration and Naturalization Service (INS) intentionally dragged Lennon's legal battle from March 1972 until July 1976. Documents later revealed that the FBI, CIA, and even the President's office were involved. INS documents later revealed letters from J. Edgar Hoover to H. R. Haldeman proved they wanted Lennon out of the country. Novelist Gore Vidal described John Lennon as a born enemy of those who governed the United States.

As with so many of our coincidental victims, books are written about the travesty of their demise.

Question ... was John Lennon the unfortunate victim of a lunatic who can't even remember shooting him? Or was he *Whacked?*

You decide.

1981

A LITTLE CONTEXT ...

The first rumblings of drugs running through the little airport in Mena, Arkansas, began in early 1981. The claim was the drug operations centered around a larger-than-life character named Barry Seal.

Seal was a commercial airline pilot who became a major drug smuggler for the Medellín Cartel. According to an FBI memo, Seal admitted to smuggling large quantities of cocaine from Colombia to the United States and used the Mena airport as part of his smuggling operation to bring the drugs in.

The drug smuggling continued for years and eventually become connected to the Iran Contra Affair. There is a significant amount of evidence that the Mena airport had been used for covert CIA operations related to the Contra rebels.

The bulk of the drug running coincided with Bill Clinton's time as Governor of Arkansas. There are many implications and some evidence of his and his administration's involvement or, in the least, guilt by looking the other way.

The Mena drug operations led to many coincidences, resulting in the deaths of a disparate amount of individuals.

Note: See Barry Seal in the pages ahead.

March 30, 1981

A DEFINITE MAYBE ...

On March 30, 1981, President Ronald Reagan completed a speech before the AFL-CIO at the Washington Hilton. Outside the hotel, John Hinckley stood with a .22-caliber Rohm R6-14 revolver. After yelling, "Mr. President, look over here," he fired six shots, one of them directly striking the commander-in-chief. That's the official line, and they're sticking to it.

Not so fast ... here is more 'official' information. An analysis of the shot sequence provided some exciting results.

Bullet One: Blasted into the skull of Press Secretary James Brady, crippling him.

Bullet Two: Struck Officer Thomas Delahanty in the back.

Bullet Three: Zipped over Reagan's head and harmlessly hit a building.

Bullet Four: Lodged in the chest of Secret Service Agent Thomas McCarthy.

Bullet Five: Careened off the bulletproof glass of the President's limousine.

Bullet Six: Well, there are some weird coincidences with Bullet Six.

Officially, bullet six is the one striking the President. But wait, journalists at the scene reported that this bullet ricocheted off the limousine. To make this theory work, we must revisit Arlen Specter's 'magic bullet theory' in the JFK assassination.

Bullet Six would have hit the limo, flattened itself like a penny, and then taken a sharp 90-degree turn through a small gap in the door and into the President's body. All this happened in a fraction of a second as the Secret Service Agent dove on top of Reagan, pinning his arms down as they landed in the back seat of the limo.

But it doesn't end there. The flattened penny-like bullet would have had to hit the rib cage, turned over, and, on its way to its resting place in his shoulder, missed his heart. As you can probably imagine ... they were selling this story, but many folks weren't buying.

Consider this ...

Judy Woodruff appeared on NBC Special Reports and said she saw at least one shot fired from the hotel overhang above Reagan's limousine. And later added that a Secret Service agent had fired that shot.

In Conspiracy Files, David Southwell and Sean Twist write, "More than one witness reported that at least one shot came from a Secret Service agent who was stationed on the overhang behind Reagan's limousine. If you inspect video footage of the shooting it is clear from the position Hinckley was standing in when he opened fire, he would have needed to shoot through a car door to hit Reagan where he did.

Hinckley was in a crowd of people when he drew his revolver. A Union President by the name of Alfred Antenucci saw the weapon and began beating Hinckley on the neck before dragging him to the ground as Hinckley kept firing.

Can anyone say, reasonable doubt? You might be thinking, but why? Who would benefit from President Reagan's demise? The first one that comes to mind is his Vice President, George H.W. Bush. You say, come on, he was dull and lifeless, this is preposterous. Well, consider this ...

We learned in Death Rattle of the Republic, Bush's father, Prescott Bush, was a supporter of Hitler. He was actually fined for his involvement. Bush the Older stated he was not in Dallas at the time of the JFK assassination, but it was later determined he was. Bush was a member of the Trilateral Commission, the Council on Foreign Relations, and a Skull and Boner, all of which flew in the face of President Reagan, who did not trust Bush the Older.

1982

A LITTLE CONTEXT ...

In 1982, Brits first learned of a secret part of their government known as the Government Communications Centre (GCHQ). It was based in Cheltenham and was responsible for covert reconnaissance missions, satellites, and other electronic means of spying.

The GCHQ came to light when one of its operatives, Geoffrey Prime, was arrested and eventually prosecuted for espionage. With the lid off the entire affair, Brits discovered that GCHQ had a pact with the American CIA, which led to their discovery of their spy.

The GCHQ was centered on the work of the British defense industry and the development of cutting-edge technology during the Cold War. It tied many projects you will read about later in the book.

What drove the need for such an outfit?

Russian defense experts, Rear Admiral Peroumnov and First Rank Engineer A. Partela wrote an essay, "A Look at the Development of Means of Electronic Warfare." In it, they had this to say ...

"The military effectiveness of electronic countermeasures, even with the emphasis on real-life experimentation, must be regarded as confirmed only under the condition that essential characteristics of the electronic weapons of the opponent have been revealed with sufficient accuracy.

But the possibility of dependably uncovering and obtaining this information is a challenging task ..."

The fact is that Western governments were engaged in an intelligence battle with Eastern Bloc countries such as Russia. As you will read ... although our governments may not want to admit it, there were casualties in that war.

March 1982

Professor Keith Bowden, a valued Marconi computer expert computer, died when his vehicle left a three-lane highway at high speed and slammed into a railway line.

His death was instantaneous and ruled an accident.

Question ... was Professor Bowden killed by their own actions? Or was he *Whacked?*

You decide.

July 27, 1982

Jack Wolfendon, a GCHQ radio operator, plunged to his death when the glider he was piloting went into a steep dive and flew right into a Cotswold hillside.

Jack was an experienced pilot not known for taking undue risks. Those close to him at GCHQ said Jack would never have deliberately flown his motorized glider into that hill because 'we had so much unfinished business to do.'

His live-in girlfriend at the time said he had acted strangely since returning from abroad.

Question ... did Wolfedon intentionally fly his glider into a hillside? Or was he *Whacked?*

You decide.

September 14, 1982

Princess Grace of Monaco, before her marriage, American actress and Hollywood star Grace Kelly died when her sports car plunged over a mountain road and fell over 150 feet.

The accident took place on September 13, and the Princess died of her injuries the following day. Her daughter Stephanie was in the car with her at the time of the accident.

There was much confusion, speculation, and what the palace described as misinformation surrounding the accident. The reports of the Princess's injuries ranged from minor to severe. There was speculation that her daughter Stephanie, who survived the crash, was driving.

There were also rumors the Princess had become involved with the Solar Temple. A group claimed they descended from the Knights Templar and possessed some mystical truth. She is said to have provided funding to them up to a point and then became disillusioned. Strange things have happened.

Question ... did the Princess of Monaco die in an accident of her own, or was her underage daughter driving? Or was she *Whacked?*

You decide.

November 1982

Ernest Brockway, an electronic specialist for GCHQ at Irton, Moor, Great Britain, was found dead at home from hanging. The inquest ruled his death a suicide.

His death, along with the earlier death of Jack Wolfendon, prompted Prime Minister Margaret Thatcher to clear the two deceased GCHQ of spying. They also released an internal memorandum telling their 7,000 employees there was no connection between the two deaths. Just a coincidence, apparently.

Question ... Did Ernst Brockway hang himself in his home? Or was he *Whacked?*

You decide.

1983

1983

Stephen Drinkwater, a clerk at the GCHQ, was found dead at home by his father.

Drinkwater was a clerk responsible for making copies of highly classified documents. He was found in his room with a plastic bag over his head. His death was ruled a suicide by asphyxiation.

Question ... did Stephen Drinkwater commit suicide by asphyxiation? Or was he *Whacked?*

You decide.

Note; Many of the deaths reported are so lacking in information they do not even have a date of death. Only a year.

March 23, 1983

A LITTLE CONTEXT ...

Ronald Reagan announced the Strategic Defense Initiative (SDI), known as 'Star Wars,' in a televised address to the nation on March 23, 1983.

The SDI was a proposed missile defense system aimed at protecting the United States from potential nuclear attacks, particularly from the Soviet Union. This initiative involved developing a space-based missile defense program that would intercept missiles at various phases of their flight, using advanced technology like space-based laser systems.

Reagan's goal with SDI was to eliminate the need for nuclear weapons and deter potential Soviet attacks, ultimately aiming to end the Cold War. The 'Star Wars' initiative greatly worried the Soviet Union. They were committed to preventing its development.

One of the defense contractors was a UK-based telecommunications and engineering firm that operated from 1963 to 1987. It originated in the Wireless Telegraph & Signal Company, founded by Guglielmo Marconi in 1897. You'll read more about Marconi's misfortune.

April 1983

Lieutenant Colonel Anthony Godley, the head of the works study group at the Royal Military College where he had been living with his wife, disappeared without a trace.

When local newspapers began inquiring about his disappearance, they found that his wife packed up and left the College within twenty-four hours, never to be heard again. The College was also mum about the situation. The Editor doing the research found that Anthony had spent the previous night at a local hotel and left without paying the bill.

In yet another coincidence, his yacht was missing and was never found.

Question ... did Anthony Godley disappear without a trace? Or was he *Whacked?*

You decide.

June 1983

Dennis Skinner, a British expat working in Moscow for ICL Corporation, was found dead in the street below his upper-level apartment. Russian authorities ruled his death a suicide.

Two days before his death, he sent the British Embassy a note stating his life was in danger and that he knew of a Russian spy in his company. Shortly before his death, he called his wife to say, *'We have a terrible enemy.'* Three hours before his death, he called the British Embassy and told them he was about to be arrested for spying.

Dr. Mary McHugh, an independent coroner, asked to preside at an inquest in England. By the time of the High Court ruling, she was on the brink of resignation. When pressed by the Daily Mail for an explanation, she said, *"I can't say where the pressure is coming from. Please don't ask. I will lose my job. So much pressure from all quarters."*

Question ... did Dennis Skinner jump to his death from his Moscow apartment? Or was he *Whacked?*

You decide.

November 1983

A LITTLE CONTEXT ...

At this point in the story, it has been twenty years since President Kennedy's assassination. And you've seen an excessive number of people tied to the events of that November day in 1963 have met their demise.

The London Sunday Times engaged an actuary to determine the odds of 18 material witnesses dying within three years of that fateful day. The actuary determined the chances of that happening would be 1 in 100,000 Trillion. If the actuary is even close to right ... the Warren Commission is a sham.

The calculation caused quite a stir and bantering back and forth. The bottom line is there are more than 18 suspicious deaths. In the first three years following the JFK ordeal, there were at least 40 suspicious deaths.

There is a spreadsheet database of people who met their Maker in coincidental circumstances. There are 104 dead witnesses out of a total of 1,400 witnesses. Of those, 71 were unnatural, 7 were suicides, 40 were homicides, 24 were accidental, 4 were from unknown causes, and 29 were suspiciously timed heart attacks.

Question ... what probability would you need to surpass reasonable doubt?

You decide.

1984

April 6, 1984

George Franks, a radio operator involved in a highly sensitive project for the GCHQ, was found dead at home. His death was ruled by hanging and suicide, at least in the beginning.

George Franks's death came four days after the GCHQ began lie detector tests on all of its employees. When the first reports came out, the news was only told that 'an employee' had committed suicide. The Press would not let up with so little information, which prompted Prime Minister Thatcher to make a statement.

She released the employee's name and claimed they were limiting information out of respect for the family. But the truth was he had no family, and his body was identified by a neighbor he rented a room from. The neighbor said he had no friends and only received two phone calls weekly. When asked from whom, he replied, *"I don't know. He talked in code."*

At the inquest, they determined he died of natural causes.

Question ... did George Franks hand himself? Or was he *Whacked?*

You decide.

1985

1985

Stephen Ole, an employee of GCHQ's most advanced listening post, was found dead at his home. He was hanging when found.

The police on the scene told the Coroner that Stephen had a piece of string twisted around his wrists in a reef knot. But he also said that Stephen could have done it himself. The Coroner rendered an open verdict, reporting that perhaps young Stephen just wanted to see what it was like to hang and maybe fall. What a coincidence.

Question ... did Stephen Oke take his own life? Or was he *Whacked?*

You decide.

March 1985

Roger Hill, a top-level researcher for Marconi Avionics, died when he accidentally shot himself with his own shotgun. His death baffled friends and colleagues.

Question ... did Roger Hill kill himself? Or was he *Whacked?*

You decide.

August, 1985

A LITTLE CONTEXT

What became known as The Iran-Contra Affair began in August of this year when Reagan administration officials facilitated the secret sale of arms to Iran. At the time of the sale, Iran was under an arms embargo. The arms sales were to be in exchange for the release of American hostages held by Hezbollah, an Islamist group in Lebanon.

The proceeds from these arms sales were then diverted to fund the Contras, a rebel group in Nicaragua fighting against the socialist Sandinista government created by the Carter administration. Sending arms to the Contras directly violated a Congressional ban, known as the Poland Agreement, on funding the Contras.

Senior Reagan administration officials, including National Security Council member Oliver North, were involved in orchestrating the arms sales and the diversion of funds to the Contras. While President Reagan was aware of the potential for the arms sales to fund the Contras, the extent of his direct involvement is disputed.

The Iran-Contra affair was ultimately uncovered by the media in 1986, leading to congressional investigations and the convictions of several Reagan administration officials. It highlighted issues around presidential power, congressional oversight, and the use of covert operations that continued to be debated in the aftermath of the scandal.

November 19, 1985

Jonathon Wash, a System X and digital communications expert working for Teleconsult, fell to his death from his hotel balcony.

Jonathon had expressed to his family just before his death his fears for his life. There were initial reports of suicide, but John Wash, the father of the deceived, has refused to accept that explanation. BBC produced a documentary on Wash's death and said, *"It's a web of official contradiction, unhelpfulness or deceit."*

At the time of his death, he was working for British Telecom Technology on a project in Abidjan, Ivory Coast, West Africa. He enjoyed his job and loved his hotel, and his father said things were going well until he called to say he was concerned for his life.

Question ... did Jonathon Wash jump to his death of his own free will? Or was he *Whacked?*

You decide.

1986

A LITTLE CONTEXT ...

A case that brought many coincidences began in 1986 when INSLAW Inc. filed suit against the U.S. government for stealing their software, PROMIS. The acronym stood for Prosecutors Management Information Systems. INSLAW sold the system to the U.S. Department of Justice.

They marketed the system as a straightforward prosecutorial management system sold to friends and foes alike.

INSLAW alleged that the DOJ had programmed a backdoor into PROMIS that allowed the U.S. to monitor them and whoever was using it. Further accusations were that the DOJ tried to harm the company by withholding payments through trickery, fraud, and deceit. This case involved allegations of the DOJ attempting to bankrupt Inslaw and murder.

An investigator named Danny Casolaro (you'll meet him elsewhere in this book) was assigned to mediate a solution between the two. During his investigation, he met Michael Riconosciuto, who claimed to have installed the back door in the program.

Intrigued, Casolaro dug deeper. As he got to know Riconosciuto, he claimed to be fighting against the globalists seeking a world government. Casalaro eventually stumbled on what became known as the October Surprise. The surprise was that Reagan's supporters persuaded the Iranians to postpone the release of hostages until after he (Reagan) won the election. This turned out to be true. Carter reached the agreement with Iran but was denied the victory lap.

The deeper Casalaro dug, the more he learned of eight men who were supposed to be behind the world government movement. He dubbed his case The Octopus. Casalaro ended up dead in a West Virginia motel where he went to meet an informant. His throat was slit, and his murder was never solved. Other murders would follow. You can now catch the movie on Netflix called The Octopus Murders. And Netflix has a four-part documentary series on the subject called American Conspiracy.

The legal battle lasted 12 years, resulting in internal reviews, Congressional investigations, and court rulings against Inslaw's claims. Following the trial, Inslaw filed for bankruptcy. In 1997, a book claimed that the NSA was behind the back door. Although the government was firm in its denial of any wrongdoing, in another stunning coincidence, disgraced FBI agent Robert Hannsen, the Soviet agent, was confirmed to have obtained PROMIS for the Soviets.

Further note: Michael Riconosciuto, the informant who claimed to have installed the back door, became a witness for INSLAW and testified on their behalf as to what he had done. Three days after his testimony, he was arrested for drug charges and sentenced to thirty years in prison. Upon his release, he was met by representatives of a movie deal. Three days later, he was *picked up and sent back to jail for a parole violation. A damned coincidence if I ever saw one.*

January 3, 1986:

Judi Gibbs was found dead, lying outside a window in her house. The Coroner ruled her death from smoke inhalation. Her house burned down with no cause ever discovered.

Ms. Gibbs appeared in Penthouse magazine in the December 1979 issue. She worked in a bordello in Fordyce, Arkansas, near Mena. The bordello reportedly ran a blackmail operation. They took pictures of clients with the girls. Word had it that there were pictures of Bill and Judi having sex, and that could have been destructive to his Presidential ambitions.

Question ... did Judi Gibbs die in an accidental house fire? Or was she *Whacked?*

You decide.

February 19, 1986

Barry Seal, a young and gifted pilot, used his own plane to run drugs from South America to the U.S., and when caught, he became a DEA informant and was found dead in his car riddled with bullets.

Seal worked with the Medellin cartel and claimed he'd earned up to $100 million and smuggled as much as $5 billion worth of cocaine into the U.S. He was caught smuggling Quaaludes into Florida in 1984. He offered to become an informant to the U.S. Attorney in exchange for going free but was again turned down.

Seal hopped in his Learjet and flew to the White House. He met with members of the Reagan administration, including Vice President George H.W. Bush's task force on crime. The task force agreed to make Seal an undercover DEA operative and set him up in business.

He was provided a military cargo plane to smuggle cocaine from Nicaragua into the U.S. as part of a sting operation. The cocaine Seal was flying came from the Sandinista government. And here is where the spark of the Iran Contra affair found life. Hidden cameras on the plane photographed the smuggling operation. The Reagan administration used the photos with the Press, using them to try and justify arming the Contras.

At the same time, Seal also worked for the CIA. They were involved in supporting Contra groups smuggling cocaine into the U.S. Allegedly, the money from drug sales funded the Contras. That meant that the CIA was backing a drug smuggling operation funneling drugs into the U.S., And much of that smuggling operation ran through Mena, Arkansas.

Seal testified on behalf of the government and was awarded a get-out-of-jail card for his efforts. He was sentenced to community service for all the crimes he committed. In a coincidence, a leak of information outed Seal Barry Seal, and the Cartel found out.

Before Seal began his public service work at a Salvation Army in Baton Rouge, Louisiana, he turned up dead in his car with multiple bullet wounds riddling his body. Mistakes were punished. At the time of his death, Seal had the personal, unlisted phone number of Vice President Bush in his wallet.

Question ... was Barry Seal killed by the Cartel for revenge? Or was he *Whacked* for what and who he knew?

You decide.

July 1986

Karl-Heinz Beckurts, a director at Siemens and an SDI contractor (Star Wars), was killed by a car bomb in Munich.

Question ... was Heinz Beckurt's murder targeted or random? Or was he *Whacked?*

You decide.

August 4, 1986

Vimal Bhagvangi Dajibhai, 24, a talented software engineer working at Marconi Underwater Systems on the guidance electronics of a torpedo called Sting Ray, was found dead at the bottom of Avon Gorge below the Clifton Suspension Bridge in Bristol, England. His death was ruled a suicide.

Vimal had fallen 245 feet to his death in the middle of the night. His car was found nearby with one half-drunk bottle of wine in the front seat and an entire bottle of the same in the back. His parents, whom he lived with, said he never drank.

His death ruling of suicide was challenged, and there were two post-mortem with a total share of irregularities. Vimal's death came as he was the only employee left in his area who knew of a heavy-weight torpedo known as Tigerfish, already used by the Royal Navy.

Question ... did young Mr. Dajibhai die by suicide? Or was he *Whacked?*

You decide.

September 1986

Gerrold von Bruanmuhl, a senior advisor in SDI (Star Wars) negotiations for the German government, was killed under suspicious circumstances.

Question ... was von Bruanmuhl a random murder? Or was he *Whacked?*

You decide.

October 1986

Arshad Sharif, 26, a top software engineer working for Marconi Defense Systems on an airborne electronic warfare system known as Zeus, died an unusual death.

Sharif used four sections of tow rope tied together. He tied one end around a tree around his neck and then sped off quickly to his death in his car. Police were stunned by the scene but ruled it a probable suicide.

The Coroner described his manner of death as unusual and complicated. A receipt for one tow rope was found, but not the four present, all new. As with Vimal Bhagvangi Dajibhai, Sharif had been driven from London, where he lived, to Bristol to die. The Coroner noted that they both worked for Marconi.

The Coroner described it as a James Bond moment, quoting Bond as saying, "This is past coincidence." His verdict on Sharif's death was recorded as 'Open.' Sharif died during the last week of his work with Marconi.

Question ... did Arshad Sharif die of a bizarre suicide? Or was he *Whacked?*

You decide.

1987

January 8, 1987

A DEFINITE MAYBE ...

It was a typical day at Loughborough University when two colleagues, months away from their Doctorates, went to a local reservoir to complete some experiments they'd been working on. One colleague went to buy lunch, and when he returned, he found his friend, 26-year-old Avtar Singh Gita, missing. He couldn't find him anywhere.

Instead of adding Singh-Gita to the thousands of missing persons the police have in files, they did something unprecedented. The police, who publicly stated foul play was not suspected, launched a search of the century.

Twenty detectives were assigned to the case. They conducted air and ground searches of the reservoir, quizzed everyone who knew him, and even brought in Scotland Yard and Interpol. All to no avail, but you have to ask why?

One of the many coincidences was that Singh-Gita knew and worked on some of the same sensitive projects that the newly deceased Vimal Bhagvangi Dajibhai and Arshad Sharif had been working on. Of course, the authorities quickly denied this.

Singh-Gita's 25-year-old wife reported that her husband was distraught when he heard about the death of Imal Bhagvangi Dajibhai. She said he had been acting strangely. Then, one of his university lecturers came forward with information that Singh-Gita had been working with a grant from the defense industry.

Two days before he went missing, police said they picked up a rumor that he and his wife were having problems, he being Sikh and she Christian. His wife denied the rumor, reminding them he had just given her a $150 wedding present.

Then, the university showed up at the couple's residence in what was described as a friendly raid. They took boxes of computer discs of Singh-Gita's research work. And, of course, his dissertation entitled "Underwater Signal Processing'.

It was strange when, four months later, in May, he was spotted in France. A local newspaper back home, The Derby Evening Telegraph, got wind of it and sent a reporter. He was working in a boutique in the red-light district. He agreed to talk to the reporter but wanted assurance that he wouldn't be dealing with the authorities.

The timing of the tip to the local newspaper became news. A police insider had shared his whereabouts with the paper. Seems they'd known all along where he was hiding out. So why the tip four months later?

It came just when there was another mysterious death (you'll read about him later) of a defense computer guru when on the way to work one day, he turned around to go the other way and, by coincidence, sped up and slammed into the side of a building where he died instantly. The news of Singh-Gita's finding overshadowed another death in the defense industry.

Avtar Singh-Gita to England and his family. He had stipulations, though. They could never ask him about his disappearance or his work at the time he went missing, and they could never mention the death of his friend, Vimal Bhagvangi Dajibhai.

January 12, 1987

Dr. John Brittan, a senior scientist at the Royal Armament Research and Development Establishment (RARDE), was found dead in the garage of his home in Camberley, Surrey. His death was ruled a suicide by carbon monoxide poisoning.

The day he passed, he prepared for work. His wife said everything was normal, and they had plans that evening. The day was cold, and his son suggested warming the car before leaving.

Dr. Brittan was found in the garage slumped over the steering wheel of his car with the car running. No pipes were running from the exhaust into the windows. His family could not agree with the suicide ruling, and it was at some point ruled an accidental death.

Later, it emerged that Dr. Brittan was working on C3i projects, the same projects David Sands, whom you are about to meet, worked on.

Question ... did Dr. John Brittan absentmindedly sit in his warming car and kill himself with carbon monoxide? Or was he *Whacked?*

You decide.

February 1987

Larry Guerin, FBI Special Agent, was killed while investigating the INSLAW case. The details of his death remain a mystery, as does the actual date. The only date available is February 1987.

Question ... did Agent Guerin die in the line of duty? Or was he *Whacked?*

You decide.

February 1987

David Skeels, a Marconi engineer, died of carbon monoxide poisoning in his own garage. His death was ruled a suicide.

Question ... did David Skeels kill himself? Or was he *Whacked?*

You decide.

February 21, 1987

Peter Peapell, a lecturer, senior scientist, and Professor of Metallurgy at the Royal Military College, was found dead in his garage under his car.

The night before his death, Peter and his wife went to a dinner party with friends. They came home after midnight, his wife went to bed, and Peter put the car in the garage. His wife admitted being overtired and didn't wake up again until 9:30 AM.

She assumed her husband was downstairs making tea but did not find him there. She stepped outside and saw the garage door was closed but could hear the car running. She rushed to the garage and found her husband dead under the car.

Mr. Peapell was found under the car, with his mouth near the exhaust pipe and near the back of the vehicle. With the door closed, there was no room to walk behind the car. The only way to slide under the car was from the back. The big question became, if this was suicide, how did Peter get under the car and then close the overhead door? Perhaps a coincidence.

His work centered on how metals behave during explosions, and he worked a great deal with titanium. He had also just returned from time in the United States. His wife could not accept that he committed suicide, and police agreed it was an odd way to do it.

Question ... did Peter Peapell miraculously get under his car, place himself with his face by the exhaust pipe, and somehow close the overhead door to kill himself? Or was he *Whacked?*

You decide.

March 1987

John Whitehead, a Marconi engineer, drowned himself in his bathtub.

The body was surrounded by pills and empty alcohol bottles. Yet the autopsy revealed no trace of drugs or alcohol. His death was never solved.

Question ... did Mr. Whitehead drown himself? Or was he *Whacked?*

You decide.

March 30, 1987

David Sands, a top scientist at Easams, a secretive Marconi subsidiary, died when his Austin Maestro slammed into a building at high speed. Authorities quickly reported that his death had nothing to do with other Marconi mystery deaths, and it was ruled a suicide.

But here comes the exciting coincidence. David Sands left home as he did every morning, heading to work. His wife said he was in a good mood and noticed nothing out of order. He drove his usual route, the A33 dual carriageway.

That is until ... he made a U-turn, accelerated to high speed, and drove straight into a brick wall of what was once the Little Chef cafe.

Easam's spokesperson said Sands was an essential and valuable employee but was not working on anything highly classified. Sometime later, one of his co-workers said David was an authority on military communications and command and control systems. He also said he'd been working on the Air Defense Command Information System (ADCIS) project. It was part of what was known as 3Ci.

His colleague further stated ... "*David Sands knew a lot.*"

Question ... did David Sands lose it on the way to work and slam his car into a brick wall to kill himself? Or was he *Whacked?*

You decide.

April 10, 1987

David Greenhalgh, a defense contracts manager at International Computers Limited (ICL), was found near death beneath a railway bridge not far from his home. The incident was immediately covered with a blanket of secrecy.

Greenhalgh had left home as usual heading to work and four hours later was found, after falling 40 feet and landing near rail lines between London and Bristol. The Woodley Police station was just over 130 yards away, but they'd seen or heard nothing.

While in Royal Berkshire Hospital, those close to him soon learned that after officers visited, they said, "*We had a visit from officers telling us that under no circumstances was this story to be released to the press.*" David was moved to different hospitals and eventually recovered.

His employer, ICL, maintained that he was just a 'salesman' and handled no classified information. Truth be told, it came out he was working on some very highly classified defense contracts. ICL announced it had won a major new, top-secret defense contract three weeks after his fall.

Question ... did David Greenhalgh jump from that bridge for no apparent reason? Or was he *Whacked?*

You decide.

Stuart Gooding, a scientific officer at the Royal Military College, died in a mysterious head-on collision while on a diving expedition in Cypress.

Stuart was reportedly being driven by a lorry driver on a mountain road when he was struck by an oncoming lorry. The driver was uninjured, and Stuart was the only one killed. The inquest to follow determined it was the fault of the deceased, in this case Stuart Gooding.

The Royal Military College had little to say and downplayed his role at the College.

Question ... did Stuart Gooding somehow cause an accident in which he wasn't driving but died in the process? Or was he *Whacked?*

You decide.

April 17, 1987

Shanni Wilson, a young Administrative Assistant working at Micro Scope, was found dead at the edge of Taplow Lake in England. Initially, the police reported her suspicious death as a suicide.

She was found face down in about eighteen an inch of water. Fully clothed, gagged, with a noose around her neck, her hand tied behind her back, and her ankles bound. Suicide? Her new Vauxhall Cavalier car was found nearby, with the door open and items strewn around the area. The only things missing were her purse and keys.

The night before, she had gone to dinner with her boyfriend, and they made plans to meet the next day. Her Mother was away for the weekend, and they had plans for when she would return. No one saw any signs of distress, and she reported she was always happy.

After an investigation, the police ruled her death a suicide. Her parents objected. A pathologist was hired by the Home office and reported the following. He declared the deceased had Shanni had tried to strangle herself, gagged herself, tied her hands behind her back, and hopped several yards in her stiletto heels to the water's edge and drowned. Now, that is one helluva coincidence.

While there were marks on her body, she was not sexually assaulted, but police had no answers as to where the bruises came from. Shanni's parents began what would be a long and unsuccessful fight for the truth behind their daughter's death.

BBC television shows CrimeWatch took up her case. They produced a show calling for witnesses to come forward. The latest police spokesman on the show proclaimed it had always been a murder investigation. But friends and family knew this was going nowhere. They were right. The police never took up the cause again once the show aired.

So why might someone murder Shanni and the police not be interested? She was just a secretary, right? Micro Scope, a computer company where she worked, denied they worked on anything for defense or confidentiality. Ten days after her death, there was an announcement from a Micro Scope partner of winning a defense contract to work on NATO software.

Two weeks after that, GEC Computers announced it was buying Micro Scope. The GEC CEO announced that it had collaborated with MicroScope for seven years on the NATO software systems. Despite their consistent denials, they were all, in fact, part of the defense establishment.

Question ... did Shanni Wilson perform an incredible magic trick and kill herself most unusually? Or was she *Whacked?*

You decide.

April 24, 1987

Mark Wisner, a computer software engineer at the Airplane & Armament Experimental Establishment (A&AEE), was found dead with nine feet of cling film wrapped around his face. His death was ruled accidental by asphyxia.

The subsequent investigation discovered Mr. Wisner was into kinky sex up to and including restricting one's air to get higher arousal. That information was debated since he held a highly classified position. Why would the authorities not have known this information before his death?

The organization denied that Wisner worked on classified projects. The truth was that he was developing the software for the Tornado warplane, which was one of the nation's most sensitive defense projects.

Question ... did Mr. Wisner die of a tragic accident while pleasuring himself? Or was he *Whacked?*

You decide.

May 3, 1987

Michael Baker, a scientist and digital communications expert at Plessey Major Systems, died when his car mysteriously ran off the road and crashed.

But there was a coincidence or two. Michael was an avid fisherman, but on this day, his Mother said he did not want to go. Two friends wanted to learn how to fish and came by, and he went against his own wishes.

On the way fishing, an accident happened. Michael was found slumped over the wheel of his car; his two passengers were uninjured. His passengers claimed they couldn't remember the accident. When asked to comment, one politely clarified that he would not comment.

Sergeant Wayman, the investigating officer, could not conclude a cause for the accident. There were no skid marks, clear and dry weather, or witnesses. Curious indeed.

At the Coroner's inquest, it was determined he died of brain damage, apparently from the accident.

Question ... did Michael Baker have a strange accident with no signs of an accident that killed him from a brain injury? Or was he *Whacked?*

You decide.

August 23, 1987

Kevin Ives & his friend Don Henry, childhood friends ages 16 and 17, were found dead on train tracks bordering the Mean, Arkansas airport. Both had been ran over by a train. Their deaths were ruled accidental from falling asleep because they were stoned on marijuana on the railroad tracks.

An upheaval ensued, and further investigation revealed that Kevin Ives died of blunt force trauma and Don Henry died of a knife in the back. It was determined that both were killed elsewhere and placed on the tracks. Their bodies had been covered with a camouflaged tarp in an apparent effort to conceal their bodies from the train conductor.

The boys had been out spotting deer. Their flashlight was found nearby. Their deaths were never ruled a murder and have never been solved. The speculation has been the two boys were out in the night and stumbled on to the alleged drug operation being out of the Mena Airport. It would be revealed some years later that, in fact, drugs were being run through the airport. It had ties to the Iran-Confra Affair, the CIA, and then Governor Bill Clinton of Arkansas.

Years later, Linda Ives, Mother of Kevin Ives, still trying to solve the case, was denied key FOIA requests, and those she received were heavily redacted. In February 2018, former World Wrestling Federation champion Billy Jack Haynes recorded a video testimony in which he claimed to have witnessed the murders of Ives and Henry while providing security for a drug trafficking drop in 1987.

Question ... were these two young boys accidentally killed by a train after they carelessly fell asleep on the tracks after covering themselves with a camouflage tarp? Or were they *Whacked?*

You decide.

1988

January 1988

Russell Smith, a Marconi lab technician, jumped to his death off a cliff in Cornwall, England. His family was shocked. The inquiry ruled a suicide.

Question ... did Russell Smith willingly jump to his death? Or was he *Whacked?*

You decide.

March 25, 1988

Trevor Knight, an engineer working for Marconi Defense Systems, was found dead in his Ford Capri with a hose hooked to the tailpipe and leading to the passenger compartment. His death was ruled a suicide by carbon monoxide poisoning.

And then the coincidences started piling up. Knight had talked with his Mother the previous day, she said, and he was happy, and they made plans for the next week. His closest was surprised, had seen no signs, and supposedly saw the suicide note turned over to police. When reporters asked his friend about the 'suicide' note, he replied, *"No comment."*

The Press asked Marconi for comment. They said they were saddened by his death, but no, he didn't work or handle anything sensitive or classified. Another coincidence later came out: Knight was not an engineer but a computer services manager.

In another revelation of sorts, Trevor Knight had worked at Marconi Underwater Systems in the previous two years, at the exact location where Vimal Dajibhai, another deceased employee, worked, and he'd worked at Marconi Defense Systems, where Arched Sharif, another deceased employee, worked. Pure coincidence, I'm sure.

Question ... did Trevor Knight decide to suck carbon monoxide to his demises? Or was he *Whacked?*

You decide.

May 17, 1988

Keith Coney, friends of Kevin Ives and Don Henry, died when his motorcycle apparently slammed into the back of a truck. Surprisingly, no one saw the accident, and the bike was not damaged.

Keith Coney was believed to have been with Ives and Henry the night of their murder. Coney told family and friends that law enforcement officials were involved in the deaths.

Question ... did young Mr. Coney die from a motorcycle accident? Or was he *Whacked?*

You decide.

August 1988

Alistair Beckham, an electrical engineer and Quality Control Manager at Plessey Naval Systems, a British defense contractor, was found dead in a shed next to his home in Vauxhall Cavalier. He apparently wired himself to the primary electric current and committed suicide by turning the power on.

Alistair had dropped off his wife to work early that day, which is a curious coincidence. They'd talked of their upcoming weekend getaway and his plans for the day, such as painting the house. He had promised to pick her up promptly at her quitting time.

When her work ended, and he didn't show, she got a ride home and found him in the shed deceased. At the inquest upon his death, it was ruled a suicide. His wife continued believing there was foul play.

Question ... did Mr. Beckham kill himself by electrocution? Or was he *Whacked?*

You decide.

August 24, 1988

Peter Ferry, a retired Army Brigadier, and current Marconi employee, was found dead in a cottage on the grounds of the Marconi plant where he worked.. Brigadier Ferry had apparently wired each of his molars to a lamp and turned the light on, electrocuting himself. The official ruling was suicide. His friends were perplexed, but the matter was closed.

Ferry was a business development manager for Marconi. Before working for them, he was a career military officer, having served three years in the United States working at the British embassy and later on defense staff. His wife remained unconvinced of the inquest's conclusions.

Question ... did Brigadier Peter Ferry kill himself in a most gruesome manner? Or was he *Whacked?*

You decide.

November, 1988

Kevin McCaskie, of Mena, Arkansas, died 3 days after making his own funeral arrangements when he was stabbed 113 times, according to the Coroner. His murder has never been solved. McCaskie is said to have had information on the Ives and Henry murders.

Question ... did McCaskie die of a simple murder? Or was he *Whacked?*

You decide.

1989

January, 1989:

James Milam was found dead, decapitated. The Arkansas State Medical Examiner ruled the death of natural causes due to an ulcer. (You can't make this up.) Mr. Milam was reportedly a witness to the Ives and Henry murders and an insider with knowledge of the drug running at Mena Airport.

Question ... did that raging ulcer cut Mr. Milam's head off? Or was he *Whacked?*

You decide.

Gregory Collins, a local Mena, Arkansas resident, died of a gunshot wound to the face. Mr. Collins was said to be a witness to the Ives and Henry murders.

Question ... was that gunshot wound to the face an accident or murder? Or was he *Whacked?*

You decide.

February 1989

Miriam Bush was found dead in a motel room just outside of San Jose, California, in December 1989. A plastic bag was around her head, and her arms were bruised and scratched. The cause of death was ruled a suicide.

Ms. Bush was a long-time secretary at the Army base in White Sands, New Mexico, when there were reports of a UFO crashing there. There was much speculation, but as time went on, many believed there was something behind hidden. Bush was thought to be a witness to whatever supposedly took place.

Question ... did Miriam Bush die of suicide? Or was she *Whacked?*

You decide.

April 1989

Jeff Rhodes was discovered dead when his body was found burned in a local trash dump. Authorities believed he had information on the deaths of Ives, Henry, and McKaskle. He died of a wound to the head. His body had been mutilated, his hands and feet had been partially sewn off. It is believed he was tortured before death.

Question ... was Jeff Rhodes a victim of simple murder? Or was he *Whacked?*

You decide.

July 1989

Richard Winters was killed in a robbery in Mena, Arkansas, which later was proven to be a setup. He had ties to the deaths of Ives & Henry.

Question ... was Richard Winters a victim of a robbery gone wrong? Or was he *Whacked?*

You decide.

The Nineties

What Did Your Government Do?

After a decade of only the invasion of Grenada in the 1980s, the bankers needed some cash heading into the 1990s. The 1990s came in with the infamous Gulf War, and that is using the term loosely. The 'war' lasted five long days; we had battles in Vietnam that lasted longer than that. But we liberated Kuwait, proving what a paper tiger Saddam Hussein really was.

To keep the money flowing, we had the Oklahoma City bombing, which was the first of several false flags to come. The first World Trade Center bombing in New York City was a precursor to the big one that would usher in the 2000s. The Los Angeles riots introduced us to the tactic of flash mobs and destruction 'triggered' by the police response to Rodney King behaving badly.

Saviors that we are in America, we couldn't seem to find our way to Rwanda to help the Tutsis, who were slaughtered en masse by the Hutus, for only God knows why. The Rwandan genocide saw nearly a million people maniacally murdered while the peace-loving United Nations stood by. Of course, there were no greenbacks for the bankers in this debacle.

It was also the decade of Arkansas moving to the White House and scandals galore. Thanks to Slick Willie, kids across the nation were introduced to oral sex and the art of lying Presidential style. We never learned what the meaning of the word 'is' is, though.

The worldwide web burst on the scene, a President was impeached, although we learned that meant nothing, and computers started appearing on everyone's desks. The stock market went crazy, with tech giants emerging, and Amazon went a decade without making a profit.

As the decade wound down, reality stole the headlines when the Columbine massacre headlined the news. Guns were the problem, or was it the Y2K disaster fueling our doom? Global cooling of the 80s morphed into Global warming thanks to Al Gore.

The mantra of the 1990s was the burgeoning global economy, the future for all. Of course, our leaders ignored our first and greatest President, George Washington, when he warned us in his Farewell Address to stay free from foreign entanglements. By the end of the 1990s, we had many foreign entanglements.

The Vietnam War, Grenada, Kuwait, Cuba, Nicaragua, and Guatemala come to mind. One thread of entanglement is a little-known airline operated by the CIA that has its tentacles in countries worldwide. Vietnam vets will remember it for the white helicopters with the little letters Air America on the side.

Air America originated when Chiang Kai-shek fought for China's survival and needed air support. A group of American pilots, known as the Flying Tigers, emerged from the OSS (CIA) to save the day. The little group of daring pilots soon morphed into Civil Air Transport, a wholly owned company financed by your tax dollars.

The airline began flying whatever aircraft the country it was serving needed. It served countries all over the world, including China, Japan, Tibet, and even the Korean War. CAT, as it was known, grew and grew and, at one point, was the largest airline operation in the world, operating under many umbrella companies.

When the OSS became the CIA, CAT became Air America. They were big in Cuba, Guatemala, Vietnam, Thailand, Laos, and other lesser-known operations. The airline was supposedly disbanded on

June 30, 1976. But don't be naive... it's alive and well with a new name.

Air America's slogan was "Anything, Anywhere, Anytime, Professionally."

Question ... can you be any more foreign entangled than that?

1990

March 1990

Jonathan Boyle, a British journalist, was investigating claims that U.S. civilian helicopters were being modified into gunships to be sold to Iraq; he was found dead, hanging inside a hotel wardrobe in Santiago, Chile.

After eight years, the authorities announced he'd been 'unlawfully killed by a person or persons unknown.' His former fiancé said, *"The British intelligence services tried to smear Jonathan suggesting he was sexually deviant."*

Question ... did Jonathon Boyle hang himself in Santiago? Or was he *Whacked?*

You decide.

June 1990:

Jordan Kettleson was discovered shot to death sitting in the front seat of his pickup truck in Mena, Arkansas. He was believed to have witnessed the train deaths of Ives and Henry. He reached out to provide information, but before he did, he was found dead.

Question ... was Jordan Kettleson a victim of a simple murder? Or was he *Whacked?*

You decide.

1991

January 22, 1991

James E. Sabow, 51, an active duty Colonel in the United States Marine Corps, was found dead of a gunshot wound in his backyard at the El Toro Marine Corps Aviation Station in California.

Colonel Sabow was third-in-command on the base and a decorated veteran of 221 combat missions during the Vietnam War. He was a career Marine who'd expressed to his family a growing concern about guns and narcotics being trafficked on the bases.

He was in good spirits on the morning of his death, planning a family barbecue that evening. His wife took the kids to school and returned within 30 minutes to find her husband deceased in the backyard. A shotgun nearby. His wife did not accept the suicide ruling to no avail. She said he was talking on the phone when she left and planned to leave for work immediately.

Question ... did Colonel Sabot die of a self-inflicted gunshot wound? Or was he *Whacked?*

You decide.

January 31, 1991

Alan Standorf, an electronic specialist with the National Security Agency (NSA), was found dead in the backseat of his car at Washington National Airport.

Standoff was a source of information for Danny Casalaro, an investigator in the INSLAW case against the Department of Justice.

Question ... was Alan Standorf a victim of random violence? Or was he *Whacked?*

You decide.

April 23, 1991

Dennis Eisman was found shot to death. His death was ruled a suicide.

He was an attorney with information on INSLAW and their case with the Department of Justice.

Question ... Did Dennis Eisman commit suicide. Or was he *Whacked?*

You decide.

August 9,1991:

Danny Casalaro, an investigative journalist, was found dead in a motel room with his wrist slit more than a dozen times. His death was ruled a suicide.

Casalaro was working on the INSLAW case when his research turned the story into one of significant magnitude involving the highest levels of the U.S. government. He was discovering information on Iran and the Iran-Contra affair. He began receiving death threats but pushed on.

He told friends he was traveling to West Virginia to meet a whistleblower. He was found dead in the hotel where he went to meet his source. His death was ruled a suicide. Experts say it is rare for someone to cut their wrists multiple times in a suicide.

Question ... did Danny Casalaro commit suicide? Or was he *Whacked?*

You decide.

1992

1992

Colonel Gerardo Huber, a high-ranking Chilean military officer, went missing for three weeks and then was found dead on the banks of a river in Santiago, Chile. His death was ruled a suicide. In a coincidence, his personal driver committed suicide around the same time.

Huber's sister-in-law said three Army officers showed up when he went missing and wanted to take custody of his three children. She refused. Colonel Huber had testified in an arms smuggling case that led back to Chilean Dictator Augusto Pinochet. It involved illegal arms deals between Chile and Croatia during the war in Bosnia.

Eventually, four Army officers were tied to his murder.

Question ... was Colonel Gerardo Huber a victim of murder? Or was he *Whacked?*

You decide.

March 1992

A LITTLE CONTEXT ...

During the 1992 Presidential race, the New York Times broke a story regarding Bill and Hillary Clinton regarding real estate investments in what was known as the Whitewater Development Corporation. The story became known as the Whitewater Scandal. Their article led to an independent investigation of Resolution Trust Corporation by investigator L. Jean Lewis.

This failed business venture aimed to develop vacation properties on land along the Arkansas River. The Clintons and James and Susan McDougal were involved in this investment, which led to investigations and allegations regarding financial improprieties and subsequent legal issues.

A few coincidences that were revealed ...

Susan McDougal received a $300,000 fraudulent federally backed loan. Some of the loans ended up in the Whitewater Development Corporation. David Hale, the principal of the company providing the loan told investigators he was pressured by Bill Clinton to provide the loan to McDougal.

Hillary Clinton denied involvement. The billing records in the case were under subpoena for two years before mysteriously reappearing in Clinton's private quarters at the White House. The true extent of Hillary's legal work was revealed.

One potential witness in the case was White House counsel Vincent Foster. His 1993 'suicide' negated his possible testimony in this case, as well as the travel-office fiasco and his filing of delinquent Whitewater Corporation tax returns.

Former Associate Attorney General Webster L. Hubbell received more than $700,000, mostly from friends of President Clinton and Democratic Party supporters. The payments came just before Whitewater investigators intensely scrutinized the former law partner of Hillary Clinton.

The original Whitewater special prosecutor was Robert B. Fiske Jr., a moderate Republican selected by Attorney General Janet Reno in January 1994.

In August 1994, a three-judge panel abruptly replaced him with a conservative activist named Kenneth W. Starr.

Starr's investigation lasted a grueling 13 months, and the results were ...

The McDougals and Arkansas Gov. Jim Guy Tucker (D) were convicted of most fraud and conspiracy charges. After his trial, James McDougal received a reduced sentence of three years for cooperating with Whitewater investigators. He died in March of a heart attack, only a few months before he hoped to be released from prison.

Susan McDougal, convicted of much lesser charges, was sentenced to two years. She started serving her sentence and was indicted on contempt of court for refusing to testify before Starr's grand jury. She was then indicted again for criminal contempt and obstructing Starr's investigation. Eventually, an Arkansas jury acquitted McDougal of obstructing justice in the Whitewater investigation and deadlocked on the two other charges, which resulted in a mistrial.

Governor Tucker, who succeeded, was convicted of conspiracy and mail fraud and was sentenced to 18 months of home detention because of poor health.

Two Arkansas bankers accused of four felony charges involving their bank and donations to Clinton's 1990 statewide campaign were acquitted when the jury deadlocked.

In case you're wondering, President Clinton testified via teleconference. And in another extraordinary coincidence, neither Bill nor Hillary were charged.

April 1992

Eugenio Barrios, a chemist who worked for the Chilean secret intelligence agency DINA, was found dead on El Pinar beach, where he washed up in Montevideo, Uruguay. He had four bullet holes in his chest, and his face and hands were removed, presumably to prevent identification.

Barrios had a long and sordid past on both sides of the aisle. He was suspected of administering poison to former Chilean President Eduardo Frei Montalva in 1982. Barrios produced sarin gas and other chemical weapons in the basement of his Santiago villa during the US-backed Pinochet dictatorship.

He was also suspected of building the bomb that killed Chilean diplomat Orlando Letelier in 1976 in Washington, DC. And is believed to be the creator of 'black cocaine,' an odorless compound that could be smuggled past U.S. border security.

After the 1973 Chilean Coup, Barrios was ordered to testify about his activities. With the help of Chilean intelligence officers, he was smuggled to Uruguay, where he lived undercover. Barrios feared for his life. On one occasion, he escaped to the Uruguayan police.

Uruguayan military intelligence surrounded the police station, where he fled and forced the police to hand him over at gunpoint. He was never seen again.

Question ... did Eugenio Barrios die a fugitive? Or was he *Whacked?*

You decide.

July 30, 1992

C. Victor Raiser II, along with his son, Montgomery Raiser, died in a plane crash along with three other passengers on a fishing expedition in Alaska.

Clinton campaign Press Secretary Dee Dee Myers said Raiser II was a significant player in the Clinton organization. Raiser had been a friend of the Clintons for a decade. He was also the finance co-chairman of Clinton's presidential campaign. Previously, he was national finance chairman of the DNC and served on the Democratic Business Council, the Center for National Policy, and the board of advisers for the Democratic Leadership Council.

Question ... were the Raiser's the victims of a private plane crash? Or were they *Whacked!*

You decide.

September 24, 1992:

Paul Tully was found dead in his room in a Little Rock hotel. The coroner ruled he apparently died of a heart attack.

At the time of his death, Mr. Tully was the Director of Operations for the Democratic National Committee. He was a close associate of Bill Clinton and headed his election campaign when he ran for Governor of Arkansas.

Question ... did Paul Tully die of a heart attack? Or was he *Whacked?*

You decide.

November 8, 1992:

Ian Spiro, a former contractor for the CIA and MI6, was found dead in a canyon outside of San Diego, California, near where he lived.

Three days before his death, his wife and two children were found murdered in their home. Spiro died of a gunshot wound to the head. The murder weapon was never found. His death was ruled a suicide.

Spriro's death remains a mystery to this day. Where is the weapon he 'suicided' himself with? Surrounded by many theories. He has been linked to Ollie North and the Iran-Contra affair. He was also a witness to the INSLAW/Clinton affair in Arkansas. And prisoner exchanges. He is also rumored to have witnessed the Inslaw Clinton affair in Arkansas.

Question ... did Ian Spiro kill himself? Or was he *Whacked?*

You decide.

December 9,1992:

Paula Grober, Bill Clinton's speech interpreter for the deaf, died in a one-vehicle high-speed car accident where she was thrown over thirty feet from the car.

She traveled with Bill Clinton for many years. And was not known as a speedy driver. There was no investigation.

Question ... did Paula die as a result of her speeding accident? Or was she *Whacked?*

You decide.

December 21, 1992:

Jim Wilhite was Vice Chairman of ARKLA Inc. and Chief Executive of Entex Inc., its subsidiary. He died from injuries incurred during a skiing accident in Aspen, Colorado.

His death occurred less than a week after ARKLA chairman Thomas McLarty resigned to become Clinton's White House Chief of Staff.

Question ... did Jim Wilhite die as a result of a freak skiing accident? Or was he *Whacked*?

You decide.

1993

February 28, 1993

A DEFINITE MAYBE ...

Attorney General Janet Reno brought Waco to American television screens. But what you may not know is on this date, former Clinton bodyguards and current ATF Agents Steve Willis, Robert Williams, Todd McKeahan & Conway LeBleu died by gunfire in the siege at Waco.

All four were examined by a pathologist, and all died from identical wounds to the left temple. All four were bodyguards for Bill Clinton. Three were guards when he campaigned for President and all while he was Governor of Arkansas. And in another stunning coincidence, they were the ONLY ATF agents killed at Waco.

March 26, 1993:

ANOTHER DEFINITE MAYBE ...

Five Navy Aviators died on this day. As reported, they all died in a crash of an E-2C Hawkeye in Italy. The incident began when a plane was 'waved off' while attempting to land on the Carrier Roosevelt. The 'wave off' was said to be caused by a 'foul deck.'

By pure coincidence, all five men had been Bill Clinton's escorts two weeks prior during the former President's visit to the Roosevelt.

Note: In what could only be described as a stunning coincidence, a few weeks later a helicopter crash took the lives of three other pilots who had flown Clinton to the Roosevelt for his visit.

April 1993

John Crawford, an attorney, died from a heart attack in Tacoma, Washington.

Crawford reportedly had information on the INSLAW case and was working with officials at the time of his death.

Question ... did John Crawford actually die of a heart attack? Or was he *Whacked?*

You decide.

May 1993

A LITTLE CONTEXT ...

Shortly after taking office President Bill Clinton fired the entire White House Travel Office staff. It was the first of many scandals under the Clinton Administration became known as TravelGate.

The group fired were long-time government travel employees. They were replaced with individuals from Arkansas who were allies and friends of the Clintons. The immediate allegations were political favoritism.

Under pressure from the White House, the FBI was called in to investigate the matter, and insiders say, to prove the firings were justified. The firings were supposedly financial, and there was a need to modernize the travel office.

However, the FBI found the decisions was more likely made to give the gold mine travelaccount to President Clinton's friend, Harry Thomason, and his travel agency. The findings led Congress to appoint an investigation committee to investigate the matter.

The investigation concluded that the firings were motivated by the Clintons' political dealings and favors. And ... nothing happened.

May 19, 1993

A DEFINITE MAYBE ...

USMC aviators Staff Sergeant Brian Haney, Marine Sergeant Tim Sabel, Major William Barkley, and Captain Scott Reynolds died in a US Marine Corps helicopter crash in Blossom Point, Maryland. The helicopter was one of a small fleet that transported the President.

Archaeologist Frank Owens and his assistant witnessed the helicopter flying over them, sensed trouble, and discovered the crash site in a clearing thirty minutes later. The local authorities arrived within minutes. The wreckage was scattered across an acre of forest.

Within an hour, a heavily armed Marine unit secured the area. Three months later, the Marines issued their final report on the crash, concluding it was caused by mechanical failure due to faulty maintenance. When Frank Owens read the report, he felt something was wrong.

In the weeks following the crash, he walked to the crash site and noticed that only some of the debris and jet fuel had been cleaned up. Frank found and collected forty-three pounds of wreckage from the site. He started his own investigation into the crash. His decision drew the attention of the press and military experts.

Journalist James Pate felt suspicious that the military did not collect all of the wreckage. He noted that with the crash of TWA Flight 800, investigators spent weeks picking up wreckage from the ocean floor to reassemble the plane as best as possible. This was not done with the helicopter crash.

The official USMC report said the crash was caused by improperly installed roll pins. The pins are two-inch metal rods that connect the transmission with the engine. The workers who installed the roll pins testified they were installed correctly. Another investigator noted that if the roll pin had been improperly installed, the helicopter would not have been able to fly in the first place.

Frank engaged electronics specialist Craig Coley, studied the flight path, and noticed that the pilot made an extreme U-turn. This meant the pilot realized something was wrong and tried to turn around to make an emergency landing. Yet, with an open field before him, the pilot kept flying and crashed into the woods. Craig wondered if the pilot's vision was impaired by something.

The team then discovered there were unusual burn marks on the victim's bodies. A burn specialist had examined the burns and could not determine what caused them. The Marine Corps claimed it was from jet fuel, but the burn specialist denied it was a cause. Then, they discovered something nearby.

A microwave weapons test facility was located within five miles of the crash site. Journalist James Pate believes that the helicopter crashed due to exposure to microwave radiation. A system allegedly developed during the 1980s that used microwave energy.was designed to disrupt electronic equipment in aircraft and missiles. The helicopter would have been far more susceptible to a microwave weapon because it would directly interfere with the flight control electronics.

Frank Owens concluded that a high-power microwave weapon was the only explanation for the crash. The gun could have blinded the pilot and disrupted the electronics. The Marine Corps considers the case closed.

Question ... did these four unfortunate Marines die in a tragic accident? Or were they accidentally Whacked?

You decide.

May 18, 1993

John Wilson, documentary filmmaker and former Washington DC Council member, was found dead by hanging. His death was ruled a suicide.

In another strange coincidence, Wilson reportedly had information on the Whitewater Scandal.

Question ... did John Wilson die by hanging, a suicide? Or was he *Whacked*?

You decide.

June 22, 1993

Paul Wilcher – a lawyer to whistleblowers Rodney Stich and Gunter Karl Russbacher, died under questionable circumstances. He was found dead, sitting on a toilet in his Washington DC apartment.

His demise came one month after delivering a letter to Janet Reno on behalf of his clients, Stich and Karl. He is said to have damning information on the drug running in Mena but more lethal than Danny Casalaro. He reportedly had information implicating now President Bill Clinton and other high-ranking government officials.

His murder was never solved. They determined he had been killed elsewhere and moved to his apartment.

Question ... was Paul Wilcher killed by an intruder? Or was he *Whacked*?

You decide.

July 20, 1993:

Vince Foster, a partner in the Rose Law Firm with Hillary Clinton, then chief counsel to President Clinton, was found deceased in Fort Marcy Park, located off the George Washington Parkway in Virginia, a short distance from Washington, D.C. His death was ruled a suicide.

His death would fuel the fires of many Clinton controversies. Foster was Bill Clinton's childhood friend and maintained a lifelong friendship. Foster was a crucial witness in the Whitewater Scandal at the time of his death. He had hired two lawyers to represent him in the upcoming Whitewater matter.

There were several significant coincidences, such as the Park Police, who investigated the matter and never found the bullet that killed him. And they couldn't explain why Foster's fingerprints weren't on the weapon found at the scene. And check these out ... the crack US Park Service Police fell a tad short on the investigation.

There were no gunshot residue samples of the decedent's hands.

A lack of complete documentation of the gunshot residues on the left hand.

A poorly diagrammed death scene with no measurements.

There was no photo log or documentation of who took what photographs or the total number of photos taken.

The death scene 35mm photos did not develop.

There was no documentation regarding the initial search of Foster's vehicle at the death scene, nor was inventory completed.

Included a photo of an unidentified briefcase next to a USPP vehicle.

Foster's pager was returned to the White House too soon, and no records were obtained regarding his pages.

The suicide weapon was processed with dust before other laboratory exams.

Inconsistent statements regarding moving and searching the body.As well as erratic and poorly documented autopsy.

Coincidences like this top ten list make me think of the old adage, *"Other than that Mrs. Lincoln how was the play."*

Question ... did Vince Foster commit suicide as the USPP wants us to believe? Or was he *Whacked?*

You decide.

August 15, 1993:

John Parnell Walker, a Whitewater Investigator for the Resolution Trust Corporation (RTC), mysteriously fell to his death from the top of an Arlington, Virginia high rise.

Mr. Walker was an investigator for the Resolution Trust Corporation (RTC) at his death. He had contacted the Kansas City RTC regional office regarding information concerning possible ties between Whitewater Development, Madison Guaranty Savings & Loan, and the Clintons.

Question ... did John Parnell Walker wander off the top floor of an apartment building and fall to his death? Or was he *Whacked?*

You decide.

September 10, 1993:

Dr. Stanley Heard, a chiropractor from Hot Springs, Arkansas, was killed in a private plane accident along with his attorney, who was piloting the plane.

Dr. Heard first met Bill Clinton fifteen years before his death. Clinton sought help from Heard in his planned run for state attorney general and shared with him his aspirations to become governor and President of the United States.

Throughout the ensuing years, Dr. Heard was a physician to Bill Clinton's mother, brother, and stepfather in Arkansas. Clinton appointed Heard to the National Chiropractic Health Care Advisory Committee when he became President. He worked with Hillary to define the chiropractor terms that were to be in her healthcare plan.

During the investigation of Vince Foster's death, he was found to be researching chiropractor malpractice cases. Under questioning, Fosters' widow, Lisa Foster, stated she had no idea he was studying that subject or why.

Fosters' lawyer was piloting a rented plane. The duo encountered problems with the original plane during their initial flight from Arkansas. They landed in St. Louis, Missouri, and rented another plane. They arrived in Washington, D.C., with no problems reported.

After the meeting, a Hillary healthcare meeting, they headed from D.C. to Topeka, Kansas. Their aircraft began to experience problems about 50 miles west of Washington, D.C. Witnesses heard the engine sputtering and the plane circling. It appeared to be heading to a nearby football field, but as it approached, it veered off and into the ground. The field turned out to be occupied.

What a coincidence to have trouble with two different planes on the same day.

Question ... did Dr. Heard die of a tragic private plane crash? Or was he *Whacked!*

You decide.

September 26, 1993:

Jerry Parks, Bill Clinton's head of security during his reign as Governor of Arkansas, was gunned down with 10 bullets at an intersection in Little Rock, Arkansas.

Parks had returned the day before from a Caribbean cruise with his wife. While on the cruise, he transacted at the Grand Cayman bank. His death occurred nine months after Bill Clinton was sworn in as President.

Parks was friends with the Clintons and provided security for the 1992 Clinton-Gore Presidential campaign headquarters in Little Rock. He was also reputed to have been involved in the Clinton Whitewater affair.

According to the *Arkansas Times*: Parks son, Gary, tried to link Clinton to the murders. He claimed that his father had collected a file on Clinton's sensual activities and that he was executed due to its contents. The article stated that Parks said to his son Gary, after seeing a newscast on Vince Foster's death, *"I'm a dead man."* His murder has never been solved.

Question ... did Jerry Parks die of a simple street murder? Or was he *Whacked?*

You decide.

November 29, 1993:

Ed Willey, Attorney and husband of Kathleen Willey, died of a gunshot wound. His death was ruled a suicide.

Willey's wife Kathleen, on the very date of his death, announced to the world that she was a victim of sexual assault from now-President Bill Clinton. Kathleen Willey was a campaign volunteer and did work closely with Clinton on the campaign trail. She further alleged that Hillary Clinton strong-armed other victims to keep their silence.

Question ... did Ed Willey commit suicide in the face of his wife's allegations against the President of the United States? Or was he *Whacked?*

You decide.

1994

January 8, 1994:

Gandy Baugh, an Attorney, jumped to his death from his tall office building. His death was ruled a suicide.

At the time of his death, by coincidence, Mr. Baugh was representing Dan Lassiter, a drug dealer and personal friend of now President Bill Clinton, in a drug case.

Question ... did Gandy Baugh commit suicide by jumping to his death from the top of an office building? Or was he *Whacked?*

You decide.

Note: Several reports of Gandy Baugh's law partner meeting a similar demise on February 8, one month following Gandy's death. I have been unable to confirm who this is or if they did, in fact, pass away.

February 1994

Stephen Milligan, a British Conservative MP Stephen Milligan, 45, was found dead in what could only be described as an awkward moment. Milligan was tied to a chair and wearing only women's underwear. He had a bag over his head and a satsuma stuffed into his mouth.

Milligan was the parliamentary private secretary to the then-Defense Minister Jonathan Aitken. There was speculation that Mr Aitken also worked for MI6. Aitken denied media reports to the contrary.

Question: Was Stephen Milligan what he was made out to be at his death? Or was he *Whacked?*

You decide.

James Rusbridger, a former MI6 agent, now journalist, was discovered hanging at his house on Bodmin Moor in Cornwall.

He was found dressed in a green protective suit, green overalls, a black plastic mackintosh, and thick rubber gloves. His face was covered by a gas mask, and his body was surrounded by bondage pictures.

Consultant pathologist Dr. Yasai Sivathondan said he died from asphyxia due to hanging 'in keeping with a form of sexual strangulation."

Question ... did James Rusbridger kill himself by accident during a sexcapade? Or was he Whacked?

You decide.

February 11, 1994:

James Bunch, a 23-year employee of the Texas Department of Human Services, died of a gunshot wound to the head. His death was ruled a suicide.

Bunch had been fired the day before after he was arrested on charges of aggravated promotion of prostitution. It turns out Bunch ran Aimes Escorts. In another strange coincidence, the same Acme Escorts that Judi Gibbs worked with died on January 3, 1986.

When authorities arrested Mr. Bunch, they found a black book with over 200 clients and their sexual preferences. His list included prominent politicians in Texas and Arkansas.

Question ... did James Bunch shoot himself? Or was he *Whacked?*

You decide.

March 1, 1994

Hershell Friday, Attorney, friend, and Clinton fundraiser, died when his plane exploded. No cause was ever determined.

Question ... did Friday die in a tragic accident? Or was he *Whacked*?

You decide.

May 12, 1994:

Kathy Ferguson, ex-wife of Arkansas State Trooper Danny Ferguson and witness in harassment allegations of President Clinton, was found dead with a gunshot wound to the head. Her death was ruled a suicide.

At the time of her death, her husband, Danny Ferguson, was a co-defendant in a sexual harassment lawsuit against President Clinton. Danny Ferguson claimed he brought Paula Jones to Clinton's hotel room. Kathy Ferguson claimed to know about the women Clinton had brought to him.

Coincidence time. The entry wound in the skull was behind the left ear, and the gun was found in the victim's right hand. That fact leads many to question the suicide ruling. (Ya think)

Question ... did Kathy Ferguson off herself? Or was she *Whacked*?

You decide.

June 23, 1994:

Stanley Huggins, an Investigator working on the Madison Guaranty Savings and Loan collapse (hint: James McDougal and the Clintons), reportedly died of suicide and was later reported as viral pneumonia.

His death came before his 300 pages of findings in the case could ever be released to the public. And those findings were never released.

Question ... did Stanley Huggins die of suicide or viral pneumonia? Or was he *Whacked.*

You decide.

June 12, 1994:

Bill Shelton, former Arkansas State Trooper and current fiancé of Kathy Ferguson, died of a gunshot wound.

Since his fiancé's death, Shelton was openly critical of the lack of investigation into her death.

He was found dead at her gravesite from a bullet wound. It was immediately ruled a suicide.

Question ... did a distraught Bill Shelton take his own life? Or was he *Whacked?*

You decide.

July 1994

Calvin Walraven, a key witness in the drug trial of Kevin Elder, son of Bill Clinton's Surgeon General, Jocelyn Elder, was found dead in his apartment ten days after testifying at the trial of the Surgeon General's son. He died by a bullet to the head, and it was quickly ruled a suicide.

You might remember Clinton appointing the ill-qualified Elder as Surgeon General. As America's head medical Doctor, she advocated for drug legalization, masturbation discussion, and contraception distribution in schools.

She blamed the conviction on entrapment and race, and they appealed to the Arkansas Supreme Court and lost, failing to prove entrapment. Her son Kevin was sentenced to 10 years in prison, but thanks to Slick, Willy only had to serve 4 months.

Question ... did Calvin Walraven shoot himself 10 days after testifying as a state witness? Or was he *Whacked?*

You decide.

October 30, 1994:

Florence Martin, a 69-year-old accountant and occasional contractor for the CIA, died of three gunshot wounds to the head. Her death was ruled a homicide.

Ms. Martin had subcontracted with the CIA to handle some accounting matters. Working out of Arkansas, she managed money in what became the Barry Seal (drug running through Mena) case.

When discovered, she had the account numbers and PIN for a bank account in Barry Seal's name in the Cayman Islands. The account had 1.4 million dollars in it. Immediately following her death, the money was moved to the Virgin Islands.

Twenty years later, a man was convicted of her murder.

Question ... was Ms. Martin simply a victim of murder? Or was she *Whacked?*

You decide.

November 11, 1994:

Caetono Catani, a Brazilian tourist and eyewitness to the sniper attack on the White House, died of an unknown infection.

Catani, by chance, filmed the October 29 sniper attack on the White House. His death came just one month before he was scheduled to return to the U.S. to testify in the upcoming trial of the shooter, Francisco Duran. Coincidence?

Question ... did a mysterious illness claim your Mr. Catani? Or was he *Whacked?*

You decide.

1995

March 29, 1995:

Robert Bates, an aircraft mechanic at the airport in Mena, Arkansas, was found dead. The coroner ruled that Bates died of a mouthwash overdose that took place over some time.

The police believe his death was a homicide.

Question ... did Mr. Bates mysteriously die of a mouthwash overdose? Or was he *Whacked?*

You decide.

April 19, 1995

Alan G. Whicher, former Overseer of President Clinton's Secret Service detail, died in the Oklahoma City bombing.

Whicher was transferred to the Secret Service field office in the Murrah Building in Oklahoma City in 1994. A warning was given to the federal agents in that building to not show up for work that day. However, Alan Whicher didn't get that memo and died in the bomb blast.

Question ... Did Mr. Whicher die by fate at the hands of Timothy McVey? Or was he *Whacked?*

You decide.

July 26, 1995:

Duane Garrett, a lawyer and radio host for KGO-AM in San Francisco, the body was found floating in the San Francisco Bay.

Garrett was also the finance chairman for Diane Feinstein's run for the Senate. He was also Al Gore's friend and helped raise funds for his campaign and ended up being a critical Democratic supporter and player.

He was investigated for defrauding investors with his failed sports memorabilia venture at his death. On the afternoon of his death, Garrett canceled a meeting with his lawyer because he had a meeting with some people at the San Francisco airport. Three hours later, he was found floating in the bay under the Golden Gate Bridge. His death remains unsolved.

Question ... did Duane Garrett meet his demise from simple foul play? Or was he *Whacked?*

You decide.

August 21, 1995

Kenneth Trentadue died while in custody at a federal facility in Oklahoma City, Oklahoma. He was found hanged in his cell. His death was ruled a suicide.

His death occurred during the investigation of the Oklahoma City bombing.

Despite the suicide ruling, The city's chief medical examiner said it was very likely Trentadue was murdered. Trentadue's brother, a Salt Lake City attorney, found out his brother's body was severely beaten and bruised. His bruises were from the top of his head to the soles of his feet. He had 41 wounds and bruises, visible in such a way as to indicate torture. And his jail cell was washed out before an investigation was performed.

Kenneth Trentadue, in what might be a deadly coincidence, closely resembles Richard Lee Guthrie Jr., an original suspect in the Oklahoma City bombing who was incarcerated at the same federal facility. An interesting tidbit, suspect Guthrie died while in custody of, you guessed it, suicide.

Trentadue's brother believes he was mistaken for Guthrie and tortured for a confession. The feds wouldn't entertain the argument, so the brother filed a civil suit against the government.

The feds denied any wrongdoing, so the family filed a civil suit. While the government rejected the claims, they offered the family a settlement of $1.1 million for their 'emotional distress.'

Question ... did Kenneth Trentadue die by suicide? Or was he *Whacked?*

You decide.

1996

A LITTLE CONTEXT ...

In 1996, while investigating the Clinton Administration Travelgate scandal, investigators discovered spying in the White House. The ensuing mess became known as FileGate.

The investigation began in 1993, when the White House improperly obtained access to hundreds of FBI files on former White House employees, including some senior Republicans. In a rare coincidence, the White House had done something improper, but not the individuals.

Two fall guys soon emerged, staffers Craig Livingstone and Anthony Marceca. They stepped forward and claimed they had requested the files, but no one believed them. Both Livingstone and Marceca ended up resigning.

Congressional investigators and independent counsel investigated the whole matter for months; like in all such investigations, everyone, including the Clintons, was acquitted of all wrongdoing.

So FileGate saw hundreds of Republican FBI files illegally looked at by someone in the Clinton White House, but like every Clinton scandal, bring out the Teflon and remember ... it depends on what the meaning of the word 'is' is?

February 29, 1996:

Sharlot Donavan, retired Tech Sergeant USAF, working in the White House Communications office, was found dead with a plastic bag over her head. Her death was ruled a suicide.

Question ... was Sharlot a victim of her own suicide? Or was she *Whacked?*

You decide.

April 3, 1996:

Ron Brown, US Secretary of State under President Bill Clinton, died when his plane crashed, along with 34 others in Croatia.

At the time of his death, Brown was under investigation for selling favors to Vietnam and selling seats on trade missions to raise funds for the Democratic National Committee. He was also viewed as a possible witness against President Clinton in his corruption investigations.

Brown's close business partner and political adviser, Nolanda Hill, was also under investigation along with Brown for a series of dubious financial transactions. Hill later claimed Brown's death spared him a great deal of humiliation" as he may have gone to jail if the investigations continued.

Reports surfaced that his autopsy revealed a bullet-shaped wound on the top of his head. The Pentagon quickly squelched the reports as there was nothing to see there. The accident was later determined to be a pilot error.

Question ... did Ron Brown unfortunately die in a tragic plane crash? Or was he *Whacked?*

You decide.

April 6, 1996:

Niko Junic, a maintenance worker at Dubrovnik Airport in Croatia where Ron Brown's plane crashed, was found dead at his home. His death was ruled a suicide.

Mr. Junic was the Mairport's Maintenance Supervisor. His team was responsible for the airport's guidance systems. Before his death, he testified that the systems were working correctly at the time of the crash.

Keep in mind that the official finding as to the cause of the crash was a pilot error, and this would have come after Junic's death. The smell of rotting fish fills the air.

Question ... did Mr. Junic, three days after the crash, commit suicide? Or was he *Whacked?*

You decide.

April 27, 1996

William Colby, retired CIA director, was reported missing by his wife on April 27, 1996. She thought he had gone canoeing. After an extensive search of nearby waters, his body was discovered nine days after his disappearance. His death was ruled an accidental drowning.

Colby was an enigmatic character people loved to hate. When he retired from government, he started writing for the Strategic Investment newsletter. His writing worried many in the intelligence community. He was known for divulging CIA secrets in the past.

Most recently, he had written of hiring handwriting experts to review Vince Foster's suicide note. He was not playing well with others in his retirement. Under President Ronald Reagan, the U.S. government began proceedings against Colby for unauthorized disclosures. He agreed to pay a $10,000 fine in an out-of-court settlement.

Many felt there was more to the story, but the FBI maintained there was no evidence of foul play. The official autopsy declared he died of a heart attack. One investigative journalist took exception to that finding; in his review, there were no signs of coming to that conclusion.

Question ... did CIA Director William Colby die of a heart attack or from exposure in a canoeing accident? Or was he *Whacked?*

You decide.

May 16, 1996:

Admiral Michael Boorda, Chief of Naval Operations under President Bill Clinton, was found dead in waters behind his home.

Boorda's body was found on a riverbank near his home, with his dinner still on the table. The medical examiner initially ruled his death an accidental drowning. While there was speculation about foul play or suicide, the coroner later determined that Boorda likely suffered a heart attack, causing him to fall into the water and drown.

Boorda served amidst several controversies, such as ...

Morale issues.

Allegations of improper management.

Wrongful privileges at the Norfolk Naval Exchange.

F-18 continuing program procurement problems.

Drug scandals at the Naval Academy.

If that wasn't enough, he was publicly criticized by Navy Secretary James Webb about Navy leaders currying favor with politicians.

Question ... did Admiral Boards die of a heart attack and fall in the water? Or was he *Whacked?*

You decide.

July 13, 1996

Richard Lee Guthrie, Jr., a confessed bank robber and white supremacist, was found dead in his jail cell one week after agreeing to testify in a federal investigation of subversion against the government. His death was, of course, ruled a suicide.

Some linked him to the Oklahoma City bombing and other right-wing conspiracies.

Question ... did Guthrie die by suicide? Or was he *Whacked?*

You decide.

August 25, 1996

Neil Moody, second husband to widowed Lisa Foster and an Arkansas judge, died when his speeding car slammed into a brick wall.

Around the time Susan McDougal first went to jail for contempt, Judge Moody's son, Neil, died in a car crash. There were reports that Neil Moody had discovered something unsettling about his stepmother's private papers.

He allegedly told Bob Woodward of the Washington Post about a blockbuster story. Witnesses to the accident said they saw Neil Moody sitting in his car arguing with another person just before his vehicle suddenly speeded into a brick wall.

Question ... did Neil Moody die of an unfortunate accident? Or was he *Whacked?*

You decide.

November 29, 1996:

John Hillyer, a cameraman for NBC, was found dead at his home. His death was ruled a heart attack.

Hillyer had been investigating a drug-smuggling operation in Mena, Arkansas, while Clinton was governor. Before the Mena investigation, Hillyer helped create a 30-minute video called Circle of Power and The Clinton Chronicles.

He told friends before his untimely death that he feared for his life.

Question ... did John Hillyer die of a heart attack? Or was he *Whacked?*

You decide.

November 29, 1996:

Barbara Wise, a 48-year-old Commerce Department employee who worked closely with Commerce Secretary Ron Brown, was found dead in her office. Despite being seen nude, bruised head to waist, her death was ruled by natural causes.

While Wise worked for the Commerce Department under Ron Brown, she also worked closely with John Huang, a controversial figure in the Whitewater scandal. Before working at Commerce Wise, I was a former executive with the Lippo Group of Indonesia. The Lippo Group was tied to Webster Hubble and alleged payoffs to the Clintons.

Question ... did Ms. Wise die of natural causes? Or was she *Whacked?*

You decide.

December 1996

Nicholas Husband, a GCHQ worker, was found dead wearing women's clothing after a bizarre sex ritual.

Mr Husband, from Tewkesbury, had a plastic bag over his face and wore a nightie and a bra. He was found dead after he failed to show up for work.

Question ... did Mr. Holland off himself in more spy agency sex rituals? Or was he *Whacked?*

You decide.

1997

January 7, 1997:

Don Adams, a small-town Arkansas Attorney, was found shot to death in his car in Springfield, Missouri.

Adams was working to help people bilked out of their life savings in land deals in Branson, Missouri. The deals involved the Clintons and their cohorts and were tied to the infamous Whitewater cases.

Question ... was Mr. Adams simply the unfortunate victim in a yet unsolved murder case? Or was he *Whacked?*

You decide.

May 15, 1997:

Gordon Matteson, friend and foe of Bill Clinton, was found with several gunshots to his body and head. His death was ruled a suicide.

Gordon Matteson was found shot to death in his car at a deserted intersection outside Little Rock, Arkansas. Matteson was reported to have been building a dossier on Bill Clinton before his death. After he died, the files were mysteriously removed from his house.

Question ... was Gordon Matteson a victim of his own suicide? Or was he *Whacked?*

You decide.

July 7, 1997:

Mary Mahoney, former White House intern during Clinton's first term and volunteer in his Presidential campaign, was found murdered while at work in a D.C. Starbucks. She was shot to death along with two coworkers.

Mary Mahoney's murder made national headlines because it was so brutal. The bodies of Mary Mahoney, age 25, and two others, Emory Allen Evans, age 25, and Aaron David Goodrich, age 18, were found in a Starbucks Coffee cold storage room by the store's assistant manager. The three coworkers had been executed at gunpoint and shot ten times.

The murders happened in the low-crime area of Burleith, north of Georgetown in Washinton, D.C. The brutal killing took place amid the pre-trial media coverage of the Paula Jones lawsuit against President Clinton.

It also came only three days after Mike Isikoff of *Newsweek* announced that a *"former White House 'staffer'* was coming out with her story of being sexually harassed while working for the President.

In the aftermath of the crime, the public and police would be hard-pressed to find answers to the murders. There was no attempt to open the safe containing as much as $10,000. The alarms at the store's two back doors never went off the night of the murders or the morning after.

Although the victims were pickpocketed, none of Mahoney's keys were missing, and the two cash registers went untouched. Mahoney's car, a silver 1994 Saturn, a gift from her grandmother, was still in the parking lot. It doesn't appear to have been a robbery.

Question ... were Ms. Mahoney and her two coworkers simply murdered? Or, were two coworkers murdered so Mary Mahoney could be silenced? Or was she *Whacked?*

You decide.

August 31, 1997

Princess Diana, former wife of then Prince Charles, was killed in a car accident in Paris. Her soon-to-be husband, Dodi Fayed, was killed in the horrific accident as well.

Princess Diana held and remains to have a special place in the hearts of millions worldwide. She was and remains a controversial figure. The controversy was why the National Security Agency admitted in 1998 to having extensive files on Diana. How extensive?

British tabloids shouted from the rooftops. "*America's spy chiefs admitted last night they snooped on Princess Diana for years— and learned some of her most intimate love secrets,*" the *Daily Mirror* screamed. *The Daily Record* stated that the NSA's surveillance had continued "*right until she died in the Paris car crash with Dodi Fayed.*"

Of course, The *Washington Post* questioned these reports and gave voice to a U.S. intelligence official who asserted that the references in the files to Diana were merely incidental. It was later learned the NSA had a comprehensive 1,056-page Diana file. They refused any disclosure 'because their disclosure could reasonably be expected to cause exceptionally grave damage to the national security" and, if released, would potentially disclose "sources and methods" utilized by the U.S. intelligence-gathering network.'

So, a former Princess somehow threatens America's national security. That seems a stretch. Readers of my last book, *Death Rattle of the Republic,* know that the Royal Family is one of the power bases behind the movement toward a world government. Her ex-husband is now King Charles.

Dodi Fayed's father, Mohamed Al-Fayed, filed a lawsuit in U.S. District Court for the District of Columbia. The elder Fayed sought access to the CIA/NSA files under the FOIA laws. They wanted the files right up to the accident that took the lives of Diana and Dodi. Of course, they did not win that lawsuit.

The investigating French authorities called for an official investigation. The driver died in the crash, along with the Princess and her lover. The only survivor was Bodyguard Trevor Rees-Jones. Nine photographers and a press motorcyclist were placed under formal investigation for manslaughter and failing to render aid to accident victims. A short while later, Judge Stephan dismissed all charges against the photographers and motorcyclists.

The decision of the investigation was the accident was caused by the deceased driver due to intoxicated driving. Convenient? Mohamed al-Fayed thinks so and doesn't believe the deaths were a result of an accident. He filed an appeal to the findings.

In what indeed is a coincidence, Richard Tomlinson, a former MI6 officer who served from September 1991 through April 1995, provided some shocking information. In August 1998, Tomlinson informed investigating magistrate Herv Stephan that Henri Paul, the chauffeur killed in the tragedy, had been on the MI6 payroll for at least three years. He also revealed that the crash resembled an MI6 plot to kill Yugoslavian President Slobodan Milosevic in Geneva. Tomlinson provided Judge Stephan with his testimony in a formal affidavit.

In a 007 twist, in September 1998, Tomlinson traveled to the United States on board a Swiss Air Flight to appear on an NBC television program to discuss his recent revelations. Upon arrival at John F. Kennedy International Airport in New York, Tomlinson was escorted off the plane by U.S. government officials who detained him for several hours. He was put on a plane back to Europe. It was later revealed that our government detained Tomlinson and prevented him from appearing on NBC at the request of MI6.

There are books written, stories published, and documents forged in this story about the death of a princess. Some disturbing happenings are challenging to explain. Only God knows who took the Princess to her death.

Question ... was Princess Diana a victim of a tragic drunk driving accident? Or was she *Whacked?*

You decide.

October 12, 1997:

Ron Miller, 58, was admitted to the hospital on October 3 for an undetermined illness. He died 9 days later. The cause of his death remains unknown.

Miller was a principal in Gage Company, an Arkansas utility company linked to a House Oversight and FBI investigation of a scheme to overcharge customers millions of dollars. The scheme being investigated included Hillary Clinton, Ron Brown, Secretary of Commerce, and White House Chief of Staff Mac McCarty.

Much has been written about this investigation, so her, Ron Miller, had agreed to cooperate with the FBI and began turning over materials. Miller was to testify before the House Committee when he became ill.

Question ... did Ron Miller conveniently die of natural causes? Or was he *Whacked?*

You decide.

December 4, 1997:

Eric Butera, police informant, was found beaten to death in what police described as a drug deal gone bad.

Butera went to D.C. police with information on the Starbucks murder of Mary Mahoney (see July 7 above). The claim is that police asked Butera to do undercover drug work with them and was murdered on an assignment.

Question ... was Eric Butera the victim of a drug deal gone bad? Or was he *Whacked?*

You decide.

1998

March 8, 1998:

James McDougal died in solitary confinement in a federal prison while awaiting his release. His death was ruled by cardiac arrest.

McDougal and his wife were partners with Hillary and Bill Clinton in a real estate venture later known as Whitewater. It came to light while Bill Clinton was in the White House. McDougal was a key witness for Ken Starr in the Whitewater investigation. He was sentenced to prison for his role in the corruption. He was a noticeable fall guy.

Question ... did McDougal die of cardiac arrest while awaiting his release from prison? Or was he *Whacked?*

You decide

March 20, 1998

Stanley Meyer (57), an American inventor well-known the world over, died suddenly after taking a drink of cranberry juice at a Cracker Barrel.

Meyer worked at NASA on the Gemini project. He was elected Inventor of the Year in *"Who's Who of America"* in 1993. In 1975, after the Middle Eastern oil embargo, Stanley Meyer dedicated his life to inventing a water fuel cell capable of turning water into an energy source for cars. Meyer shared the reasoning behind the process in his documentary *"It Runs On Water."* He said, *"It became imperative that we must try to bring in an alternative fuel source and do it very quickly,"*

The water fuel cell purportedly split water into components, hydrogen and oxygen. Then, the hydrogen ignited to generate energy, reconstituting the water molecules. According to Meyer, the device required less energy to perform electrolysis than the minimum energy requirement predicted or measured by conventional science.

Meyer was open about speaking out about the government.

"There is a move to try to force the countries to accept that they would sign over their natural resource rights. If you signed over your natural resource rights, you have taken over the countries without firing a shot. This is to help bring in a one-world government. The number one thing that would defuse the entire episode to be able to maintain us is to bring an alternative energy source in that we can sustain and maintain not only in the industrial base of this country but the world."

Meyer made a demonstration before Professor Michael Laughton, Dean of Engineering at Mary College, London, Admiral Sir Anthony Griffin, a former controller of the British Navy, and Dr. Keith Hindley, a U.K. research chemist.

After returning to the States, he and his twin brother Stephen attended a business meeting with two Belgian investors, Philippe Vandemoortele and Marc Vancraeyenest.

The meeting was at a Cracker Barrel restaurant in Grove City, Ohio. Stephen Meyer recounted the events of March 20, 1998: *"Stanley took a sip of cranberry juice. Then he grabbed his neck, bolted out the door, dropped to his knees, and vomited violently."* I ran outside and asked him, *'What's wrong?'"*

He said, *'They poisoned me.'* That was his dying declaration.

A three-month investigation into his death concluded that he died from a brain aneurysm.

Question ... did Stanley Meyer die of a brain aneurysm? Or was he *Whacked?*

You decide.

March 29, 1998:

Johnny Lawhorn Jr., an auto mechanic with his own shop in Little Rock, Arkansas, died in what was described as a mysterious car accident where his car was found embedded into a utility pole.

Johnny Lawhorn's accident happened soon after his discovery of an extensive check from Madison Guaranty Savings and Loan made out to Bill Clinton. It was found in a car at his repair shop.

Question ... did Johnny die by running his car into a utility pole? Or was he *Whacked?*

You decide.

July 26, 1998:

Lieutenant General David J. McCloud died while piloting his private plane. The cause of the crash was never determined.

McCloud served as the director of the Joint Chiefs of Staff Force Structure, Resources, and Assessment Directorate, or J-, during a portion of Clinton's presidency8. He later became the commander of Alaskan Command and the 11th Air Force.

While unsubstantiated, it is believed McCloud was part of a group of 24 flag officers that sought to arrest Clinton for treason under the Uniform Code of Military Justice while he was President

Question ... did General McCloud die in a tragic plane crash? Or was he *Whacked?*

You decide.

August 1, 1998

Christine M. Mirzayan, a 29-year-old intern at the National Academy of Sciences, was murdered and beaten to death with a heavy object near Georgetown University. The medical examiner determined that she died from blunt head trauma, with a skull fracture and brain injuries.

Mirzayan's death sent shockwaves through the scientific community, as she was described as a rising star with a promising career ahead of her. Her murder remains an unsolved cold case over 20 years later.

Question ... was government intern Christine Mirzayan randomly killed? Or was she *Whacked?*

You decide.

November 17, 1998:

Charles Miller, Vice President of Alltel, was found dead of two gunshot wounds in a pit a few hundred yards from his home on his ranch. His death was ruled a suicide. At the crime scene, police discovered two different weapons and multiple shots fired from them.

Miller was an executive with Alltel and a member of its board of directors. Alltel is the successor to Jackson Stephens' Systematics. This company provided the software for the White House's 'Big Brother' database system and was behind the administration's plan to develop the secret computer Clipper chip to bug every phone, fax, and email transmission in America.

Question ... was Mr. Miller the victim of his own suicide? Or was he *Whacked?*

You decide.

November 20, 1998

Galina Starovoitova, a prominent Russian politician and human rights activist, was shot multiple times in an ambush-style attack as she was walking up the stairs to her apartment building in St. Petersburg, Russia.

Her personal assistant was also critically injured in the attack but survived. Starovoitova was a member of the Russian parliament, known for her outspoken advocacy of democracy, human rights, and opposition to extremism.

She was known to have faced numerous threats due to her activism.

Question ... was Ms. Starovoitoya a victim of the high crime in Russia? Or was she *Whacked?*

You decide.

1999

March 1999

Kevin Allen, a linguist at GCHQ, was found dead in bed by his father at his home in Cheltenham.

He had a plastic bag and a dust mask over his mouth. An autopsy revealed his death was due to asphyxiation.

Question ... did young Kevin Allen kill himself? Or was he *Whacked?*

You decide.

March 19, 1999

Corporal Eric S. Fox, a crewman for Marine One, the Presidential Helicopter, was found dead in his car, a shot to the back of his head. It was not declared a suicide.

Corporal Fox served Marine One during the first Clinton administration. Police stated evidence would point to suicide, but it was never declared to this day. Due to several members of the Clinton administration suffering coincidences leading to their deaths, there remains speculation about Corporal Fox.

Question ... did Corporal Eric Fox off himself? Or was he *Whacked?*

You decide.

April 26, 1999

Jill Dando, a top News Anchor for BBC, was shot execution-style on the front step of her home in broad daylight.

Jill Dando was killed early in the morning after returning to her home in southwest London. Dando arrived home around 11:30 AM. Within seconds, she was dead. With keys in hand, she was attacked from behind and slammed on the hard floor. A single bullet was then fired into the left side of her head. She died instantly.

The United Kingdom's Metropolitan Police did their absolute utmost to try to solve the shocking crime. Indeed, it was a high-profile murder, and the police launched a massive investigation. They tracked 191 CCTV cameras and conclusively proved no one followed her home. Over 5,000 people were interviewed, and 2,500 statements were taken. In cases like this, an investigation of this scale is refreshing. Unfortunately, the murder wasn't solved.

A local nearby well was eventually arrested and convicted of Dando's murder. However, on appeal, the case was overturned, and the accused was ultimately acquitted. The police were embarrassed and back to square one. They briefly pursued the murder, which could be linked to Dando's work on BBC's Crimewatch show. The show could have pissed off an unknown criminal who did the dirty deed. That theory was quickly dismissed.

At this point, some information came in that the authorities wanted to offer a discount. Jill Dando was murdered on April 26. Three days earlier, on April 23, NATO forces struck Radio Television of Serbia, where 16 employees were killed by carefully targeted bombs.

The theory, based on information coming in, was that Dando was a prominent media figure, Great Britain was the face of NATO, and a Serbian warlord by the name of Željko Ražnatović had Dando taken out in retaliation. Raznatovic was wanted by several agencies, including Interpol.

To this day, no one has been further apprehended in Dando's murder. In January 2000, Ražnatovi'was assassinated. His killer remains unknown, although rumors suggest that the culprit was attached to U.S. intelligence.

Question ... was Jill Dando murdered in a random killing? Or was she *Whacked?*

You decide.

July 16, 1999

John F. Kennedy Jr., Carolyn Bessette Kennedy, and Carolyn's sister, Lauren Bessette, died when the plane JFK Jr was piloting off the coast of Martha Vineyard, Massachusetts.

The plane young Kennedy was piloting dropped into the Atlantic Ocean short of the runway he was heading towards. The Coast Guard did not immediately find their bodies, which is questionable in that where the plane went down is not really deep water.

The bodies were all recovered five days after the crash and cremated the same day on July 21, 1999. Immediate cremation is always a red flag when dealing with these 'coincidences.' The Kennedy family has had more than their share of strange, disputed, and coincidental tragedies. JFK Jr. was no exception.

So, let's look at this case. Senator Daniel Moynihan announced retiring from his Senate seat representing New York. John F Kennedy Jr. expressed interest in claiming the seat. But he wasn't the only one interested in the Moynihan seat.

Hillary Clinton, then First Lady, knew Bill's time in the limelight was ending, and she did not want her career to end. Although living in Washington, DC at the time, and having moved there from Arkansas, she filed

for Moynihan Senate seat in New York state just 10 days before JFK Jr.'s plane went in the drink on July 6.

The detractors are everywhere, but the coincidence is front and center. The media quickly critiqued Kennedy as an inexperienced pilot who shouldn't have flown that night. His flight instructors said he was more than qualified and known to be a deliberate and severe pilot.

Question ... did John John take his wife and sister-in-law to their deaths with him due to a pilot error? Or was he *Whacked?*

You decide.

July 27, 1999:

Daniel Dutko, the former Vice Chairman of Finance for the Clinton-Gore Campaign, died in a mountain biking accident while attending a Democratic fundraiser in Aspen. It seems he forgot to wear the biking helmet he was known for always wearing. He fell and hit his head twice.

Dutko's death is curious because he was in Aspen to attend a fundraiser attended by President Clinton. He also served as vice chairman of finance for the DNC in 1996. During that time, thousands of dollars were reportedly funneled from a Chinese military officer to Bill's re-election campaign.

That same year, the Clinton administration also reversed a State Department policy that categorized satellites as 'munitions,' making it easier for China to launch American satellites and even acquire sensitive technology. Oh my, it's just another Clinton coincidence.

Question ... did Daniel Dutko die of an accident on his bicycle? Or was he *Whacked?*

You decide.

WHACKED!

The Two Thousand's

What Did Your Government Do?

The first decade after the turn of the century is the decade of madness. It began with the New Year coming in with a whimper as the fear-mongering Y2K crowd fell flat on its face. It also ushered in the Presidency of Bush the Younger, who won a contested election by one hanging Chad.

September 11, 2001, brought terrorists to America with planes flying into buildings, which ignited wars and rumors of wars far and wide. It was soon Shock and Awe in the streets of Baghdad in the hunt for weapons of mass destruction (WMD) we knew weren't there.

Bush the Younger beat the Older to Baghdad, then came the serious 'oh shit.' What do we do now with a country destroyed? To the cheers of the bankers, we were Afghanistan-bound. Our foreign entanglements would strangle us before he was gone.

We had our first African American President, Barry Soetoro, aka Barack Obama. He ushered in his Presidency with a pledge to fundamentally change America and immediately embarked on a world apology tour like no other. He worked two terms in office, successfully reducing America to a paper tiger on the world stage.

With the war in the background and the rise of Big Tech, the world has changed faster than ever before. Google, Amazon, Facebook, and YouTube became household names. Gaming went big time with PlayStation 2, and Wii lit a fire as the industry grew.

Following the Slick Willie disaster with Monica, our moral decline picked up speed at this time. God sent a message a few times, but no one listened. The Indian Ocean earthquake and tsunami claimed over 230,000 lives, and Americans got a first-hand look live on TV as Hurricane Katrina wreaked havoc in New Orleans while Mayor Ray said all was fine.

In the end, nothing will top the story of the decade and a President bullied by two of his aides. George the Younger and his two arsonists, Dick Cheney and Donald Rumsfeld poured gas all over the middle east for reasons of their own.

Their case for war was weak and shady at best. A Senate Intelligence Committee report was scathing in its criticism of this aspect of the White House's case for war. It emphatically found that Iraq and al-Qaeda's statements that they were working together were not substantiated, and statements regarding Iraq providing al-Qaeda with weapons of mass destruction were false.

The Senate Committee cited numerous CIA reports that did not corroborate the White House propaganda leading up to the war. Despite all the lies, no one went to jail, and quite frankly, that's why the likes of Bush, Cheney, Rumsfeld, et al. continue to deceive us. We, the people, have been buried and covered up.

We live in a time where it pays to be a skeptic. The list grows longer, and one day, I am confident we'll find the truth about the giant false flag of all ... 9-11.

2000

January 15, 2000

Željko Ražnatović, a Serbian warlord wanted across Europe, was assassinated in Belgrade, Serbia, by a lone gunman.

Ražnatović, also known as Arkan, was a bad guy and hated by many. In the attack, his bodyguard was also killed, and two women with them were wounded. Speculation at the time centered around a Serbian organized crime hit. But the subject was a lousy guy implicated in the death of BBC journalist Jill Dando.

The U.N. International Criminal Tribunal had indicted him for crimes against humanity committed during the Yugoslav Wars that took place in the 90s.

Question ... did Raznatovic die at the hands of one of his many enemies? Or was he *Whacked?*

You decide.

April 8, 2000

Four Marine helicopter pilots died along with 15 others in the crash of a US Marine Osprey near Tuscon, Arizona.

Witnesses said the Osprey burst into flames in flight before crashing. The Osprey aircraft has had a questionable history since its inception. The Marine Corps determined this crash was not caused by the plane but by human causes.

The coincidence is that the four Marine pilots mentioned above were former pilots of Marine One, the chopper that flies the President. They flew during President Clinton's time in office.

Question ... did the four Marine pilots die as a result of pilot error? Or were they *Whacked?*

You decide.

April 18, 2000

Carlos Ghigliotti was found dead sitting at his home office computer desk.

Ghigliotti was found dead in a decomposing state, meaning he'd been dead for some time. The death was initially ruled a homicide and later changed by the Coroner to natural causes, probably a heart attack.

He was a crucial figure in the congressional investigation of the Branch Davidian and subsequent look at what happened in Waco. The 42-year-old was a respected expert in the field of thermal imaging.

He had been retained by the House Government Reform Committee to analyze surveillance video of the Branch Davidian assault. He told friends he had discovered damaging information that did not support the government's position.

Question ... did Carlos die of a heart attack? Or was he *Whacked?*

You decide.

June 5, 2000

John Millis, a former CIA operator and current Staff Director of a Special Congressional Committee, was found dead in a motel room from an apparent gunshot wound. His death was immediately ruled a suicide.

At the time of his death, he was leading a committee to investigate the Clinton administration's approval of arms shipments from Iran to Muslim forces in Bosnia. Before his current work, he had been involved in an investigation regarding alleged CIA cocaine smuggling.

Fairfax (V.A.) Police received an anonymous call that a man was threatening suicide in a local motel. When they arrived, they found Millis dead.

Question ... did John Millis commit suicide? Or was he *Whacked?*

You decide.

June 10, 2000

Tony Moser, a short 10 days after being named a full-time columnist for the Democrat-Gazette newspaper and two days after writing a stinging indictment of political corruption in Little Rock, was killed while crossing the street in Pine Bluff, Arkansas.

Moser was an anti-corruption journalist and critic of the Arkansas Democratic Party and its political machine. The article he wrote two days prior exposed the looting of programs designed to obtain money from deadbeat parents to then give to their children.

Police in Little Rock concluded no charges would be filed against the driver of the 1995 Chevrolet pickup that hit Moser as he was walking alone. Police ruled out foul play because the driver was found sober, and there was no sign of excessive speed.

Question ... did TonyMoser die of a random accident? Or was he *Whacked?*

You decide.

July 3, 2000:

Frank Lynn, a scientist at the Army Research Lab (a black site) at Aberdeen Proving Grounds in Maryland, died of an apparent gunshot wound. His death was ruled a suicide.

Lynn was one of ten whistleblowers who provided proof that lab secrets were provided to China during the Clinton Administration.

Question ... did Frank Lynn die of suicide? Or was he *Whacked?*

You decide.

August 2000:

Robert Deas, a scientist at the Army Research Lab (same as Frank Lynn above) at Aberdeen Proving Grounds in Maryland, died in a mysterious car accident while traveling to Canada.

Deas was one of ten whistleblowers who provided proof that lab secrets were provided to China during the Clinton Administration.

Question ... did Robert Deas die from a legitimate car accident? Or was he *Whacked?*

You decide.

November 20, 2000:

Charles Ruff, White House counsel who defended President Clinton in his impeachment trial, was found dead at home by his wife.

There are multiple stories regarding how he was found. One is he was found lying outside his shower. Another is that he died of a heart attack. In the end, authorities declared he had died of a heart attack.

Question ... did Charles Ruff die of a heart attack? Or was he *Whacked?*

You decide.

2001

November 12, 2001

Dr. Benito Que, a cell biologist, was found dead outside his laboratory at the Miami Medical School in Miami, Florida.

Dr. Que had been working on infectious diseases, including HIV, which was controversial at the time. The story gets murky from here. The Miami Herald said his death occurred as he headed to his car in the parking lot. Police first said he was probably the victim of a mugger.

The local media discovered information that Dr Que had been beaten by four men with baseball bats. Officials claim that it was recanted and declared that Que died of a heart attack. Once the Police declared his death natural, they interestingly refused to provide any more comments.

Question ... did Dr. Que die of a heart attack? Or was he *Whacked?*

You decide.

November 23, 2001

Dr. Vladimir Pasechnik, a microbiologist for Biopreparat, a bioweapon production facility in Russia before the collapse of the Soviet Union, was found dead near his home in Wiltshire, England.

Dr. Vladimir Pasechnik defected to England in 1989, bringing with him the first detailed information to the West regarding the incredible scale of the Soviet covert biological warfare program. His defection did not go well back in the Soviet Union.

However, Dr. Pasechnik made a successful life for himself, and by the time of his death, he had started his own company. His son told authorities that his father always lived in fear the KGB would reach him. The officers determined he died of a stroke.

Question ... did Dr. Vladimir Pasechnik die a natural death? Or was he *Whacked?*

You decide.

November 24, 2001

Dr. Yaakov Matzner

Amiramp Eldor

Avishai Berkman, coincidentally, the same day Dr. Wiley went missing, three other microbiologists were killed. The Doctor died when their Swissair flight from Berlin, Germany, to Zurich, Switzerland, crashed on its landing approach. In total, 22 people died, and 9 survived.

The three deceased were ...

Dr. Yaakov Matzner, 54, dean of the Hebrew University School of Medicine.

Amiramp Eldor, 59, ran the Hematology Department at Ichilov Hospital in Tel Aviv and was a world-recognized expert in blood clotting.

Avishai Berkman, 50, Director of the Tel Aviv Public Health Department.

Coincidences can be strange, and they cover the world.

Question ... were these three gentlemen simply the victims of an unfortunate commercial plane crash. Or were they *Whacked?*

You decide.

December 12, 2001

Robert M. Schwartz, one of the nation's leading researchers on DNA sequencing, was found dead by neighbors.

Schwartz lived alone in a secluded northern Virginia farmhouse. He was cofounder of the Virginia Center for Innovative Technology. Coworkers at his company reported they had not seen him, and he must have uncharacteristically skipped work. The center's President, Anne Armstrong, said, *"We're all stunned."*

His death was ruled a homicide. He had an X carved in the back of his neck. While there is controversy concerning his death. Three days after the murder, on December 15, Police announced they had the killers. Police revealed that he had been killed with a two-foot sword in a 'planned assassination.' They express that the reason for the X remains a mystery.

They arrested Kyle Hulbert, 18, Michael Pfohl, 21, and Katherine Inglis, 19. The following day, the media was reporting an intriguing story on Inglis. In January 2001, she reported to the Naval Recruit Training Command Center in Great Lakes, Illinois. Navy officials said she had suddenly left on May 28, never returning. Suspect Pfohl was telling people right before the assassination that he wanted to be in the covert world of Special Forces.

Question ... was Robert Schwartz a simple victim of a random murder? Or was he *Whacked?*

You decide.

December 14, 2001

Set Van Nguyen, a microbiologist at the Commonwealth Scientific and Industrial Research Organization's Animal Disease Establishment of Geelong, Australia, was found dead under questionable circumstances.

Nguyen's death came 48 hours after DNA researcher Robert Schwartz was mysteriously murdered. Police in Victoria, Australia, stated: "Set Van Nguyen, 44, appeared to have died after entering an airlock in a storage laboratory filled with nitrogen. His body was found when his wife became worried.

He was killed after entering a low-temperature storage area where biological samples were kept. He did not know the room was full of deadly gas, which had leaked from a liquid nitrogen cooling system. Sounds legit, right? Probably. But read on.

Question ... did another scientist, Set Van Nguyen, meet an untimely death by accident? Or was he *Whacked?*

You decide.

December 20, 2001

Dr. Don C. Wiley, on November 24, 2001, the FBI announced that it was investigating the disappearance of a Harvard biologist because he researched potentially lethal viruses, including Ebola. He had attended a conference in Memphis, Tennessee, where he was last seen.

Due to the nature of Dr. Wiley's work on infectious diseases, there was originally a concern that terrorism might be involved.

On December 20, 2001, his body was found in the Mississippi River. The Shelby County medical examiner ruled that Dr. Wiley's death was an accidental fall from a bridge. He also determined that foul play was not involved, and the case was closed.

Question ... did Dr. Wiley die from a simple slip from a bridge? Or was he *Whacked?*

You decide.

A DEFINITE MAYBE ...

Seven scientists worldwide suffered life-ending coincidences from November 23 to December 20, 2021. This is something to consider. Reuters News Service stated that Wiley's death had 'triggered alarm bells due to the current bio-warfare fears' and the nature of his work.

Another United Kingdom newspaper, The Times, reported on an initiative Israel and her allies led. The article reported that they were working on a

biological weapon designed to kill specific types of people. The Times reported that the intent was 'to use the ability of viruses and certain bacteria to alter the DNA inside their host's living cells.'

It further stated that the scientists were trying to engineer deadly microorganisms that attack only those with distinctive genes. It was a highly controversial plan to provoke death by racial profiling.

We need to look to Wuhan, COVID-19, and the deadly vax attack to see the Reuters and Times reports are not only believable but probable. Pay attention as you read on to many microbiologists who met an early fate.

2002

January 25, 2002

J. Clifford Baxter, formerly vice chairman of Enron, was found shot dead in his Mercedes-Benz in a suburb of Houston, Texas. Authorities ruled his death a suicide. Baxter reportedly confronted Enron's management team, CEO Jeff Skilling, about the company's corrupt transactions. After that encounter, he resigned in protest.

The pistol used to kill Baxter used rat shot, an unusual type of ammunition, untraceable by forensics. Baxter also had strange, unexplained wounds on his hands and shards of glass on his shirt.

The police handling of the crime scene raised alarms. They moved the body and all the evidence, including the gun, before ever taking photographs of the crime scene as required by law. There was no autopsy performed on Baxter's body. Later, when this was challenged, an autopsy was ordered, but his body was already being prepared for burial by a funeral home.

The case became one of U.S. history's most significant corporate fraud cases. Congress initiated hearings to investigate Enron. Baxter was crucial to the case because of his close relationship with Enron's CEO and could have provided valuable information about the company's criminal activities.

When talking with a former business associate after agreeing to testify before Congress and two days before his death, Baxter told him he might need a bodyguard afterward. He was found dead two weeks before he was set to testify,

Question ... did Mr. Baxter, a key witness in the Enron case, commit suicide? Or was he Whacked?

You decide.

January 28, 2002

Alexi Brushlinski, a microbiologist and member of the Russian Academy of Science, was murdered in what Russian authorities in Moscow dubbed a bandit attack'.

Question ... did another microbiologist bite the dust from random street violence? Or were they *Whacked?*

You decide.

February 10,2002

Katherine Smith, a 49-year-old Tennessee DMV worker, was found burned to death in her 1992 Acura Legend on a rural Tennessee highway.

Following the attack on the Twin Towers, investigators stated that Ms. Smith admitted to providing five Middle Eastern men with fraudulent identification cards. She provided aid to six suspects.

The first, Kahled Odtllah, 31, drove from New York to Memphis on September 11, the day of the attack. Sakher Hammad, 24, possessed a visitor's pass for the World Trade Center. It was dated September 5, 2001. His cousin, Abdelmuhsen Mahmid Hammad, 31, was charged with trying to obtain a false license. The other suspects were Mostafa Said Abou-Shahin, 25, Abdelmuhsen Mahmid Hammad, 31, and Mohammed Fares, 19. All were suspects in the September 11, 2001 attacks on the World Trade Center.

Katherine Smith was cooperating with authorities and was scheduled to testify in open court the day after she was murdered.

Question ... was Ms. Smith randomly burned to death in her car? Or was she *Whacked?*

You decide.

February 11, 2002

Victor Korshunov, 56, a noted microbiologist and head of the Microbiology Faculty at Russian State Medical University, was hit over the head and killed as he tried to enter his home in Moscow.

Question ... was Victor Korshunov randomly murdered at his home? Or was he *Whacked?*

You decide.

February 15, 2002

Ian Langford, 40, a Russian senior research associate at CSERGE (University of East Anglia's Center for Social and Economic Research) in the United Kingdom, died under mysterious circumstances. His death is confirmed, but no details are available even today.

Langford's death came just three days after the death of fellow researcher Victor Korshunov. His most recent work was as a senior researcher assessing risk to the environment.

Question ... Did Ian Langford die of natural causes? Or was he *Whacked?*

You decide.

March 24, 2002

Dr. Steven Mostow, one of the United States' leading infectious disease experts and the associate dean at the University of Colorado's Health Sciences Center, died when his plane crashed near Centennial Airport. It killed him and his passengers, Denver car dealer Kent Rickenbaugh, his wife, and his son.

While investigators said the crash was being investigated from six to eight different angles, the cause of the crash has never been determined.

They were killed in a plane crash near Centennial Airport.

Mostow was an early advocate for widespread flu vaccinations and, more recently, had been deep in talks with U.S. intelligence officials on the threat of bioterrorism. Some called him a crusader.

Question ... was Dr. Mostow killed in a plane crash accident? Or was he *Whacked?*

You decide.

David Wynn-Williams, an astrobiologist with the Antarctic Astrobiology Project and the NASA Ames Research Center, died when hit by a car while jogging near his home.

This is the same day Dr. Mostow noted above, but it is half a world away in Cambridge, England. At the time of his death, he was studying how microbes of a potentially hostile nature adapt to living in extreme environments.

Question ... was David Wynn-Williams killed when hit by a car? Or was he *Whacked?*

You decide.

August 21, 2002

Vladimir Golovlev, a co-chairman of the Liberal Russia party, was shot dead while walking his dog near his Moscow home.

Golovlev had recently switched from the Union of Right Forces (SPS) party to the Liberal Russia party, founded by the exiled tycoon Boris Berezovsky.

Before his death, Golovlev had been stripped of his parliamentary immunity so prosecutors could press corruption charges against him while he was still a member of the SPS party.

No one has ever been convicted for Golovlev's murder.

Question ... was Golovley a victim of another Moscow murder? Or was he *Whacked?*

You decide.

October 25, 2002

Paul Wellstone, 58, a United States Senator representing the state of Minnesota, known for his staunch anti-war views, died along with his wife, his daughter, three campaign staff members, and a pilot were killed when their charter plane crashed in a northern Minnesota forest.

On October 3, Senator Wellstone gave his most crucial career speech. The day before, the Senate leadership had introduced the resolution backed by then-President George W. Bush to invade Iraq. Wellstone opposed the resolution vehemently. When he and his family perished in the plane crash, it was twelve days before the Senate was to vote on the Iraq invasion resolution.

While the exact cause of the crash has never been determined, the NTSB said the probable cause was pilot error. Notably, the two pilots were very experienced with their aircraft.

As we all know, the Senate subsequently passed the resolution.

Question ... Were Paul Wellstone and his entourage victims of a plane crash? Or were they *Whacked?*

You decide.

2003

April 17, 2003

Sergei Yushenkov, a long-time Russian politician and co-chairman of the Liberal Russia Party, was shot several times in the chest after getting out of his car near his apartment building. His attacker escaped the scene after the shooting, leaving a pistol by his body.

Yushenkov was known for his opposition to Russia's wars in Chechnya. He was also aligned with the liberal, pro-Western political party Liberal Russia. Those close to Yushenkov could find no apparent motive for the murder.

Question ... was Sergei a simple victim of murder? Or was he *Whacked*?

You decide.

July 3, 2003

Yuri Shchekochikhin, a Russian investigative journalist and lawmaker, died after a sudden 16-day illness.

Shchekochikhin died in a Moscow hospital after developing symptoms consistent with radiation poisoning or a severe allergic reaction, including skin peeling, hair loss, and organ failure. Following his death, his medical records were classified as a 'medical secret.' His relatives were denied access to them.

In another Russian совпадение or coincidence ... Before his death, Shchekochikhin had been investigating high-level corruption cases. In particular, the 'Three Whales' smuggling scandal that involved the Russian security services shortly before his death.

His employer, Novaya Gazeta newspaper, believed he was poisoned to prevent him from uncovering more about the corruption cases he was investigating. Shchekochikhin had planned to travel to the United States to meet with FBI investigators just days before his sudden illness and death.

The Prosecutor General's Office repeatedly denied requests to open a murder investigation into Shchekochikhin's death, citing a lack of evidence of foul play.

Question ... did Shchekochikhin die of a rare infection while hospitalized? Or was he *Whacked?*

You decide.

July 18, 2003

Dr. David Kelly, a British biological weapons expert, reportedly died while walking in the woods and slitting his own wrists while doing so. His death was ruled a suicide.

The British press reported that Dr. Kelly was the Chief Scientific Officer for the British Ministry of Defense. He was the senior adviser to the proliferation and arms control secretariat and the Foreign Office's Non-Proliferation Department. From 1994 to 1999, Kelly was also the senior adviser on biological weapons to the U.N. biological weapons inspection teams (Unscom). Thus, Kelly was viewed as preeminent in his field worldwide.

Kelly had expressed grave doubts about the claims being made that Saddam Hussein possessed significant numbers of weapons of mass destruction (WMD). His views were at odds with British Prime Minister Tony Blair. Shortly after his death, PM Blair joined forces with President Bush over the invasion of Iraq, but I am sure that is nothing but a coincidence.

Ten years after David Kelly's death, The Guardian ran an article that made it quite clear many prominent people weren't buying the suicide story the establishment had been selling.

Question ... Did vibrant and active David Kelly take his own life on that walk in the woods? Or was he *Whacked?*

You decide.

November 18, 2003

Robert Leslie Burghoff, a prominent microbiologist, died when a hit-and-run driver jumped the sidewalk and ran him over in Houston, Texas. He was pronounced dead at the scene.

Burghoff's death came four months to the day after David Kelly, as noted above. At the time, he studied recent virus outbreaks onboard cruise ships and their potential links to terrorist activity.

Question ... did Burghoff die of a simple hit-and-run? Or was he *Whacked?*

You decide.

2004

A DEFINITE MAYBE ...

The story begins in Belgium in August 1996. A 14-year-old girl vanished while at a public pool. An eyewitness reported seeing her being forced into a suspicious van owned by Marc Dutroux. Police searched the Dutroux home and found nothing. Two days later, Dutroux and his wife shocked investigators by confessing.

The couple then led investigators into their basement dungeon. It was a horrifying scene, but they found the missing girl was still alive a week after her kidnapping. Then Dutroux led Police to the dead bodies of two more girls who had been held captive in another home. As you read the rest of this story, think of Jeffrey Epstein and Ghislaine Maxwell

These revelations happened in 1996, and the Belgian public was outraged. Nothing happened, and people began to speak of a cover-up. What was taking so long? The poor police handling of the case was evident. Dutroux wasn't put on trial until 2004.

During the silent eight years between confession and trial, the rumor mill was in overdrive. Word on the street was that Dutroux was the tip of an ugly iceberg of underage sex involving high government officials. Citizens smelled a cover, and the first judge overseeing the case, the first judge overseeing the case, Jean-Marc Connerotte, was dismissed after participating in a fundraiser in support of the parents of one of the murdered girls.

After eight years of stalling, the dismissal outraged the Brussels citizens. 300,000 people marched through Brussels in protest. Citizens believed the delay was deliberate to protect the people who were highly placed in defending the accused.

As the trial began, Dutroux was joined by his now ex-wife Michelle Martin, a drug addict named Michel Lelievre, and Michel Nihoul, who, it had been rumored for years, provided sex parties for senior officials and business leaders. The public believed he was also part of a pedophile network tied to those in power, extending up to and including the royal family.

Then began a series of coincidences beyond belief.

Judge Connerotte's testimony shook the court. He stated that murder contracts had been taken out against those overseeing the investigation to prevent broader inquiries into Dutroux's underage sex ring.

In truth, 20 potential witnesses had died before they could give testimony in court. Most under mysterious circumstances.

Bruno Tagliaferro, a scrap metal merchant, told prosecutors he knew Dutroux and that he had crucial information about the car in which two of the victims had been kidnapped. Then, he turned up dead. Authorities said he died of a heart attack. His wife steadfastly refused to accept the heart attack scenario. She sent tissue samples of his body to the U.S., which showed that he was poisoned.

Shortly after the report from the U.S. regarding the poisoned tissue samples, Mrs. Tagliaferro was found dead, burned to death in bed at home by her teenage son.

Hubert Massa, a top prosecutor known for getting death sentences in tough trials, died suddenly before the trial started in what was ruled a suicide. Of course, he left no suicide note.

Simon Poncelet, one of the investigating policemen, was shot dead while on duty. His murder was not solved.

A sex club owner associated with Michel Nihoul was shot dead.

When the trial finally happened, the defense argued that Dutroux acted for others, not himself. He was procuring them for clients. He was given a life sentence for his crimes. Those with the name Dutoux were so disgusted by his actions that they applied to legally have their names changed.

Question ... do you think there are sex rings for the rich, beautiful, and powerful? Think hard.

February 15, 2004:

Father John Minkler, a priest in the Albany (N.Y.) Archdiocese was found dead in his home by his sister. His death was first ruled a heart attack and later changed to suicide.

Father Minkler was the whistleblower who exposed a massive pedophile ring in Albany (N.Y.) Archdiocese. After his allegations were made public by a local newspaper, he was called into a meeting. There, it was demanded that he recant his allegations. He refused.

Two days later, he was found dead. His allegations were later proven to be true.

Question ... was Father Minkler a victim of his own suicide? Or was he *Whacked?*

You decide.

July 3, 2004:

Dr. Paul Norman, the chief scientist for chemical and biological defense at the British Ministry of Defense's laboratory at Porton Down, Wiltshire, died when the single-engine Cessna 206 aircraft he was piloting crashed in the county of Devon.

Dr. Norman was from Salisbury, Wiltshire, England, married with a fourteen-year-old son and a twenty-year-old daughter.

Air Accident Investigation Branch officials sealed off the crash site and examined the aircraft's wreckage. Then, the wreckage was removed to the AAIB base at Farnborough, England.

The authorities called the crash firmly ruled accidental.

Question ... did Dr. Paul Norman die in an accidental plane crash? Or was he *Whacked?*

You decide.

August 2004

Professor John Clark, head of the science laboratory that created Dolly the cloned sheep and founder of three spin-off firms from Roslin: PPL Therapeutics, Rosgen, and Roslin BioMed, was found dead hanging in his holiday home. In another coincidence, his death came six weeks after Dr. Norman noted above.

Clark led the Roslin Institute in Midlothian, Scotland, one of the world's leading animal biotechnology research centers. He was crucial in creating the transgenic sheep that earned the institute worldwide fame.

Question ... did Professor Clark suddenly hang himself? Or was he Whacked?

You decide.

December 10, 2004:

Gary Webb, 49, an Investigative Journalist best known for his 1996 series Dark Alliance, died of two gunshot wounds to the head. His death was ruled a suicide by the Coroner.

Gary worked for years to expose the ties of a northern California drug ring to the CIA. He worked for the San Jose Mercury until his final Dark Alliance series ran. His work caused a stir that brought attacks from The Washington Post, the New York Times, and the Los Angeles Times.

His tireless work proved a link between several government agencies, drug dealers, and the cocaine epidemic of the 1980s in America. He also proved the drugs were directed at black and minority neighborhoods, especially in Los Angeles.

He was let go by the San Jose Mercury because of pressure from their owners. He began receiving death threats and had his home broken into several times. He refused to stop telling the truth.

Question ... did Gary Webb die by suicide when he put not one but two bullets in his head? Or was he *Whacked?*

You decide.

2005

January 7, 2005

Jeong H. Im, a Korean Professor of research at the University of Missouri, was found dead in the trunk of his burned car. He had multiple stab wounds that were determined to be the cause of his death.

Professor Im was seen on camera walking from his office to the parking garage. A short while later, firefighters were summoned to the garage with reports of a car on fire. The firefighters extinguished the blaze and found him in the trunk of his charred automobile.

Eight years after the murder, Police identified the killer through DNA left at the scene. The killer had died by suicide by that time.

Question ... was Professor I a victim of a random madman? Or was he *Whacked?*

You decide.

May 2005

David Banks, 55, an Australian bioscientist, was killed in a plane crash in Queensland. His death was ruled a tragic accident.

Banks was a principal scientist with Biosecurity Australia and, in his work, had just started a study of the Northern Australia quarantine strategy.

Question ... did David Banks die in a plane crash? Or was he Whacked?

You decide.

May 15, 2005

Li Fuxiang, a Chinese national and head of China's foreign exchange regulatory body, jumped to his death from the seventh story of a hospital when he returned from his foreign assignment in the U.S.

Fuxiang had been serving in the U.S. during the Clinton and Bush Administrations. Upon his return to China, he was mysteriously hospitalized with no explanation. While in the hospital, he jumped to his death. Chinese officials ruled his death suicide. Before jumping to his death, he had no known health problems.

Question ... was Li Fuxiang a victim of his own suicide? Or was he *Whacked?*

You decide.

2006

October 7, 2006

Anna Politkovskaya, a prominent Russian journalist and human rights activist, was shot dead at point-blank range in the elevator of her apartment building in central Moscow.

Politkovskaya was known for her critical reporting on human rights abuses, particularly in the Chechen Republic. She was outspoken in her criticism of Putin's government.

Politkovskaya was on her way home from visiting her mother at the hospital when she was shot. At the time, Politkovskaya was preparing to become a grandmother, as her daughter Vera was pregnant and she was also in a new romantic relationship.

She was killed on President Vladimir Putin's birthday. The killer has never been found. The statute of limitations expired in October 2021.

Question ... was Ms. Politkovskaya a victim of a random murder? Or was she *Whacked?*

You decide.

November 1, 2006

Alexander Litvinenko, a former Russian security agent and critic of President Vladimir Putin, fell seriously ill shortly after meeting with two Russian intelligence agents, Andrey Lugovoy and Dmitry Kovtun, at a London hotel. He was hospitalized and died three weeks later.

A British parliamentary report and the European Court of Human Rights concluded that Litvinenko was deliberately murdered by Russian state agents acting on behalf of Putin. Russian authorities and Putin deny the allegations.

An autopsy revealed Litvinenko was intentionally poisoned with the radioactive isotope polonium-210, a rare and highly toxic radioactive substance, in his body. The polonium-210 found in the autopsy was traced back to a nuclear reactor in Russia. Russia continued in its denial.

Question ... did Alexander Litvinenko get sick after his meeting and die? Or was he *Whacked?*

You decide.

2007

January 31, 2007

Donald Young, a member of Trinity United Church of Christ and friend of former President Barry Soetoro (aka Barack Obama), was found dead by his roommate, having suffered multiple gunshot wounds to the head. The Cook County Medical Examiner ruled Young's death a homicide.

I would remind the reader that 2007 was the run-up to the election that placed Barry Soetoro in the White House. The media reported much about his belonging to the church of the controversial Reverend Jeremiah Wright.

Norma Jean Young, Donald's mother, revealed to The Globe that her son was openly gay and was a close personal friend of Barack Obama. Young was planning to attend graduate school to become a school principal. He wasn't known to have any enemies. Mrs. Young also said the Chicago Police Department, her former employer, was not much interested in solving the case of her son's death.

And then there were the rumors at the time, like the one that Mr. Young and Mr. Soetoro were in the same bed. True? We'll never know, but the mere mention of such a thing significantly distracted the chosen one as he raced to the White House.

Question ... was excellent Mr. Young a victim of one of the many thugs roaming the streets of Chicago? Or was he Whacked?

You decide.

2008

April 15, 2008:

Deborah Jeane Palfrey, 52, a Washington DC Madam who operated one of the most secretive escort services in the United States, was found hanging with a nylon rope around her neck in a shed behind her mother's mobile home in Tarpon Springs, Tampa, Florida.

Palfrey's business was known as Pamela Martin and Associates. In 2004, the IRS and the United States Postal Inspection Service opened an investigation into Palfrey's prostitution connections. She was found guilty by a jury of money laundering, mail fraud, and racketeering on April 15, 2008.

Wayne Madsen, a former NSA analyst, and Navy intelligence officer, speculated that one of the key motives behind the DC Madam's demise was the information her call girls picked up from Washington's elite.

Some information she reportedly picked up related to our government's complicity in the 9/11 attacks. Madsen, who spoke personally to Palfrey numerous times, recalls one conversation.

A note from 2016:

"For the first time, the former D.C. lawyer, Madam Deborah Jeane Palfrey, says her sealed escort service includes information related to the 2016 Presidential election. She states the records contain customer names, addresses, and social security numbers, not just their telephone numbers.

For the past two weeks, Montgomery Blair Sibley — whose license to practice law in D.C. was suspended in 2008 — has attempted to modify several 2007 restraining orders that prohibited him from releasing Palfrey's phone records."

In a coincidence, a 2016 Supreme Court bid to release Deborah Palfrey's phone records was denied.

Question ... did Ms. Palfrey hang herself outside her mother's trailer? Or was she *Whacked!*

You decide.

Note: This sounds like the Jeffrey Epstein case. The government won't release his 'list' either. It's just a coincidence, I am sure.

April 17, 2008:

Lieutenant Quarles Harris Jr., 24, a contractor for The Analysis Corporation, was discovered dead inside his car.

The Analysis Corporation is funded by the State Department. It relays intelligence briefings and handles sensitive material related to U.S. government officials. John Brennan, former CIA Director, was the CEO of Analysis at the time of his death.

In 2008, you may remember an access breach and the theft of information connected to the passports of U.S. Presidential candidates Barry Soetoro (aka Barack Obama), Hillary Clinton, and John McCain. It seems the chief suspect was Lt. Harris.

Harris was shot to death inside his car in front of the Judah House Praise Baptist Church in Washington, DC. A Washington Times article said that a police officer was the first on the scene of the murder. The article read, *"Commander Anzallo said a police officer was patrolling the neighborhood when gunshots were heard, then Lt. Harris was found dead inside the vehicle, which investigators would describe only as a blue car."*

His murder has never been solved. No suspects have arisen.

Question ... did young Lieutenant Harris die from a random attack? Or was he *Whacked?*

You decide.

July 29, 2008

Bruce Edwards Ivins, an American microbiologist and the prime suspect in the 2001 anthrax attacks that killed 5 people and sickened 17 others, died of an overdose. His death was ruled a suicide.

Following the anthrax letter attacks and a lengthy FBI investigation, federal prosecutors were preparing to charge Ivins for the anthrax mailings. They claimed to have DNA from the letters that matched a flask of spores. Ivins worked at USAMRIID.

On July 27, 2008, Ivins was hospitalized after an apparent overdose of acetaminophen. He died on July 29 from an intentional overdose, in what was ruled a suicide. No formal charges were filed against Ivins.

Since then, friends, family, colleagues, and Congress have questioned the FBI's findings. Anthrax spores actually have a footprint, so to speak, and the spores in question were, in fact, not traced to Ivins. The case has never been solved.

Question: Did Bruce Edward Ivins, a respected and experienced microbiologist, off himself when the FBI accused him? Or was he *Whacked?*

You decide.

August 13, 2008

Bill Gwatney was shot in the head and died at the scene.

Gwatney was a Superdelegate in the 2008 primaries. His vote against Hillary Clinton and for Obama was crucial for her surprising loss. The Police identified a man named Tim Johnson, a young man who had never met Gwatney and had no police record.

Question ... was Gwatney the victim of a random murder by a guy whom he never met? Or was he *Whacked?*

You decide.

Tim Johnson, on the very same day, accused murderer of Bill Gwatney, died in a shootout with Police.

In what may be a coincidence, Johnson led the Police on a high-speed chase. They stopped him with a PIT maneuver, and he was killed in the subsequent shootout with the Police.

Question ... did Tim Johnson simply die in a police shootout? Or was he *Whacked?*

You decide.

August 19, 2008:

Barry Jennings, 53, died on September 11, 2001, from what authorities called natural causes. Jennings worked for the New York City Housing Authority, where he was Deputy Director of the Emergency Services Department.

Barry was one of the key witnesses to the collapse of World Trade Center Building 7. Jennings testified that an explosion trapped him and Michael Hess, New York City Corporation Counsel, in the Building. He further stated that a string of calculated explosions occurred throughout the Building until firefighters saved them.

The only formal announcement of his death was a single statement at his workplace that stated, "regretted to report the passing of ... Barry Jennings on August 19, 2008." Short and sweet. No cause of death was given, no autopsy or death certificate had even been released, and no witnesses to his death had come forward.

Question ... did Barry Jennings die of natural causes? Or was he *Whacked?*

You decide.

November 2008

Harwin Strydom, a Cape Town, South African citizen tired of the rampant gangs ruling the city, agreed to testify, something few at the time would do. Days before he was set to testify against the leader of 28s Gang, the most lethal in town, he was gunned down.

George "Gewald" Thomas was arrested and charged fifty-two times, including attempted murder, weapon charges, murder, and more. The trial was stretched out over four years. Many witnesses were intimidated, disappeared out of fear, or worse. Harwin Strydom was determined to do what he could to stop the madness.

Strydom's bravery allowed the South African government to convict the gang leader, and Thomas is currently serving seven life sentences and another 175 years in prison.

Question ... was Harwin Strydom the victim of an unsolved murder? Or was he *Whacked?*

You decide.

December 19, 2008:

Michael Connell, 45, was a Republican strategic consultant who dealt with computer algorithms, website designs, and I.T. management; died when the 1997 Piper Saratoga aircraft was piloting crashed two miles from the Akron-Canton, Ohio Airport.

According to CBS News, Connell's article listed a trail of accomplishments credited to him. He co-founded Gov Tech Solutions with his wife, Heather. With the company, they pursued government contracts. His clients eventually included everything from the White House to several Republican-led Congressional committees and members' websites.

In 2004, Connell attained some notoriety for helping with the website of Swift Boat Veterans for Truth. An organization aimed at attacking Democratic presidential nominee John Kerry.

Connell had a central role in building the I.T. infrastructure of the White House. In that role, he worked closely with Karl Rove, which came with the controversy over missing White House emails about firing U.S. Attorneys and sending emails on servers other than the White House.

He was subpoenaed to testify in an alleged voter fraud case at an Ohio federal court. Despite exit polls showing Democratic nominee John Kerry's lead of more than 4 percent, Mr. Bush won the state's vote by 2.5 percent.

WOIO correspondent Blake Chenault quoted an anonymous close friend of Connell's who reported twice in the past two months that he had canceled flights because of suspicious problems with his plane. He had also been receiving death threats.

Question ... did Mr. Connell die from his own unsafe flying habits? Or was he *Whacked?*

You decide.

December 19, 2008:

Stephanie Tubbs Jones, a young Democratic Representative, set to be a Superdelegate in the 08 Ohio primaries, died of what was ruled a cerebral hemorrhage. An autopsy revealed she died of a brain bleed.

Jones was excited about the upcoming Democratic Convention but was troubled by the pressure to agree to vote for Obama. The night of her death, she was pulled over for DUI. The cop found her incapacitated. He took her to the hospital, where she died.

Her death was officially ruled a result of a brain bleed.

Question ... did Ms. Jones die as a result of her drinking, which led to a brain bleed? Or was she *Whacked?*

You decide.

December 23, 2008

Rene-Thierry Magon de la Villehuchet, the cofounder and CEO of Access International Advisors, was found dead in his office in New York City.

His body was discovered with lacerations on his arms with a box cutter and sleeping pills nearby. His death was ruled a suicide.

Magon de la Villehuchet had lost over $1 billion of his clients' investments that were placed with Bernard Madoff. Who was later found to be running the largest Ponzi scheme in history?

Question ... did Magon de la Villehuchet commit suicide? Or was he *Whacked?*

You decide.

2009

January 2009

Adolf Merckle, a German investor and billionaire, threw himself in front of an oncoming train and died as a result. Merckle was involved in a deal to short Volkswagen stock. The deal failed miserably.

Question ... did Adolf Merckle die by his own hands? Or was he *Whacked?*

You decide.

February 12, 2009

Beverly Eckert, a widow of 9/11 victim Sean Rooney, died, along with 48 others, when her Colgan Air Flight 3407 went down shortly after takeoff from Newark Airport in Newark, New Jersey.

Eckert lost her husband on 9-11 and became a fierce advocate of the 9-11 'Truth' movement. Eckert attended a Washington, DC, meeting at the Eisenhower Executive Office Building.

President Soetoro (aka Obama) was present at this meeting, including several family members of 9/11 victims. Eckert had personal contact with him and demanded that he issue another investigation into the 9/11 attacks.

She was known to make a lot of people uncomfortable. In her 2003 manifesto, *My Silence Cannot Be Bought ...*

She wrote,

"I've chosen to go to court rather than accept a payoff from the 9/11 victims compensation fund. Instead, I want to know what went so wrong with our intelligence and security systems that a band of religious fanatics was able to turn four U.S. passenger jets into an enemy force, attack our cities, and kill 3,000 civilians with terrifying ease. I want to know why two 110-story skyscrapers collapsed in less than two hours and why escape and rescue options were so limited.

The victim's fund was not created in a spirit of compassion. Instead, Congress acknowledged that it had tampered with our civil justice system in an unprecedented way. So I say to Congress, big business, and everyone who conspired to divert attention from government and private-sector failures: My husband's life was priceless, and I will not let his death be meaningless. My silence cannot be bought."

The plane was headed to Buffalo when it crashed. The plane's black boxes were recovered at the crash site, revealing critical information. Neither the air traffic controller nor the pilot voiced or demonstrated any urgency indicating an emergency.

The NTSB said the captain's inappropriate response to the activation of the stick shaker caused an aerodynamic stall, resulting in the crash. This doesn't match their statement, and neither has demonstrated urgency. When a plane stalls, there is extreme shaking, and it soon falls out of the sky. There is time for the black box to record a pilot's response.

Question ... did Colgan Air Flight 3407 suffer a stall in flight, resulting in the death of Beverly Eckert? Or was she *Whacked?*

You decide.

April 28, 2009

Michael H. Doran, 51, an American lawyer who spearheaded work with families of 9/11 victims to garner compensation from the 9/11 fund, died when his plane crashed with him at the controls.

Michael Doran and fellow lawyer Matthew Schnirel, 26, were returning to Buffalo, New York, from a deposition in Cleveland, Ohio. Shortly after leaving Cuyahoga County Airport, the plane entered a wooded area. There were no survivors.

An NYDailyRecord.com article quoted local sources saying, "Doran was an experienced pilot who had owned several other aircraft." The NTSB or others have never listed a cause of the crash.

Question ... did Michael Doran and his fellow attorney die from a legitimate plane crash? Or was he *Whacked?*

You decide.

July 15, 2009

Natalya Estemirova, a prominent Russian activist, journalist, and human rights leader, was abducted from her home in Grozny, Chechnya. Witnesses reported seeing her being forced into a car while shouting she was being kidnapped. Her body was later found with gunshot wounds to the head and chest.

Estemirova was a Board Member of The Memorial, a human rights organization. The organization accused the Chechen government, and President Kadyrov denied any involvement in the murder.

Russian President Dmitry Medvedev condemned Estemirova's murder and promised a thorough investigation. To this day, no suspects have ever been identified.

Question ... did Ms. Estemirova die of a random kidnapping and murder? Or was she *Whacked!*

You decide.

November 10, 2009

Dr. Ramin Pourandarjani, a young (25) Iranian Doctor who testified in the aftermath of the riots regarding the 2009

Presidential elections, was found dead under mysterious circumstances.

When incumbent President Mahmoud Ahmadinejad defeated a strong opposition candidate, protests erupted across Iran. The masses believed the election was rigged. Police arrested over 4,000 Iranians in what became known as the Green Revolution.

The Iranian Police weren't very nice to the protestors, and many were beaten and injured. One Doctor called in to help, and that person was Dr. Ramin Pourandarjani. Pourandarjani tried to give medical care to one protester who died in prison from multiple blows to the head.

The Iranian Parliament heard about the protestor's death and wanted it explained to them. The good Doctor was honest, and his testimony was vital in forcing Ayatollah Khamenei to close the prison where it occurred. The prison was closed, but the Ayatollah apparently wasn't pleased.

Dr. Pourandarjani was arrested by Iranian authorities shortly after his testimony. Off to jail, interrogated, and humiliated, he was eventually released on bail. Then, Iranian authorities threatened to strip him of his medical license and imprison him indefinitely if he disclosed anything more about the incidents at the prison.

The young and promising Doctor returned to his family and friends and immediately reported he was receiving threats against his life. And in one of those seemingly ever-present coincidences, he was found dead. And everyone knew.

Iranian authorities first said the cause of death was from injuries sustained in a car accident. Then it was due to a heart attack and then to suicide, and then to poisoning. The truth? Pourandarjani had eaten a salad before his death. The salad was later found to be laced with a lethal dose of a medication. Iranian authorities refused to allow the family to investigate further.

Question ... did Doctor Pourandarjani die from one of the array of ways the Iranian authorities claimed? Or was he *Whacked?*

You decide.

November 16, 2009

Sergei Magnitsky, 37, a Russian tax advisor, reportedly died in prison. His death was first ruled by malnutrition. It was later changed to him having been beaten to death.

Sergei Magnitsky was a whistleblower who exposed Russian corruption and human rights violations. After coming forth, he was arrested and imprisoned. He was found dead in prison one week before the year the government had to try him. He was never charged with a crime.

Question ... did Sergei die of malnutrition? Or was he *Whacked?*

You decide.

The Twenty Ten's

What Did Your Government Do?

The decade beginning in 2010 would prove pivotal in the ongoing destruction of America. We'd get a second dose of Barry Soetoro's Marxism in America and more of the growing pretend world of the mainstream media.

The 'make believe' began with so-called pro-democracy protests in the Arab World, and before we knew it, the media dubbed it 'The Arab Spring.' Hillary Clinton, as our Secretary of State, cheered the crazies on while giving the bulk of our strategic uranium away to Putin in Russia.

Husband Bill made a fortune on the speaking circuit, getting 100 thousand dollars for a one-hour speech. It was money laundering at its best. Their Clinton Foundation became a family affair that gave 10% of their billions in donations to help others. But the Teflon Family continued to slither away.

After years of Where's Osama sightings and our refusal to take him out, Obama announced a daring raid by Navy Seals that killed public enemy number one in Abbottabad, Pakistan, on May 2, 2011. But rather than let the world see the spoils of war, the government claimed out of respect for Muslims that his body was taken to a US Navy ship, and one of the FBIs most wanted was buried at sea.

President Barry's social agenda arrived on the scene, with same-sex marriage taking center stage and becoming legal. The #MeToo Movement wrecked the lives of many a man for alleged crimes way beyond the statute of limitations.

After aka Obama's reign of destruction, Hillary was destined to be the finisher of America in the 2016 election. In a shock heard around the world, abrasive, arrogant, and effective Donald Trump became the 45th President of the United States, setting off a firestorm of opposition that knew and knew no bounds. The Deep State Trump vowed to destroy waged a war that is still raging.

Despite the assault, Trump managed to increase employment, lower inflation, and make America not only energy independent but also an oil exporter. Despite his success, as the decade concluded, Trump was the most hated man on the planet thanks to a partnership of government, media, and education giants like Facebook and Twitter.

The end of the decade brought a stolen election, news of a coming mysterious outbreak from a bat cave in China, and Al Gores' revenge when the world suddenly declared our climate was about to melt us all. And our once independent media, the backbone of a free country, sang the tune of the globalist masters now calling the shots.

America now had a propaganda arm to make Pravda look like a high school paper in the old Soviet Union. The Deep State owned our entire media. Unofficially, it began in the 1950s. That is when the CIA started what is known as Operation Mockingbird.

Operation Mockingbird was a covert program aimed at influencing and controlling media outlets domestically and internationally. The government initially wanted to shape public opinion and disseminate propaganda against communism. It may have started out that way?

The CIA recruited journalists, put them on the agency's payroll, and instructed them to write stories that aligned with the CIA's political agenda.

Through this network of complicit journalists and publications, the CIA was able to manipulate news coverage and distort the truth, feeding the American public a skewed version of reality.

Operation Mockingbird is alive and well and has destroyed public trust in all forms of journalism.

2010

A DEFINITE MAYBE ...

When you research mysterious deaths in the cloak-and-dagger world, some common coincidences seem to happen. After the fact, many of these individuals suddenly appear to have fetishes, a taste for porn, a taste for weird tastes, and more. Anything to discredit the individual.

The other ordinary coincidence is many seem to have a penchant for leaping from buildings, committing suicide in bizarre ways, and consistently, suddenly having mental health issues. The key is to look for commonalities between coincidental deaths.

A former MI6 officer turned Author told The Independent on Sunday:

"I am on verbal record to my own family, close friends, and select lawyers that if anything ever happened to me – a straight man and a positive thinker – it would likely be made to look either like a suicide or that I died dressed like a woman.

"Over the years, it seems to me a favourite way of presentation. I, of course, am not suicidal in any remote way nor do I like to dress so. When I read in the press about Gareth Williams, women's clothes, and a wig, it all fits the usual scenario."

Keep your eyes wide open.

March 26, 2010

Nancy Schaeffer, Georgia State Senator, and her husband of 52 years, Bruce Schaeffer, were both found dead of gunshot wounds. The deaths were ruled a murder-suicide.

During her second term, State Senator Schaeffer came into possession of damaging information on prominent people in Georgia. Those people purportedly participated in and benefited from activities involving human trafficking that involved Child Protective Services. It is also loosely tied to the PizzaGate fiasco in D.C.

She took the information to her fellow Republican Senators, who quickly rejected her and her information. They then worked to ensure she was not reelected. Once out of the Senate, she became President of another organization and continued her quest for Justice.

Upon discovery of the bodies, the State reconstructed and alleged her husband shot her and killed himself. However, the gun used in the killing was not his personal weapon but an unregistered, untraceable gun.

After pressure from news organizations questioning the suicide ruling, the Georgia Bureau of Investigation (GBI) reopened the case. The GBI would not pursue a criminal investigation, and all items seized from the house the night of the deaths have been destroyed. Another coincidence?

Question ... did Nancy Schaeffer and her husband die in a murder or suicide? Or were they *Whacked*?

You decide.

August 16, 2010

Gareth Williams, a super-fit, a world-class code-breaking mathematician with MI5 and GCHQ, was found dead in his apartment tucked into a sports bag.

Gareth Williams was an up-and-coming operative for British intelligence and failed to show up for work one Monday morning, and the nation's top spy agency didn't bother to look for him for a week. When they did, they found him dead, stuffed in one piece inside a sports bag.

The police tried to replicate the fete of being in a gym bag and zipping oneself up, but it could not be reproduced. Rumors began surfacing that Williams had a women's lingerie fetish, that he may have been a double agent, and other what the media termed regular rumors regarding death.

Question ... did Gareth Williams stuff himself inside that gym bag and zip it up to commit suicide? Or was he *Whacked?*

You decide.

December 31, 2010:

John Wheeler, 66, defense industry consultant and former government official in the Reagan, Bush, and Bush administrations and Chairman of the Vietnam Veterans Memorial Fund, was found dead at the Cherry Hill Landfill in Wilmington, Delaware.

On December 30, Wheeler was spotted disoriented and wearing only one shoe in a New Castle, Delaware parking garage. On December 31, his body was discovered by a landfill worker as it fell from a Waste Management trash truck into a pile of trash at the Cherry Island Landfill in Wilmington.

The Newark Police Department ruled Wheeler's death a homicide, though the cause of death was not released.

Question ... did Mr. Wheeler die of a simple homicide? Or was he *Whacked?*

You decide.

2011

July 13, 2011:

Danny Jowenko, 55, a Dutch demolition expert who opened an independent investigation into the September 11 attacks on the World Trade Center, died in a single-vehicle crash in the village of Serooskerke, Netherlands. The official report is he lost control of his car and hit a tree. His dog was in the passenger seat and survived.

In 2006, he produced numerous YouTube videos showing discrepancies regarding the NIST final report on the World Trade Center. He also produced eyewitness video evidence. His ongoing belief was that 9/11 took place under the guise of a terrorist attack but was indeed connected to controlled demolition. Jowenko gave an interview reasserting his faith in the demolition theory and was found dead three days later.

Question ... did Danny Jowenko die in a car accident? Or was he *Whacked?*

You decide.

2012

January 2012

A DEFINITE MAYBE ...

Huawei, a telecommunications equipment company with close ties to the Chinese government, has raised serious concerns. In a Congressional Report to be released this year, it was revealed that Huawei and ZTE, another Chinese company, built back doors to their technology. These back doors could potentially give the Chinese government access to US systems, posing a significant cybersecurity threat that cannot be ignored.

Moreover, Huawei has been accused of engaging in unethical practices such as stealing intellectual property and trade secrets. In 2017, Huawei was found guilty of stealing trade secrets from T-Mobile, a clear violation of trust and fair competition. In 2020, they were charged with racketeering conspiracy and conspiracy to steal trade secrets, further highlighting their disregard for ethical business practices.

And that isn't the end of their dirty tricks. The US government charged Huawei with violating sanctions on Iran and North Korea. They did this by using fake names for secret subsidiaries in these countries. In 2019, their CEO was charged with fraud. Their equipment was first restricted entry into the US, then banned in most instances. The battle with Huawei culminated in 2022 when the FCC banned the sale or import of their equipment due to national security risks.

Note: Read how one young American was lost to the war with Huawei, and no one was willing to do anything about it. See Dr. Shane Todd in the pages ahead.

March 1, 2012:

Andrew Breitbart, 43, a conservative journalist and founder of Breitbart News, died, according to authorities, of a heart attack.

Breitbart was involved in the early stages of the Huffington Post and the Drudge Report before creating Breitbart News. In our woke world, Breitbart News has been described as misogynistic, xenophobic, and racist by academics and journalists. That's woke code for 'they tell the truth.'

Breitbart was not a wallflower and played central roles in political controversies, like Anthony Weiner's sexting scandal, the firing of Shirley Sherrod, and the ACORN 2009 undercover videos.

On the night his problems began, he was at a Los Angeles hotspot called the Brentwood. He kept to himself and left before midnight. He collapsed a short time later and was pronounced dead on March 1. Witness Christopher Lassiter told journalist Paul Huebl,

"There was a thick white band around his forehead all the way around his hairline, bright red face, thick, thick white band – made me make a double-take."

Question ... did Andrew Breitbart die of the reported heart attack? Or was he *Whacked?*

You decide.

April 20, 2012

Michael Cormier, 61, a Los Angeles Coroner's Technician who assisted in the private autopsy of Andrew Breitbart, who died after a short illness.

But ... as you know by now, there is more to the story, which is tied to the Andrew Breitbart case noted earlier. On March 4, 2012, Los Angeles Coroner's Technician Michael Cormier received a phone call to assist with a private autopsy for a celebrity case. While Michael worked for the Coroner's Office, he started a side business, MAC Autopsy Services LLC, which enabled him to take side jobs for extra cash.

Dr. David Posey of Glen Oaks Pathology Group conducted the private autopsy. Dr. Posey was highly regarded, and his website said he'd personally conducted more than 3,000 autopsies. Michael worked for Glen Oaks Pathology Group many times before. He often performed the entire autopsy while Dr. Posey observed, and this case was to be no different.

When Michael arrived home after this autopsy, he said he had a souvenir for his brother, Ed Cormier. Michael said, *"Look who I worked on,"* and handed Ed a security crypt toe tag with BREITBART ANDREW written along with a case number.

On April 13, Michael began feeling sick and soon had severe diarrhea and vomiting. Two days later, on April 15, he attended a planned cancer walk and fell ill again. On April 18, Michael went to dinner with friends and couldn't finish his meal. He tried to enjoy a night out to dinner with friends and couldn't finish his meal. Michael went to Kaiser Hospital with chest pains and was released the following day with medication.

Two days later, in the early morning hours of April 20, paramedics were called to his home. He was immediately transported to St. Joseph's Medical Center. When brother Ed found out Michael was in the hospital, he called and suggested they test for poison. The doctors found heavy metals in Michael's blood, later confirmed to be arsenic.

In yet another coincidence, Michael Cormier died that day. KTLA TV reporter Elizabeth Espinosa was the first to report his death. She also broke the news of Andrew Breitbart's preliminary autopsy results. They were published by L.A. Coroner's Office Chief of Operations Craig Harvey. Breitbart's death was officially declared of natural causes due to the onset of heart failure.

Then things got interesting ...

Tuesday, April 24: Four days after Michaels's death, Detective Steve Castro of North Hollywood Homicide arrives as an investigator for the case. It turns out that the Burbank Police Department failed to report Michael's death from arsenic poisoning until that day. Detective Castro told Ed Cormier that if he had not called the hospital about the possibility of poisoning, then the arsenic wouldn't have been found.

Blogs and talk shows began claiming a conspiracy that Cormier had conducted the autopsy on Breitbart and was killed because of it.

Then came the official denials. LAPD Homicide Supervisor Detective Rich Wheeler and L.A. Coroner's Assistant Chief Ed Winter released statements that Cormier had no connection to the Breitbart case.

On April 30, Assistant Chief of the Los Angeles Coroner's Office Ed Winter held a press conference. It stated that Michael Cormier never assisted on the Andrew Breitbart autopsy because only doctors worked the case, and foul play was never suspected. He concluded, *"Mr. Cormier was not the attendant on Mr.*

Breitbart's case, nor did he handle or investigate any of the cases."

On May 9, LAPD Detective Rich Wheeler relayed a similar statement to TheDailyBeast.com —*"He (Cormier) had nothing to do with the autopsy or anything to do with the case ... That story is based on rumor and innuendo."*

Michael's brother, Ed Cormier, was hearing none of it. He wanted explanations. On September 6, 2012, Ed learned that two different doctors from the L.A. Coroner Office, Dr. Ortiz, the Coroner who performed Michael's autopsy, and Dr. Rangan, a Toxicologist, had requested advanced tests on Michael's stomach contents but were informed that advanced testing couldn't be performed. When Dr. Ortiz was told that these advanced tests couldn't be performed, he said,

"Therefore, my conclusion based on available data is that the decedent died from severe acute arsenic poisoning of unknown origin. The clinical presentation and the level of arsenic detected in the blood and stomach are consistent with a large, recent intentional exposure."

Ed Cormier would not give up his quest for justice and truth. Dr. Ortiz said he would try to get the names of those who said they couldn't perform the tests. Those calls never came from Ortiz or anyone in the L.A. Coroner's office.

Fast forward to April 23, 2014, after more than a year of waiting, the Interim Chief reached out to Ed via email that there were no stomach contents to be tested since his stomach was pumped at the hospital.

Ed returned an email correcting Anderson, pointing out the 2300ppm of arsenic. Dan Anderson replied that the stomach contents were destroyed per their retention policy on March 25, 2013. Ed persisted, and Anderson responded, giving dates for discarded items. He then told Ed that was to be expected since his brother spent several days in the hospital.

Ed's last communication reads as follows ... "

"Thanks, Dan. However, your recollection is not correct. Mike did not spend several days in the hospital, only several hours. His stomach was not pumped. Submitted stomach contents contained 2300ppm of arsenic, according to a lap report emailed to you on 5/9/2012. We need the stomach contents. Do you have it, Dan?"

Ed never gave up on the truth. The entire affair is described in his book The Breitbart Coroner.

As you can see, making sense of some of these coincidences requires a decoder ring that the Deep State never provides.

Question ... did Michael Cormier accidentally ingest enough arsenic to kill himself? Or was he *Whacked?*

You decide.

June 24, 2012

Dr. Shane Todd, a brilliant young American electrical engineer working for a Chinese electronics company and living in Singapore, was found dead in his apartment the day before his scheduled return to the States for a new job. His death was immediately ruled a suicide by Singaporean Police.

Dr. Todd had shared his concerns about the company he was working for in Singapore. As told to his parents over a Christmas holiday, his company, IME, was involved in some shady dealings he felt put him in jeopardy of violating federal law and worse. He made plans to leave the company upon his return.

Upon news of his death, a suicide, his family immediately flew to Singapore. The police there described a scenario of the crime scene that was nothing like what they found visiting his apartment. His close friends did not believe he was suicidal, and the suicide note provided by his parents did not match their son in writing or wording.

Thus began their years-long battle to find the truth. In his personal belongings, they found what they believed to be a compact speaker. When they were home sorting through his material, they realized it was a hard drive. They sent it away to an expert to have it forensically analyzed.

Their findings were shocking. The company was involved in some shady dealings in the defense field and was in talks with Huawei, the Chinese tech firm having its own problems with the US government. They also found that the hard drive had been hacked and the date removed after their son's death.

The family has conducted a years-long battle for the truth. Their journey has taken them to Congress, the FBI, the Singapore government, and Chinese authorities, all to no avail. Frustrated, they had a top medical scientist review the autopsy findings, and he concluded Dr. Todd was a victim of homicide.

Question ... did Dr. Shane Todd, a bright young electronics engineer with a new job waiting, commit suicide the night before his flight home? Or was he *Whacked!*

You decide.

Note: In this story, we can see the lengths governments will go to cover up a dirty deed. Dr. Todd's parents pursued the truth around the world at great personal expense, engaged their Congress members, and ended up on 48 Hours Mystery, all to no avail.

September 11, 2012

A DEFINITE MAYBE ...

On this date in Benghazi, Libya, well over 100 Islamic jihadi's attacked the US diplomatic compound, setting fire to the main building. The group Ansar al-Sharia claimed responsibility for the attack. The onslaught lasted off and on for three days.

When the dust settled, US Ambassador J. Christopher Stevens, his tech guy Sean Smith, and two former US Spec Ops men, Tyrone Woods and Glen Doherty, were dead. Ambassador Stevens was dragged through the streets, tortured, and killed. Smith was strangled, and Woods and Doherty died fighting to the death.

Then, Secretary of State Hillary Clinton immediately put out a press release that the attack was in response to an anti-Islamic video placed on the Internet the day prior. The announcement was met with skepticism, and the world knew something was amiss.

Congressional investigators uncovered the fact the State Department was running guns through Libya to rebels seeking the life of Libyan leader Muammar Qadaffi and those in Syria after President Bashar al-Assad. The ugly truth is that our own State Department was operating behind Ambassador Stevens's back, refused his requests for increased security, and four Americans are dead.

Investigators with the House Armed Services Committee issued a scathing report condemning the White House's action or inaction. It was found that the head of the US African Command, General Carter Ham, had informed and provided CCTV video to Defense Secretary Leon Panetta and Joint Chiefs 'Chair Martin Dempsey immediately that it was a terrorist attack and nothing to do with the video.

Panetta and Dempsey quickly met then-President Barry Soetoro (aka Barack Obama) at the White House. Within hours, the entire senior White House staff knew the truth behind the cause of the attack. Yet, two weeks later, President Barry was spinning his lies during an appearance on "The View."

Investigators found that Hillary's State Department had their hands on seven reports before the attack warning them of what was coming. They even found that former Guantanamo inmates from the War on Terror, all released by Barry, were involved. In the end, investigators were stymied, yet the White House still refused to cooperate with witnesses and provide documents.

If that isn't bad enough, as the FBI was unleashed to investigate Benghazi after an avalanche of public outcry, 15 material witnesses, Libyans, turned up dead before FBI investigators could interview them. Now, that is one helluva 'coincidence right there. 15 direct witnesses to what took place and why they met their maker before they could say an official word.

Is it just another coincidence that 15 innocent people met their ultimate fate after crossing paths with Hillary Clinton and Barry Soetoro? You'll have to decide.

November 10, 2012

Alexander Perepilichny, a wealthy, successful Russian businessman and investment banker who traveled the world, died mysteriously while jogging near his private estate in Great Britain.

It seems Perepilichny had a fatal flaw ... telling the truth. As a young and successful investment banker, he saw some disturbing things. He began his own investigation into fraud in the Russian economy.

He uncovered one of the biggest taxpayer thefts in history. Since it involved Swiss banks, he gave a series of documents to Swiss officials. The documents caught the Russian mafia and its government conspiring to steal $230 million in a massive money laundering scheme from the Russian treasury.

Swiss prosecutors responded by freezing the Swiss bank account of a Russian government official worth $11 million. And that's when the coincidences began.

Perepilichny began to receive death threats. He fled Russia for Britain, where he secretly moved to a private estate. He sought to live a private life. He did until he went jogging and was found a short time later dead on the road.

As is typical in many coincidences, he had no injuries on his body. He also had no medical conditions. The autopsy following his death revealed the presence of a rare poison in his stomach related to the deadly Gelsemium genus of plants. Russian authorities ruled his death by natural causes.

After his death, an anonymous close acquaintance told the press that Perepilichny's had been put on a hit list. The perpetrators wanted him dead. Perepilichny was actively providing information to investigators probing the case when he died. Most know Russia's domestic intelligence agency, FSB, may have played a role.

Question ... did Alexander Perepilichny die of natural causes while jogging near his home? Or was he *Whacked?*

You decide.

2013

A LITTLE CONTEXT ...

2008, the world suffered a major financial collapse, and the repercussions and blamestorming were alive and well for many years. There were several conspiracy theories regarding the growing number of 'suicides' in the banking industry. Early on, it appeared that these claims were wild speculation. As time progressed, pieces and pieces of the vast coincidence began to look more and more like a vast criminal conspiracy.

When the skies of coincidence cleared, it gave birth to what is known as the LIBOR interest rigging scandal. The LIBOR is the London Interbank Offered Rate. The scandal involved a scheme by bankers to manipulate the rates, a benchmark interest fundamental to the global financial system. It was a big deal.

A few things were subsequently discovered ...

Between 2005 and 2009, the British bank Barclays manipulated LIBOR submissions to gain profits and limit losses from derivative trades.

Barclays also made dishonestly low LIBOR submissions between 2007 and 2009 to dampen market speculation about its financial viability during the economic crisis.

In October 2008, central banks, including the Bank of England, intervened on a large scale to pressure banks to manipulate LIBOR by submitting artificially low rates to restore calm to financial markets.

Note: This intervention was not disclosed to juries when some traders were later prosecuted for LIBOR manipulation.

The scandal revealed systemic issues with LIBOR, including that it relied on banks to honestly report their borrowing rates when they had incentives to underreport them. This undermined the accuracy and integrity of a benchmark used for trillions of dollars in financial transactions. Several people lost their jobs and received criminal sentences, and banks failed worldwide.

In a stunning coincidence, more than forty international bankers allegedly killed themselves over two years in the wake of the LIBOR scandal. Three of these allegedly unrelated suicides shared common threads related to Deutsche Bank. These three banker suicides were in New York, London, and Siena, Italy. They took place within 17 months of each other in 2013 & 2014 in what investigators labeled 'unrelated suicides.'

Sadly, these massive events are forgotten when the investigations are complete.

March 6, 2013

David Rossi, 51, communications director at the world's oldest bank, Italian Monte dei Paschi di Siena, fell to his death from three stories.

The bank where Rossi worked was on the verge of disaster due to massive losses in the 2008 financial crisis.

The New York Times said of his death ...

"A devastating security video shows Rossi landing on the pavement on his back, facing the building—an odd position more likely to occur when a body is pushed from a window. The footage shows the three-story fall didn't kill Rossi instantly.

For almost 20 minutes, the banker lay on the dimly lit cobblestones, occasionally moving an arm and leg. As he lay dying, two murky figures appear. Two men appear, and one walks over to gaze at the banker. He offers no aid or comfort and doesn't call for help before turning around and calmly walking out of the alley.

About an hour later, a co-worker discovered Rossi's body. The arms were bruised, and he sustained a head wound that, according to the local medical Examiner's report, suggested there might have been a struggle before his fall."

Question ... did David Rossi jump to his death as an act of suicide? Or was he *Whacked?*

You decide.

March 7, 2013

Calogero Gambino, a senior Deutsche Bank regulatory lawyer, died from suicide at his home in Brooklyn, New York.

At his death, Gambino negotiated legal issues for Deutsche Bank related to the alleged manipulation of the London interbank offered rate, or Libor.

Question ... did Mr. Gambino commit suicide? Or was he *Whacked?*

You decide.

A DEFINITE MAYBE ...

Three scientists have been identified, of which there is little information. The three died within the space of three months in early 2013.

The three are ...

***Professor Seymour Laxon**, a climate scientist at the University College of London, died falling down a flight of stairs while attending a New Year's Eve Party. A colleague, Professor Wadham, reported in the weeks after Professor Laxon's death, that he believed he was targeted by a lorry that tried to force him off the road. He reported the incident to the police. As a note, Laxon's work was as the director of the Centre for Polar Observation and Modeling at the University College London. His research pioneered the use of satellite altimetry to study sea ice.*

***Dr. Katharine Giles**, also a climate scientist at the University College London, died when she was in a collision with a lorry when cycling to work in London.*

***Dr. Tim Boyd** of the Scottish Association for Marine Science is thought to have been struck by lightning while walking in Scotland.*

None of these coincidences means they were Whacked rather than victims of unfortunate circumstances, but the known facts make you wonder.

June 18, 2013:

Michael Hastings, a journalist for Rolling Stone magazine, died in a highly suspicious single-vehicle auto accident.

Hastings was best known for breaking stories critical of Secretary of State Hillary Clinton. One of the emails leaked during the 2016 Democratic Convention confirmed that Hillary had received Hastings' damning investigative report of the attack on the Benghazi consulate 5 months before his death.

In the weeks before his death, he told friends that he was afraid for his life.

Question ... did Michael Hastings die in a strange auto accident? Or was he *Whacked?*

You decide.

July 2013

Carsten Schloter, the CEO of Swisscom, died by suicide. There is little information on his death. Swisscom was in the middle of the 2008 financial meltdown.

Question ... did Mr. Schloter commit suicide? Or was he *Whacked?*

You decide.

July 25, 2013

Barnaby Jack, 35, a New Zealand hacking expert and computer programmer

was discovered dead by his girlfriend at his San Francisco apartment.

Jack was a renowned hacker who had demonstrated vulnerabilities in medical devices and ATMs. At the 2010 Black Hat Computer Security Conference, Barnaby hacked two ATM machines, causing them to release cash. He also showcased hacking medical devices such as pacemakers and insulin pumps.

In October 2011, at the McAfee Focus 11 event, Barnaby successfully hacked insulin pumps under the employment of McAfee Security. He did so without prior knowledge of the device's serial numbers and accomplished this feat using a high-grade antenna. He was a big deal in the hacking community and high tech.

He was scheduled to present research on hacking pacemakers at the Black Hat security conference a week after his death.

The San Francisco Medical Examiner's Office determined that Barnaby Jack's cause of death was acute mixed drug intoxication involving a combination of heroin, cocaine, and prescription drugs. When his girlfriend found him unresponsive in his bed, there were multiple bottles of beer and champagne in the garbage can. The Examiner believed this indicated an accidental overdose.

Question ... did Barnaby Jack foolishly die of a drug overdose? Or was he *Whacked?*

You decide.

August 2013

Pierre Wauthier, the chief financial officer of Zurich Insurance, was found dead in his home in what was believed to be a suicide. As with many others, little information exists about his passing.

Zurich Insurance was involved in the 2008 financial meltdown.

Question ... did Wauthier die by suicide? Or was he *Whacked?*

You decide.

August 8, 2013

Melaney Parker, a young woman, recently married who had plans to move to Austin and pursue graduate studies, was found dead after being hit by a train in Marfa, Texas, in Presidio County.

Her death was quickly ruled a suicide by Presidio County Judge Cinderela Guevara. Melaney's mother, Liz Parker, questioned how the investigation into her daughter's death was handled by Judge Guevara. The Judge did not order a rape kit or an autopsy and instead ruled Melaney's death a suicide based only on a toxicology report.

Liz Parkers expressed concerns that the possibility of foul play was not adequately investigated. She shared that her family found half of Melaney's broken eyeglasses some distance from where her body was hit by the train. The family felt the evidence at the scene suggested Melaney may have already been deceased when struck by the train.

However, Judge Guevara told Liz Parker that she ordered a toxicology report because the cause of death was 'obvious.'

Ms. Parker's death is relevant when compared to how Judge Guevara handled even a high-profile case, the death of Supreme Court Judge Antonio Scalia. *(See February 12, 2016)*

Question ... did young Melaney Parker die in an unusual suicide? Or was she *Whacked?*

You decide.

November 2013

Dr. Andrew Moulden, a researcher of vaccines, died in a mystery.

Dr. Moulden died of a heart attack or a suicide, depending on the sources reporting. Information on his death remains a mystery to this day.

A colleague of Dr. Moulden, who, for obvious reasons, wishes to remain anonymous, reported to Health Impact News that they had contact with him two weeks before he died in 2013. Dr. Moulden told the source and a few trusted colleagues in October 2013 that he was about to break his silence. He would release new information that would significantly challenge the vaccine business and hit Big Pharma hard.

Dr. Moulden had been silenced but was ready to come back.

Question ... did Dr. Moulden die of a heart attack or suicide? Or was he *Whacked* because he was anti-Big Pharma?

You decide.

2014

January 2014

William Broeksmit, a former Merrill Lynch employee who was co-CEO of Deutsche Bank AG, was found dead, hanging in his London home.

Deutsche Bank AG was involved in criminal investigations resulting from the 2008 worldwide financial meltdown.

Did Mr. Broeksmit commit suicide? Or was he *Whacked?*

You decide.

Gabriel Magee, a former vice-president of Corporate and Investment Bank Technology at JPMorgan, fell from the top of the bank's London offices.

JP Morgan was investigated for criminal wrongdoing due to the 2008 financial meltdown.

Did Mr. Magee commit suicide? Or was he *Whacked?*

You decide.

July 17, 2014

Glenn Thomas, a leading consultant in Geneva and expert in AIDS and Ebola Virus, was on board a Boeing 777-200 aircraft on Malaysia Airlines Flight MH17, which went down on the border between Ukraine and Russia, killing 298 people on board.

Glenn Thomas was the media coordinator for the World Health Organization and was one of 100 people on board a plane heading to an AIDS Conference in Australia. Thomas was involved in the investigations that revealed the issue of trial operations of AIDS and Ebola vaccines.

A Dutch-led investigation determined that the aircraft was shot down by a Russian-made surface-to-air missile fired from separatist-held territory in Ukraine.

Question ... was Glenn Thomas a victim of a Russian shoot down? Or was he *Whacked?*

You decide.

October 19, 2014

Serena Shim, a Lebanese-American journalist working for Press T.V., reporting in Turkey near the border with Syria, died in a mysterious automobile accident.

Shim reported that ISIS agents were being taken across the border into Syria from Turkey. The report was not welcome in Turkey. That meant the world would know they were secretly supporting ISIS. The Turkish government accused her of being a foreign spy.

Shim was no wallflower and came out with a courageous reply. She said ...

"I am very surprised at this accusation. I've even thought of actually approaching Turkish intelligence, and because I have nothing to hide, I've never done anything aside from my job, and I'd like to make that apparent to them. However, I am a bit worried because, as you know, and as the viewers know, Turkey has been labeled by Reporters Without Borders as the largest prison for journalists. So I am a bit frightened about what they might use against me."

Serena Shim issued that statement on October 17, 2014. She was killed in a car crash two days later under very suspicious circumstances. Shim was 29 years old at the time of her death.

Question ... did Serena Shim die from a legitimate automobile accident? Or was she *Whacked?*

You decide.

2015

January 9, 2015

Alberto Behar, 47, a robotics expert and scientist at NASA's Jet Propulsion Laboratory for 23 years, died instantly when his single-engine plane nosedived shortly after takeoff Friday from Van Nuys Airport.

Mr. Behar had a wealth of knowledge of instruments for the Curiosity rover on Mars and other extreme environments. Behar was responsible for a device that detected hydrogen on the planet's surface as the rover moved. He was a valuable asset to NASA.

Although Behar was an experienced pilot and instructor of airplanes and helicopters, and the weather conditions were evident at the time of the crash, the National Transportation Safety Board determined that the engine lost power due to insufficient fuel, leading to a stall and crash. Curious, surely?

Question ... Did Alberto Behar take off with no fuel in his tanks, killing himself? Or was he *Whacked?*

You decide.

January 18, 2015

Alberto Nisman, an Argentine prosecutor investigating the 1994 bombing of a Jewish community center in Buenos Aires, died of a gunshot wound to the head. It was initially ruled a suicide.

The suicide was changed by a federal judge, who determined that Nisman was, in fact, murdered. Nisman accused the former Argentine President, Cristina Fernández de Kirchner, of covering up Iran's alleged involvement in the 1994 bombing. In another one of those pesky coincidences, he was found dead just hours before he was set to testify about these allegations.

A 2017 police report concluded that Nisman was beaten, drugged, and then shot in what appears to have been a staged suicide.

Question ... was Alberto Nisman simply murdered? Or was he *Whacked* for what he knew and was about to testify?

You decide.

February 27, 2015

Boris Nemtsov, a leader, and critic of President Vladimir Putin, was shot multiple times, with four of the shots hitting him in the head, heart, liver, and stomach, as he was walking across the Bolshoy Moskvoretsky Bridge near the Kremlin.

In an unbelievable coincidence, Nemtsov was shot just hours after he had very publicly called for a march against Russia's involvement in the conflict in Ukraine. Nemtsov's Ukrainian girlfriend, Anna Duritskaya, was with him when he was shot but was not physically harmed. She was the sole eyewitness to the murder.

Two Russian men were eventually arrested and confessed but later recanted, claiming torture. The person who ordered him shot has never been revealed.

Question ... did Boris Nemtsov die of a random murder? Or was he *Whacked?*

You decide.

June 15, 2015

Dr. Teresa Sievers, a famous alternative medicine Doctor and local celebrity in Bonita Springs, Florida, was found dead in her home after not returning to work after a vacation. She was bludgeoned to death.

After a tip came to police from Illinois, they arrested her husband and eventually two accomplices. The motive, they believe, was her life insurance. While it appears Ms. Sievers was probably a victim of her husband and his cohorts, her death is also connected to several more mysterious holistic doctor deaths around this time.

Question ... was Dr. Teresa Sievers a victim of murder at the hands of her husband? Or was she *Whacked* for her attacks on Big Pharma?

You decide.

June 19, 2015

Dr. Jeffrey Bradstreet, the owner of a practice specializing in the treatment of autistic patients, is reported to have shot himself in the chest after his offices were raided by US FDA agents and North Carolina law enforcement agents.

Three days before his death, agents exercised a search warrant to gather information about the use of GcMAF with autistic patients in his clinic. Human GcMAF holds great promise in the treatment of various illnesses, including cancer, autism, chronic fatigue, and possibly Parkinson's.

Since 1990, 59 research papers on cancer treatment have been published on GcMAF, 20. Big Pharma is often accused of not liking simple solutions to health problems.

By coincidence, I am sure, his death came 4 days after Dr. Sievers.

Question ... did researcher, medical pioneer, and Doctor Jeffrey Bradstreet become so distraught over the FDA barging that he put one in his chest? Or was he *Whacked?*

You decide.

June 21, 2015

Dr. Bruce Hedendal, a private chiropractor and Harvard PhD in nutrition, was found dead in his car on Father's Day. His death was ruled by natural causes.

His death shocked his family and friends who knew him as fit and healthy. He had run a distance competition the day before his death. He actually won a Gold Medal that day.

Family members and friends remained suspicious as the years passed.

Question ... did Dr. Hedendal die of natural causes? Or was he *Whacked* for his views and work in alternative medicine?

You decide.

Walter Scheib, the former White House executive chef who served under President Bill Clinton, was reported missing on June 16, 2015, after he left for a hike in the mountains near Taos, New Mexico.

His body was found on June 21, 2015, submerged in a mountain drainage near a hiking trail. An autopsy determined that Scheib's death was an accidental drowning.

Question ... did Mr. Scheib wander off a hiking trail, fall into a ditch, and drown? Or was he *Whacked?*

You decide.

June 26, 2015

Dr. Baron Holt, a 33-year-old chiropractor and alternative healer, Doctor to Olympians and UFC fighters, dropped dead on the street while on a business trip to Jacksonville, Florida. The cause of death was not determined.

Dr. Holt was known to be fit, healthy, and very active. He had no known medical issues. He had a large and thriving medical practice with over 500 patients and even traveled to the Olympics to treat certain athletes.

He worked to help those who struggled with medical bills and preached recovery over profits.

Question ... did Dr. Baron Holt die of natural and unknown causes? Or was he *Whacked* as an enemy of Big Pharma?

You decide.

July 20, 2015

Dr. Lisa Riley, a 34-year-old osteopath and alternative medicine from Lee County, Georgia, died of a gunshot wound to the head.

Her death was clearly murder, but the police handling of the investigation was suspicious. Her husband, Thomas Riley, was initially charged with her murder but was eventually released without charge. Her murder had never been solved.

Question ... was Dr. Lisa Riley a simple victim of murder? Or was she *Whacked?*

You decide.

July 21, 2015

Dr. Nicholas Gonzalez, a physician known for his alternative cancer treatments, died suddenly. His cause of death was ruled from cardiac issues.

Dr. Gonzalez developed a nutritional approach to treating cancer patients involving a strict diet, supplements, and pancreatic enzymes. Despite his unorthodox methods, Dr. Gonzalcz maintained a medical practice in New York City for over 30 years.

Ty Bollinger, a friend, and fellow Doctor of alternative cancer treatment, wasn't buying the heart attack ruling. He said he and Gonzalez shared a common skepticism of the media and a common desire to spread the truth about cancer. Bollinger said Gonzales was the foremost expert on cancer.

Question ... did Dr. Gonzalez die of a heart attack? Or was he *Whacked* because he was a thorn in the side of Big Pharma?

You decide.

July 22, 2015

Dr. Mary Louise Yoder, a 60-year-old chiropractor in Whitesboro, New York, died after a short, unexpected illness. After autopsy, her death was ruled by poisoning.

Dr. Yoder became ill at the office three days before her death. She had diarrhea and vomiting. Her condition worsened overnight, and she was taken to the St. Luke's emergency room, where she was admitted to the ICU, where she suffered multiple heart attacks and died.

The autopsy revealed Dr. Yoder died from colchicine poisoning, which she had no reason to be using. The investigation eventually led to the arrest of Kaitlyn Conley, a receptionist at Dr. Yoder's practice, who was convicted of manslaughter for poisoning her with colchicine3.

No motive was ever determined.

Question … was Dr. Mary Louise Yoder murdered by a random nut job? Or was she *Whacked?*

You decide.

July 29, 2015

A LITTLE CONTEXT …

On July 29, 2015, Health Impact News ran an article titled "Is the U.S. Medical Mafia Murdering Alternative Health Doctors Who Have Real Cures Not Approved by the FDA?" There were reports that five holistic doctors had met untimely and suspicious deaths within 30 days and that five more were still missing. But that's just the beginning.

Another week brought a report of two more doctors found dead under suspicious circumstances. That's which 7 inside a month. Now, within 90 days, eleven doctors have been found dead under suspicious circumstances. Then, a twelfth holistic doctor, Marie Paas, turned up dead due to an apparent suicide. In a 2016 Natural News article titled "Wave of Holistic Doctor Deaths

Continues, as Florida Chiropractor Suddenly Dies Despite Being Hearty and Healthy.'"

Correspondent Julie Wilson wrote,

"A wave of mysterious deaths continues to plague practitioners in the field of holistic medicine, including chiropractors, herbalists, and other alternative healers, with the latest fatality involving a licensed chiropractor who also worked as a full-time teacher.

Dr. Rod Floyd, Associate Professor and Faculty-Clinician with the Palmer College of Chiropractic at the Port Orange, Fla. campus, had just celebrated his and his wife's 37th wedding anniversary when he abruptly passed away in his home late last month."

A June article in Truth Theory magazine read, "50 Holistic Doctors Have Mysteriously Died In The Last Year, But What's Being Done About It?" The story was intriguing and highlighted thirty-four deaths within the previous year.

What does all this mean? First, if it's even partially true, someone out there wants natural medical practitioners around. Secondly, why is this only reported in publications we've never heard of?

Coincidences are hitting holistic medicine hard.

September 15, 2015

Dr. Mitchell L. Gaynor, a pioneer in integrative oncology, famous for combining traditional cancer treatments with alternative medicine, was found at his home in Hillsdale, New York. He died of a gunshot wound to the chest at age 59. His death was ruled a suicide. No one, including his family, found him suicidal.

Dr. Gaynor founded Gaynor Integrative Oncology in Manhattan and served as Director of Medical Oncology at New York Presbyterian Hospital. His alternative treatments included therapies like music, meditation, nutrition, and supplements.

His natural methods of treating cancer were popular, and he had been practicing for several decades. He also studied and offered similar natural remedies for obesity, aging, gene degeneration, and diabetes. He was also the Author of several best-selling books on alternative medicine.

Question ... did Dr. Gaynor commit suicide at the height of his career? Or was he *Whacked* as an enemy of Big Pharma?

You decide.

November 5, 2015

Mikhail Lesin, 57, a prominent Russian politician who served under President Vladimir Putin as Russia's Minister of Press and Media, was found dead in his hotel room at the Dupont Circle Hotel in Washington, DC, by a maid.

Lesin was known for his cruelty in media capabilities. He was instrumental in bringing Russian national T.V. channels under Kremlin control and setting up the global media outlet R.T. (formerly Russia Today)

Initially, Lesin's family said he died of a heart attack. Still, after a year-long investigation, the Washington medical examiner determined that the cause of death was blunt force injuries to the head. The medical Examiner also found that Lesin had sustained a fractured hyoid bone in his neck, which could have been caused before or after his death.

The circumstances around Lesin's death were highly suspicious, with no apparent signs of forced entry or foul play initially. Lesin had fallen out of favor with the Kremlin elite, and official sources described his death as mysterious. Media sources sought autopsy results, but the D.C. Medical Examiner's Office declined due to D.C. law, which says only the family can see the autopsy results.

Question ... was Mikhail Lesin a victim of a simple homicide? Or was he *Whacked?*

You decide.

2016

February 12, 2016;

Justice Antonin Scalia, 79, U.S. Supreme Court Justice, was found dead while on a weekend quail hunting trip with friends.

Justice Salia attended the event at Cibolo Creek Ranch in Marfa, Texas. on behalf of an invite from President Reagan's former National Security Adviser and the ranch owner, John Poindexter.

Scalia joined an evening party on February 12 with thirty-five fellow guests of the Cibolo Creek Ranch and retreated to his bedroom around 10 p.m. On February 13, the Justice's body was found by John Poindexter, who immediately contacted Presidio County Sheriff Danny Dominguez to report the death. And here come the coincidences. According to Sheriff Dominguez, Poindexter wouldn't give him the name of the deceased and requested the investigation be turned over to the U.S. Marshals Service. Poindexter then told Sheriff Dominguez, *"He then stated to me that this death was way beyond my authority."*

When authorities arrived, they found his breathing machine on the left side of his bed but not connected to him. The scene was described as orderly, with no signs of a struggle. Scalia's head was propped up by three full-sized pillows and a loose pillowcase over his face.

The Police Report stated, *"The top pillowcase appeared to have shifted at some point in the night due to the weight of his pillow, causing the pillowcase to slide down and cover his eyes."* I guess that is one interpretation of the scene. There is nothing to see here.

Coincidence alert ... No autopsy was conducted on Judge Scalia. Local Judge Guevara proclaimed Judge Scalia's death to be of 'natural causes' after speaking via telephone to the U.S. Marshals.

Declaring a cause of death over the phone is permitted in the State of Texas.

Before ruling on the cause of death, Judge Guevara originally made a confusing statement regarding Judge Scalia's cause of death. Note that she was the center of a controversial ruling on the death of a young woman named Melaney Parker. See entry in this book for August 8, 2013, Melaney Parker.

Question ... did Justice Scalia die of a heart attack? Or was he *Whacked?*

You decide.

March 3, 2016

Berta Caceres, a Human Rights Activist from La Esperanza, Honduras, was found dead in her home while sleeping.

In a strange coincidence, Ms. Caceres had named Hillary Clinton as responsible for the Honduran coup that toppled democratically elected President Manuel Zelaya. After the coup, Honduras became one of the most violent places in the world. At the time of her death, Hillary was Secretary of State and was running for President.

Question ... did Ms. Caceres drop dead? Or was she *Whacked?*

You decide.

June 22, 2016

John Ashe, a former U.N. Ambassador from Antigua and Barbuda and President of the United Nations General Assembly, died of asphyxiation when a barbell fell on him in his home gym.

His death was a freak accident. He died from traumatic asphyxia with laryngeal cartilage fractures after a barbell fell on his neck while he was working out at his home in Dobbs Ferry, New York.

He was awaiting trial on federal corruption charges. He was accused of accepting over $1 million in bribes from Chinese businesspeople.

The Chinese man worked closely with Bill and Hillary Clinton in a stunning coincidence. There's nothing to see here. Oh, one final note. Ashe was scheduled to testify against the Clintons on June 23, 2016. They dodged a bullet when Ashe's hand slipped off those barbells.

Question: Did John Ashe's slip in the weight room cost him his life? Or was he *Whacked?*

You decide.

July 10, 2016

Seth Rich, a Voter Expansion Data Director for the Democratic National Committee (DNC), died of two gunshot wounds to the back while walking from the White House to his home. Police said it was a botched robbery, but in another coincidence, nothing was stolen. His wallet, money, and personal items were all found at the scene.

One of the exciting things that came from the investigation was this little statistic. In 2016, DC had 301 homicides and 205 shootings that resulted in a homicide. In a remarkable coincidence, poor Seth Rich was the only homicide in 2016 of a white male, even near the vicinity of the Bloomingdale neighborhood where he met his maker.

To put a little perspective on this case, coming into the 2016 election, Wikileaks published damaging information about Hillary Clinton, the candidate for President. Seth Rich soon became suspect number one. Rich was also a potential witness in an upcoming DNC fraud trial. That's two strikes against the young up-and-coming staffer.

Question ... did young Seth Rich die a victim of a random robbery? Or was he *Whacked?*

You decide.

July 25, 2016

Joe Montano, 47, former Chairman of the Democratic National Committee (DNC), died of a heart attack.

Montano stepped aside to install the infamous Debbie Wasserman Shultz as Chairman. Montano left and went to work for Tim Kaine. Montano died shortly after the Wikileaks DNC email dump.

Question ... did Joe Montano die of a heart attack? Or was he *Whacked?*

You decide.

August 16, 2016

Gareth Williams, an international British MI6 agent, was found dead in his London bathtub. His body was naked, padlocked, and stuffed into a 32 x 19-inch duffel bag. His death was ruled a probable suicide.

The U.K. Sun newspaper credited Gareth Williams with the illegal hacking of secret data on Bill Clinton.

His death remains one of Britain's most mysterious unsolved cases. Officials still maintain his death was a suicide. Opponents of the suicide ruling point out there were no palm prints on the edge of his bathtub, and his DNA was not found on the lock. And in yet another coincidence, all messages left by Williams on the voicemails of his friends and family were deleted in the days following his death.

Question ... did MI6 agent Williams stuff himself in that duffle bag and die? Or was he *Whacked?*

You decide.

August 1, 2016:

Viktor Thorne, Author, was found dead on a Pennsylvania mountaintop from a gunshot wound. His death was ruled a suicide.

In what may be the irony of ironies, Viktor Thorne is the Author of three books. The three books are a trilogy on Bill and Hillary Clinton: The Sex Volume, The Drug Volume, and The Murder Volume. They are all well-documented, written, and informative.

Question ... did Victor Thorne go off on a mountain and shoot himself? Or was he *Whacked?*

You decide.

August 2, 2016

Shawn Lucas, a process server, died unexpectedly from what was ruled a drug overdose. In another set of coincidences, one, Mr. Lucas was not a drug user, and two, the bruises and cuts on his face and back weren't noted in the police report.

Shawn Lucas's fifteen minutes of fame came when he live-streamed a video of him serving a lawsuit on the Democratic National Committee. The lawsuit concerned the misconduct of DNC Chairwoman Debbie Wasserman. The video went viral on social media.

The allegations were the DNC suppressed the votes of Bernie Sanders to allow Hillary Clinton to win the nomination. A short time after the video went wild on social media, Wikileaks dumped emails proving the allegations, and Wasserman resigned.

Question ... did process server Shawn Lucas, whose friends claim they never used drugs, die of a drug overdose? Or was he *Whacked?*

You decide.

August 15, 2016

John Jones, the International lawyer, was found dead. His death is shrouded in secrecy and was ruled a suicide.

John Jones QC was the lawyer for WikiLeaks founder Julian Assange.

He was the head of the international criminal law team at Doughty Street Chambers and was known for representing high-profile clients.

Jones specialized in war crimes, counter-terrorism, and extradition cases. He acted as Assange's lawyer when Sweden attempted to extradite him for questioning regarding rape allegations.

How many times can I say this ... in a remarkable coincidence, his death came one month after Julian Assange released a batch of incriminating Hillary Clinton emails.

Question ... did high-powered lawyer John Jones commit suicide in a manner no one to this day knows? Or was he *Whacked?*

You decide.

2017

July 14, 2017

Klaus Eberwein, Haitian director General of the government's Economic Development Agency, Fonds d'assistance Conomique et Social, died in a Miami hotel room of a gunshot wound to the head. His death was ruled a suicide.

Eberwein was due to appear before the Haitian Senate Ethics and Anti-Corruption Commission. The inquiry regarded the misappropriation of Haiti earthquake donations in concert with the Clinton Foundation. In addition, he was to testify in a Senate hearing regarding the same subject the day after his death.

Since Eberwein was a fierce critic of the Clintons and their foundation, it was widely believed that he would testify in the Senate hearing that the Clinton Foundation misappropriated Haiti earthquake donations from international donors.

Before this event, Eberwein told friends his life was in danger since his public comments on the Clinton Foundation's activities in Haiti.

Question ... did Eberwein kill himself? Or was he *Whacked?*

You decide.

May 14, 2017

Peter W. Smith, an investment banker and Republican supporter, was found dead in a hotel room located in Rochester, Minnesota.

When found, Smith was five hours away from his Lake Forest, Illinois home. A plastic bag attached to a helium pump covered his head. His cause of death was initially reported to be of natural causes. His official cause of death was ruled a suicide.

Smith contributed to investigations related to Democratic candidates and is known to have funded investigations into the 1993 Troopergate scandals. Troopergate was where Arkansas state troopers claimed President Bill Clinton had extensive marital affairs while Governor of Arkansas.

In 2017, the Wall Street Journal quoted Smith saying he was in contact with Russian hackers in 2016 about accessing emails about Hillary Clinton. Smith was also known to be close to General Michael Flynn.

Question ... did Peter Smith kill himself? Or was he *Whacked?*

You decide.

2018

August 23, 2018

Dr. Fahmy Malak, former Arkansas chief medical Examiner under Governor Bill Clinton, was found dead at his home in Florida. His death was ruled a suicide.

Question ... did Dr. Fahmy Malak commit suicide? Or was he **Whacked?**

You decide.

December 9, 2018:

Gerald Cotton, 30, founder and CEO of QuadrigaCX, Canada's largest cryptocurrency, while on his honeymoon in India, is said to have died suddenly of complications from his Crohn's disease.

After his death, it became public knowledge that Cotten had been operating QuadrigaCX as a Ponzi scheme. He was using customer funds for personal expenses, having purchased multiple properties, luxury cars, a yacht, and a plane.

His customers were also shocked to learn that he was the only person with access to the exchange's cold storage wallets, which contained around $190 million in customer funds. They also had to endure the pain of finding out that before founding QuadriggCX, he had a history of other online scams and fraud schemes dating back to when he was 15.

Question ... did Gerald Cotton die of Crohn's disease? Or was he *Whacked?*

You decide.

2019

August 10, 2019

Jeffrey Epstein, a convicted pedophile, financier, and prostitute for the stars, is found dead in his cell at Rikers Island. The coroner ruled the death a suicide. Epstein had a broken neck.

Jeffrey Epstein, what more must we say about this bottom feeder? The people of the Serengeti have heard of this guy. Bottom line, he was in jail on new charges related to his island, the Lolita Express, and various scams for the rich and famous.

And from Disney land to those folks in the Serengeti, we all knew Epstein would never go to trial. His client list was a who's who of the world's upper echelon. His client list was not released and will never be released. At the top of the list were President Clinton and Prince Andrew, to name only two clients. Epstein was in solitary confinement, two guards were assigned suicide watch, and they say he committed suicide. Turns out they didn't do their jobs and were missing when he supposedly hung himself in his cell.

Question ... did Jeffrey Epstein die at his own hands by hanging? Or was he *Whacked?*

You decide.

August 23, 2019

Zelimkhan Khangoshvili was a former platoon commander for the Chechen Republic of Ichkeria during the Second Chechen War; fighting against Russian forces was deemed a criminal by Russia and Vladimir Putin. He was murdered in Berlin, Germany.

Khangoshvili was considered a terrorist by the Russian government and was wanted in Russia. He survived multiple assassination attempts before fleeing to Germany in 2016. The German government arrested Vadim Krasikov, who used a false identity to get close to the victim and carry out the killing.

Krasikov was believed to be a Russian FSB operative. Russia has denied any involvement.

Question ... was Mr. Khangoshvili a victim of random violence in Berlin? Or was he *Whacked?*

You decide.

November 2019

Ross Alderson, an Australian living in Canada, was previously a director of anti-money laundering investigations at the British Columbia Lottery Corporation (BCLC).

He was one of the people responsible for monitoring and stopping money laundering schemes in the Canadian province. He worked for the BCLC as an investigator for seven years, from 2008 to 2015.

He then became the BCLC director and worked until he resigned two years later, in October 2017. Alderson had repeated his concerns about money laundering in casinos. He continued voicing his concerns to authorities and soon became ill.

In late 2019, a Commission of Inquiry was eventually established in British Columbia. Alderson offered to become involved, but the Commission summoned him and did not respond.

To this day, Anderson has not responded, nor has he been seen again.

Question ... did Ross Anderson disappear of his own volition? Or was he *Whacked?*

You decide.

The Twenty Twenty's

What Did Your Government Do?

When we rang in the New Year, bringing 2020 to life, we had no idea what was happening to the world. An election had been stolen in the dark of night, an imposter was president, and Barry Soetoro, aka Barack Obama, entered his third term as president illegally.

On January 6, 2021, a coup took place, and the communist regime began show trials against President Trump that continue to this day. The new government then pursued and falsely charged over 400 Americans for insurrection when it was all clearly a setup.

For the first time in World history, martial law was instituted worldwide over a supposed pandemic when it was a plandemic all along. At the beginning of this decade, the Globalists behind the move for a one-world government ushered in the beginning of a Chinese-style technocracy.

During this time, society has been flipped upside down. Men are women, women are men, and kids can choose their gender, and kindergartners are taught by drag queens. Lying is reality, and truth is absent from the scene. Drug addicts like George Floyd are held up as examples for all to see.

So far, it's an era where police are wrong, criminals are good, and when you see something you want, our leaders in D.C. say, 'take it.'

Riots destroy our cities, but the guilty are forgiven, and gaslighting goes mainstream with the help of our media.

Spy balloons from China cruise our prairies, people are paid not to work, and crooked D.A.s and Judges use lawfare to further their Marxist agendas. But nothing comes close to the egregious lockdowns, online schooling, and Draconian vaccines aggressively pushed on the world's peonies.

COVID-19 is the biggest hoax perpetrated on a people in the history of the world. The problem? People worldwide can't imagine their leaders would do them so wrong. As discussed in *Death Rattle of the Republic*, people in the West, the free world, can't imagine the evil in people of power.

When governments the world over ordered a home lockdown, masks for everyone, and an untested vaccine ... shockingly, the vast majority of people joined in, lockstep and mindless, staying home, wearing masks, reporting neighbors, all the while believing our leaders that we were about to be wiped out by a virus from a bat cave. And life has never been the same and never will.

Pleasing people worldwide followed like lemmings because it had to be accurate; our leaders wouldn't lie. Let me introduce you to Operation Sea-Spray.

Operation Sea Spray was a secret 1950 U.S. Navy biological warfare experiment in San Francisco. The Navy released deadly bacteria, Serratia marcescens, and Bacillus globigii, airborne off the coast of San Francisco. The Navy 'believed' the bacteria released to be harmless. They wanted to see if the city was vulnerable to a bioweapon attack.

The month following the release, 11 residents of San Francisco checked into a hospital. Many had a severe but rare urinary tract infection. One patient, Edward J. Nevin, died three weeks later from a heart valve infection. The Kevin family filed a suit against the government, and the case was kicked out of court. How long did the Navy continue spraying? We may never know.

In 1977, the Senate held hearings in which Army bio lab folks admitted that between 1949 and 1969, 239 open-air tests of biological agents were conducted, all of which they believed to be harmless. They also admitted to performing such tests in New York and Washington, D.C. Do you trust them?

If you do, you are probably okay with taking the COVID-19 MnRA vaccine, driving insurance actuaries crazy worldwide. Evil is alive and well and being perpetrated by Satan every minute of every day somewhere in our magnificent world. Get real.

2020

February 7, 2020

Dr. Li Wenliang, an ophthalmologist working in Wuhan, China, and whistleblower during the coronavirus epidemic, died, according to authorities from the Coronavirus.

Wuhan Central Hospital confirmed his death after a series of conflicting reports about his condition. The 33-year-old Doctor was the first to raise the alarm about the Coronavirus in late December. Li attempted to warn his colleagues using the Chinese social media platform Weibo.

His posts went viral, and he expressed worries about being punished. Within days, he was summoned by Chinese officials and forced to sign a letter admitting he had made false comments and that he had severely disturbed the social order. Unfortunately, Dr. Li was allowed to return to work and contracted the virus. In an interview with Pear Video, Dr. Li's Mother said her son had been stable for several weeks, and his condition only deteriorated in the last 2 days.

Question ... did Dr. Wenliang die from the coronavirus? Or, was he *Whacked?*

You decide.

February 8, 2020

Fang Bin, a Chinese reporter and COVID whistleblower who filmed and broadcast early images from Wuhan, China, disappeared and was never heard from again.

As a citizen of Wuhan, Fang Bin saw the early infections and how quickly the virus was spreading. He saw the deaths and noticed the Chinese government was lying about the situation. He produced videos and uploaded them to social media, which were viewed worldwide.

On February 1, 2020, Fang Bin was arrested for the first time. This was in response to his video showing soldiers piling corpses into a van in front of a hospital in Wuhan. He was later released, but not for long.

Fang Bin didn't stop his videos. His last post showed a picture of a paper with this written on it. Resist all citizens, hand the power of the government back to the people." After that post, police visited his flat, and Bin has never been seen since.

Question ... did Fang Bin run away from home? Or was he *Whacked?*

You decide.

February 21, 2020:

Phillip Haney, the DHS whistleblower and author, was found dead, lying near his car outside of the town he was visiting for a speaking engagement the next day. He was found with one gunshot to the head.

Phil Haney was a friend of mine. We met on the speaking circuit. He was a prominent, high-profile, and outspoken whistleblower from the Department of Homeland Security (DHS). He had spent over two decades in DHS and was a stellar and dedicated employee until he came forward with a complaint.

Under the Barry Soetoro (aka Obama) administration, Haney developed a database that was effective in identifying terrorists as they headed to the U.S. on our airlines. The database was in demand throughout DHS, and one fine day, he was called in and ordered to destroy it. And who gave the order? None other than one President Soetoro (aka Obama).

Haney blew the whistle and was immediately accused of high crimes and misdemeanors. He testified in Congress, wrote the book See Something Say Nothing, and began traveling the country at his own expense, spreading the word about what was happening to our security apparatus. We met when we brought him to Montana to speak.

Phil was an outspoken critic of the Soetoro (aka Obama) Administration, the Council on Islamic American Relations (CAIR), and Islam, and the feeling was mutual. Haney lost his longtime wife a year before his death. At the time of his death, he was engaged to be remarried in a month. He was working on what friends called' a blockbuster expose on DHS' and was finalizing his manuscript.

Haney was found dead on a rural roadside in California. His death was immediately ruled a suicide. There was an outcry from many directions, and the local Sheriff assured everyone he would thoroughly investigate the case. Months went by, and more months. He eventually confirmed his earlier finding of suicide.

And the manuscript ... no one knows.

Question ... did Phil Haney, soon to be married with a new book near completion of a new promising book, kill himself the night before his speaking engagement? Or was he *Whacked?*

You decide.

April 24, 2020

Dr. Natalya Lebedeva, head of the emergency medical service at Star City, the primary training base for Russia's cosmonauts, died when he fell from a hospital.

The hospital was within the Federal Biomedical Agency, which says it was 'a tragic accident' that had occurred. They did not elaborate further.

Question ... did Dr. Lebedeva jump to her death? Or was she *Whacked?*

You decide.

May, 2020

Yusen Zhou, a top military scientist for the Chinese Communist Party (CCP), died when he fell from a building in Wuhan, China.

Little information comes from China; if there is, it needs to be more credible. However, in another shocking coincidence, Yusen Zhou took a dive in Wuhan two months after filing a patent on the COVID-19 virus.

Question ... did Yuen Zhou jump to his death on his own volition? Or was he *Whacked?*

You decide.

May 1, 2020

Dr. Yelena Nepomnyashchaya, the acting head Doctor of a hospital in Krasnoyarsk, Russia, died after falling from a window at her hospital.

Nepomnyashchaya fell from a fifth-floor window during a conference call where she opposed treating COVID-19 patients. The local health ministry denied that her fall was related to the conference call but admitted the circumstances around her death were suspicious.

Question ... did Dr. Nepomnyashchaya get frustrated, throw down the phone during the conference call, and jump to her death? Or was she *Whacked?*

You decide.

Dr. Alexander Shulepov, an ambulance doctor in Voronezh, Russia,

fell from a second-floor window of the Novousmanskaya Hospital in Voronezh, where he was being treated for COVID-19.

He suffered a severe skull fracture and was left in serious condition after the fall. He lived but never fully recovered.

Question ... did Dr. Shulepov jump from his hospital room? Or was he *Whacked?*

You decide.

December 7, 2020:

Brenda Vaughan, a former Merch sales executive who became a whistleblower regarding the COVID-19 vaccines, was found dead at home by her young son.

Brenda became a renowned whistleblower regarding vaccines. She founded the website LearnTheRisk.org, which exposes the adverse health effects of vaccines and other medical interventions. Her activism didn't go over very well. She made a chilling video of the many times her house had been broken into and the death threats she received.

The Santa Barbara coroner ruled she died of natural causes, although no one doubted her family's claims she had no known health problems.

Question ... did Brenda Vaughan die? Or was she *Whacked?*

You decide.

2021

January 2021

Dr. Huang Yanling a Chinese virologist working at the Wuhan lab and a critic of the governments handling of COVID-19, went missing from the hospital where she was reportedly being treated for COVID.

She remains a missing person.

Question ... did Dr. Yanling disappear of her own accord? Or was she *Whacked!*

You decide.

June 12, 2021

Christopher Sign, 45, an award-winning journalist and Alabama News Anchor, happily married with three small children, was found dead at his home. Police responded to a 911 call and determined his death was an apparent suicide.

Chris Sign was a local celebrity. He was a former college football player who had been a news anchor and reporter in Alabama and Arizona. But what gave him instant fame was his 2016 breaking story about the controversial tarmac meeting between former President Bill Clinton and Attorney General Loretta Lynch.

His fifteen minutes of fame cost him dearly. He authored a book on the subject, Secret on the Tarmac. His family reported receiving death threats and described what happened after the exposure as 'his life became a living hell.'

The Coroner maintained his ruling of suicide.

Question ... did Christopher Sign commit suicide? Or was he *Whacked?*

You decide.

July 7, 2021

Jovenel Moïse, President of Haiti (along with his wife), was assassinated in their residence in Haiti.

President Moise was involved in an election controversy that was ultimately settled with the help of U.S. Secretary of State Hillary Clinton. The elections were questionable from beginning to end and were settled on behalf of his opponent, Michel Martelly.

Following the Haitian earthquake, the Clinton Foundation became involved in a high-level dispute regarding the misappropriation of funds. There was an ongoing investigation, and it was well known that President Moise was not a supporter of the Clintons or their foundation.

In another of those damned coincidences, after Moise death, the investigation into the Clinton Foundation went nowhere.

Question ... was President and Mrs. Moise whacked by disgruntled Haitians? Or was he really *Whacked?*

You decide.

October 9, 2021

Jacob Dugyu, a German internet hero who designed the 3D-printed FGC-9 pistol caliber carbine, was found dead in his driveway by German police.

The German police found Dugyu dead when they arrived to raid his home. The German authorities were unhappy with Dugyu's designs and his vast internet following. They raided his home for financial transactions related to his weapons designs.

Authorities maintain Jacob Dugyu was dead when they arrived. They immediately announced his death was from natural causes and added 'without any doubt.'

Question ... did an Internet hero and weapons designer kill himself in his driveway? Or was he *Whacked?*

You decide.

2022

April 27, 2022

Val Broeksmit, son of a Deutsche Bank executive who committed suicide in 2014 and a Deutsche Bank whistleblower himself, was found dead in a high school parking lot.

Broeksmit found emails from his father (while at Deutsche Bank) that he claimed showed questionable loans by Deutsche Bank to Donald Trump. He also claimed the emails showed it involved Russia.

The information Broeksmit provided led to what became known as the infamous Russian collusion, Fusion GPS, and Christopher Steele show. Shortly after the news was made public, Broeksmit disappeared.

He remained unseen until a few days before his death.

Question ... did Val Brocksmit kill himself? Or was he *Whacked?*

You decide.

May 2, 2022

Mark Middleton, former aide to President Bill Clinton, was found hanging from a tree with a shotgun blast to his chest.

Middleton was known as the guy who ushered Jeffrey Epstein to the Oval Office to see the President. He has ushered Epstein 7 of the 17 times he visited the President.

The Sheriff who investigated the death reported he found Middleton hanging from a tree by an electric cord. And that the deceased had a gaping wound to the chest, which the Sheriff believed was indicative of a shotgun blast. Coincidentally, no gun was ever recovered.

The death was ruled a suicide.

Question ... did Mark Middleton hang himself from a tree and shoot himself in the chest with a gun no one found at the scene? Or was he *Whacked?*

You decide.

June 27, 2022:

Michael Stenger, former Sergeant at Arms of the U.S. Senate at the time of the events on January 6, 2021, was found dead. The official cause of death has not been revealed.

Michael Stenger was in charge of security at the Capital on January 6. He had been criticized for the events of that day. Testifying in a DHS hearing, Stenger called for an investigation into the professional agitators he had found in the crowd that day.

In an interesting coincidence, he died hours before he was scheduled to testify before the January 6th Committee on Capital Hill.

Question ... did Michael Steiger die of natural causes? Or was he *Whacked?*

You decide.

August 23, 2022

Steven Hoffenberg, an associate of Jeffrey Epstein. was found dead, decomposing in his Connecticut home. The cause of death has not been determined.

Hoffenberg ran Tower Financial Corporation in the 1990s. He was convicted of running a Ponzi scheme and spent time in federal prison.

Epstein worked for Hoffenberg but was widely recognized as the brains behind the Ponzi scheme. Epstein did no jail time.

Question ... was Hoffenberg a victim of natural causes? Or was he *Whacked?*

You decide.

September 1, 2022

Ravil Maganov, the Chairman of the Russian oil company Lukoil, died after falling from a window at the Central Clinical Hospital in Moscow.

Maganov was a close associate of Lukoil's founder, Vagit Alekperov, who resigned as the company's president months earlier amid sanctions over Russia's invasion of Ukraine.

He was being treated at the hospital for a heart condition when he accidentally fell from a sixth-floor window and died from his injuries. Russian media reports cited an 'informed source' who said Maganov fell to his death.

Lukoil, Russia's second-largest oil producer, confirmed Maganov's death but only said he passed away following a severe illness.

Question ... did Ravel Maganov jump to his death all by himself? Or was he *Whacked?*

You decide.

October 28, 2022

Nikolai Mushegian, a crypto billionaire, was found dead lying on a beach in Puerto Rico.

Mr. Mushegian was an early developer of MakerDAO, the most prominent decentralized finance protocol. In his final Tweet, he stated the CIA and Mossad were after him and going to frame him as being in a pedophile ring.

The Coroner ruled the death to be by drowning from strong undertow currents. He was found on the beach, not in the water.

Question ... did Mr. Mushegian die from drowning? Or was he *Whacked?*

You decide.

November 22, 2022:

Javier Biosca, a crypto billionaire, was found dead in Estepona, Spain, after jumping from his 5th-floor hotel room. Surprise, surprise, his death was ruled a suicide.

He was under investigation by the Spanish government for scamming over 400 Spanish investors out of millions.

Question ... did Mr. Biosca jump to his death all by himself? Or was he *Whacked?*

You decide.

November 23, 2022:

Tiantian Kullander, a crypto-billionaire, co-founder of the Amber Group, and founder of KeeperDAO, a decentralized finance protocol.

He unexpectedly and mysteriously died in his sleep.

No other details have been made available.

Question ... did Tiantian Kullander die in his sleep? Or was he *Whacked?*

You decide.

November 25, 2022

Vyacheslav Taran, a Russian billionaire and founder of the Forex Club Company, died in a helicopter crash near Villefranche-sur-Mer, France.

Question ... did Mr. Taran go down in flames by accident? Or was he *Whacked?*

You decide.

December 30, 2022:

Park Mo, a South Korean crypto-billionaire, was found dead in front of his house. No further details of his death have been made available.

Park Mo was also vice president of Vidente, the largest shareholder of the South Korean cryptocurrency exchange Bithumb.

Question ... did Park Mo happen to drop dead in front of his home? Or was he *Whacked?*

You decide.

2023

January 20, 2023

Melanie Andress-Tobiasson, a Nevada Justice of the Peace, was found dead of a gunshot. Her death was ruled a suicide.

Ms. Andress-Tobiasson was a Justice of the Peace when she went to the Metro Las Vegas police with allegations there was a ring operating in the area trying to persuade children of judges to participate in prostitution. Her daughter was a witness to the charges.

The Metro Police did not respond. She went to the FBI, which led to an investigation by the Metro Police, who accused her of judicial misconduct for going to the FBI.

At the time of her death, she was embroiled in a legal battle with the City of Las Vegas.

Question ... did Ms. Andress-Tobiasson kill herself? Or was she *Whacked?*

You decide.

March 3, 2023

Dana Hyde, a prominent D.C. Attorney and former State Department Advisor for Presidents Clinton and Soetoro (aka Obama), and Dana was also a member of the 9-11 Commission, died from injuries incurred while flying in a private jet with her family and others.

No one else on the plane was injured. The accident remains under investigation.

Question ... was Dana's death just a random accident? Or was she *Whacked?*

You decide.

May 23, 2023

Carolyn Andriano, once a victim of Jeffrey Epstein, died of what was ruled an accidental drug overdose.

Before her death, Carolyn Andriano was a 36-year-old mother of five. She and her husband and family were moving to North Carolina to start over. She was not known to be on drugs of any kind at the time of her death.

As a victim of Epstein. she was also a victim of Ghislaine Maxwell, Epstein's pimp. When Maxwell was brought to justice, Andriano testified against Maxwell at her trial, which subsequently put her in jail. At the trial, Maxwell denied knowing Andriano.

Question ... did Carolyn Andriano die of a drug overdose? Or was she *Whacked?*

You decide.

May 30, 2023

Dr. Arne Burkhardt, a renowned German pathologist, died at his home of unknown causes.

In another stunning coincidence, Dr. Burkhardt and a colleague presented evidence from their autopsies that the mRNA COVID-19 vaccines were damaging individuals who had taken them.

Their work was challenged and very unpopular with the German government. They were censored and berated in newspapers at home and abroad.

Question ... did Dr. Arne Burkhardt die of unknown causes? Or was he *Whacked?*

You decide.

May 31, 2023

Dr. John Forsythe, an ER Doctor at a hospital in Missouri and a crypto billionaire, was abducted and later found dead floating in a lake with bullet wounds.

Dr. Forsythe started a crypto coin business as part of his medical practice. His crypto business was very successful, and he became a multi-millionaire. Cryptocurrency is new, risky, and watched closely by the government.

The good Doctor had reported threats and claimed to have been previously abducted about his crypto business. His death remains under investigation and unsolved.

Question ... was Dr. Forsythe killed because of his crypto business? Or was he *Whacked* because of it?

You decide.

July 22, 2023

Anton Cherepennikov, 40, a Russian millionaire involved in probes by the U.S. government, was found dead in his office. His death was ruled out due to cardiac arrest.

Cherepennikov got sideways with the U.S. Treasury over his business dealings. He was being investigated for developing software to steal financial assets worldwide.

He was known to be in excellent health at the time of his death.

Question ... did Anton Cherepennikoy die of cardiac arrest? Or was he *Whacked?*

You decide?

July 23, 2023

Tafari Campbell, personal chef to former President Barry Soetoro (aka Barack Obama), died in a drowning at the former President's estate on Martha's Vineyard.

Campbell and an unnamed friend went paddle boarding on a small pond near the estate. Campbell fell off his board, and the Secret Service protection had boats, but none of the ships were serviceable at the time of the drowning.

The President showed up shortly after the incident. He was first reported to be a strong swimmer but later became weak.

His companion has not been identified. His death was ruled an accidental drowning.

Question ... did Tafari die by accidental drowning? Or was he *Whacked?*

You decide?

August 23, 2023

Yevgeny Prigozhin, the head of the Wagner mercenary group in Russia, was killed when the private jet he was traveling on crashed.

Prigozhin led a brief mutiny against the Russian military leadership in June 2023. His actions were considered the biggest challenge to Putin's authority during his 23-year rule.

The plane crashed about 185 miles north of Moscow. U.S. and Western officials believe the crash was likely caused by an intentional explosion. Russian authorities confirmed Prigozhin's death after conducting DNA tests on the bodies recovered from the crash site.

Question ... did Prigozhin die in an unfortunate plane crash? Or was he *Whacked?*

You decide.

November 27, 2023

Efrain 'Stone' Reyes, the last cellmate of Jeffrey Epstein, died from an illness while at his Mother's home. His death was ruled to be from COVID.

Reyes shared a cell with Jeffrey Epstein. The day following his being moved to another cell, Epstein reportedly committed suicide.

Question ... did the deadly COVID claim, Efrain Reyes? Or was he *Whacked?*

You decide.

2024

January 11th, 2024

Gonzalo Lira, an American journalist living in Ukraine and being held in jail for criticizing their President, died in a Ukrainian prison reportedly from pneumonia.

Gonzalo Lira was living in Ukraine when the war with Russia started. As a journalist, he was highly critical online of Ukrainian President Vladimir Zelensky and President Biden and his administration.

He was arrested and held in a notoriously rotten Ukrainian prison. The Biden administration declined to intervene. Lira was tortured and left to die in prison, where he contracted pneumonia and was not offered medical treatment.

Question ... did Gonzalo Lira die of pneumonia? Or was he *Whacked*?

You decide.

February 11, 2024:

Angela Chao, CEO of Chinese-owned Foremost Group, sister of former U.S. Transportation Secretary Elaine Chao, and sister-in-law to Senate Minority Leader Mitch McConnell, was found dead in her sinking vehicle in a pond on a ranch in Johnson City, near Austin, Texas.

A Blanco County Sheriff's Office statement to the Austin American-Statesman said when they reached the scene, she had succumbed to drowning. It is being investigated to determine if foul play was involved. Her car ended up in a pond on a ranch owned by her husband's corporation. Her husband's corporation is the Foremost Group, owned and controlled by the Chinese Communist Party (CCP).

Question ... did Angela Chao die in a tragic accident on her ranch when she drove her car into a pond? Or was she *Whacked?*

You decide.

February 16, 2024

Alexei Navalny, a prominent Russian opposition leader and critic of Vladimir Putin, died unexpectedly while serving a 19-year sentence in an Arctic penal colony in Russia.

According to Russian authorities, Navalny suffered 'sudden death syndrome' after taking a short walk and feeling unwell. He collapsed and never regained consciousness. Navalny's family and associates have alleged that the Kremlin was responsible for his death, though the Kremlin has denied any involvement. Russian authorities claim he died of natural causes; no autopsy results have been confirmed.

Question ... did Alexei Navalny drop dead? Or was he *Whacked?*

You decide.

March 9, 2024

John Barnett, a whistleblower who worked for Boeing for over thirty years, was found dead in his pickup truck parked in his hotel parking lot after failing to appear to testify in a federal case against his former employer.

Barnett testified that he had raised serious concerns involving safety and production standards, but management did nothing. The issues were related to a series of problems with Boeing planes. Barnett was scheduled to provide further testimony the next day.

The Coroner ruled he died by a self-inflicted gunshot to the head.

Question ... did John Barnett shoot himself? Or was he *Whacked?*

You decide.

March 21, 2024

Brian Malinowski, Manager of the Bill & Hillary Clinton International Airport in Little Rock, Arkansas, died on this date two days after he was shot in an ATF predawn raid of his home.

Malinowski was a respected and successful citizen with no criminal record. ATF Agents raided the Malinowski home to 'serve 'a warrant. After blocking the Malinowski home front door camera, they knocked the front door down, unannounced, with body cameras off, and yelled into the home.

Upstairs, asleep, Malinowski and his wife are startled awake. Malinowski springs to his feet to confront the intruders. How would he know they are ATF Agents? Coming down the steps, he gets a glimpse of the intruders and fires a warning shot from his shotgun into the floor.

The ATF Agents opened fire, mortally wounding Malinowski. He was brain dead and passed two days later. When called before Congress for answers, ATF leaders did not provide them. One day, we will know the truth of why Brian Malinowski was executed.

Question ... was the raid on the Malinowski home, with lethal force, justified in the killing of this citizen? Or was he *Whacked?*

You decide.

May 2, 2024

Joshua Dean, a former Quality Control Director for a Boeing subsidiary and whistleblower, died suddenly after a four-day illness shortly after testifying before a Congressional inquiry.

Joshua Dean claimed he was fired after working at Boeing for several years because he disclosed information about safety violations during plane construction.

Dean suddenly fell ill and was hospitalized for four days. His condition continued to deteriorate with an apparent unidentified infection. On day 4, he was placed on life support and was pronounced dead of what authorities describe as a stroke.

Question ... did Joshua Dean come down with a mysterious infection that led to his stroke and death. Or was he *Whacked?*

You decide.

May 25, 2024

Angelo Onorato, Architect and husband of Francesca Donata, an Italian member of the European Parliament, was found in his Range Rover, parked along Via Minutilla in Palermo, Italy. His death was immediately ruled a homicide.

As a member of the European Parliament, Ms. Donata was highly vocal and rabid about the European Parliament's response to COVID-19. She stood up against mass vaccinations and other undemocratic measures. She has been a lightning rod of the Left in Europe.

Authorities are mere days after the discovery of his body, not claiming suicide. His wife and 21-year-old daughter found him and have taken the position he did not commit suicide. Evidence at the scene supports murder.

Question ... did Angelo Onorato die from a simple murder or suicide? Or was he *Whacked?*

You decide.

Who Knew?

The Power of Coincidence in the Hands of the Government?

Remember that CIA manual for Russian operatives? If it happens once, it's a coincidence; twice, you better be looking over your shoulder. We, the people, need to be looking over our collective shoulders.

In my last book, Death Rattle of the Republic, we learned that evil has been growing in our Republic for over a hundred years. The communists' long march culminated in the infamous insurrection on January 6, 2021. The insurrection was a brilliantly executed coup that marked the end of the Trump Administration.

The message of Whacked! Is a communist will stop and nothing, including murder, to achieve their utopian ends. As citizens, we need eyes wide open, knees on the ground in prayer, and hope in God above, for the days ahead will be hard. It is essential to realize the people now leading our government are evildoers who have no regard for our once-great Constitution.

Think about what you've just read. In case you need a refresher, here are specific incidents to consider.

The JFK Assassination: In the three years following his assassination, 18 people connected to the events of that day died. The suspect, Oswald, his shooter, Ruby, and 18 material witnesses.

Of those who died, there were 8 murders, 2 suicides, 3 heart attacks, 3 accidents, and 2 by natural causes.

The Warren Commission: It was established to get to the bottom of the JFK assassination. During the investigation, 29 associates of the Commission died within a short period. There were 8 murders, 6 accidents, and 1 suicide, and 5 killed under questionable circumstance.

The Church Committee: It was established by Senator Frank Church to investigate the CIA. New Orleans District Attorney Jim Garrison began his own investigation of the JFK assassination when the Warren Commission was doing a whitewash. Of the people involved in these two investigations, 21 associates died. There were 10 murders, 3 accidents, and 4 killed under questionable circumstances.

The House Select Committee on Assassinations: It was established in the House of Representatives to investigate the Kennedy, King, and Lennon assassinations. People related to this committee experienced 20 deaths. There were 8 murders, 1 suicide, 1 accident, and 5 heart attacks the week they were to testify.

Watergate: The aftermath of this debacle saw 30 of our fellow Americans lose their lives through the power of coincidence. The coincidence of being involved in our nation's historic circumstance of the events in our nation.

Whacked! documents the price people pay for standing for right and fighting wrong. Just like the veterans of our many foreign wars need to be remembered, so too must the victims who died standing for the truths we claim to honor.

Those who established our nation and gave us the greatest Constitution the world has known paid many a price. Many gave their lives and fortunes so that we may enjoy life in a nation like no other. Many continue to pay that price, but not enough. The days of dying on your sword for your good name, your values, and your nation are behind us.

The Bible tells us that if you know the truth, the truth will set you free. That is true. Knowing the truth that God lives and His Son,

Jesus Christ, is our Savior frees us from the fear of what is coming, however terrible it may be.

Knowing and accepting the truth about what has happened in America and what kind of people are now leading us astray will free us from the fantasy that everything will be fine after the next election.

A wise man once told me that you cannot solve the current problem with the same level of thinking that got you into it in the first place. Here are eight truths to accept right now if you hope to move forward and prepare for what is coming ...

The world's wealthiest, old-guard bankers and their foundations control everything.

We do not have an elected President and will not after the coming election.

As currently constituted, Congress will not change a thing, and any newly elected members who try will be compromised. It is all theater.

The Republican Party is no more. They only pretend. America has a UniParty, and it is far left.

Our Justice system has been totally compromised. It has been weaponized against the truth. It is weaponized by the DOJ, the FBI, and the courts. That is not going to change.

The invasion of our southern border is planned, purposeful, and financed by number 1 above. The purpose is to destroy Western culture once and for all. The same thing happens to Europe, New Zealand, Australia and Canada.

Climate change is the latest crisis created by 1 above to take control of the planet. Conspiracy theory? I hardly read their words. They are that brazen today.

My future, your future, and all of our futures will be modeled on the society currently operating in Communist China. That future is very near—within five to ten years at the most.

Sobering? Negative? Depressing? Guilty as charged. A typical response I get is, *"Well, aren't you Mr. Sunshine and Sprinkles."* I am if you don't get it. I spent two years of my life, from age 19 to 21, running around the jungles of Vietnam as a Marine Sniper. Our teams were two to five men, and we'd be out ten days back three and do it all over again.

We didn't survive to live another day by having a positive mental attitude. We didn't endure the hardships by believing our enemy played by the same rules we did. And it didn't help us to look on the bright side because there wasn't a bright side. We survived and succeeded by being real, by dealing with reality in every step of every day, one after another.

It's been said that if we don't learn from history, we're doomed to repeat it. History is clear where we're headed. We need only look to Lenin, Stalin, Mao, Hitler, Mussolini, the crackpot in North Korea, Castro, Ho Chi Minh, Pol Pot, Chavez, and countless other communists. Their utopias turned out to be the killing fields for over 200,000 million of their fellow citizens who once supported them.

Oh, but you think that could never happen here. This book is to let you know it is already happening here. These people are amongst us. Take the Clintons, for instance. Bill and Hillary have left a trail of destruction behind them the size of a Cat 4 tornado. A total of 85 of our fellow citizens met their maker, being just two degrees of separation from the infamous pair. Were they all Hacked? Probably not, but my money is on at least 80%, a coincidence.

Think about your own life. How many people do you know who died by murder, suicide, or under unexplained or unusual circumstances that are within two connections of you? I'm 78 years old, have lived in 10 states, traveled to 20 foreign countries, moved 17 times in our 55 years of marriage, and I know one person who was murdered. I know of a couple of suicides, and nobody was even sentenced to jail. Unusual circumstances.

And being a civilized society, we don't *Whack* everyone. Only the ones they know they can get away with. Today, the popular term is to 'cancel' someone. That means to destroy them publicly in any way possible. It's like being *Whacked!* without actually dying.

Here are just a few people who've been 'canceled. How about Julian Assange? He once crossed Hillary by releasing an email where she said, "Can't we just drone this guy? She was talking about him when he ran Wikileaks. He's been in exile or jail, running for his life ever since.

Of course, there is General Michael Flynn, My Pillow guy Mike Lindell, Sidney Powell, Roger Stone, Brett Kavanaugh, and the list goes on. They've put the most effort into canceling Donald Trump, and his guts and grit make him impossible to cancel. Who knows what fate he eventually faces for not going away quietly? In Mao's America ... not following the party line is punished.

We're at the end, the bottom line. We, the people, are in deep trouble. Quit learning and quoting the Constitution. Those in power don't follow it, and we collectively do nothing while they ignore it. We are engaged in an epic battle between good and evil. If you're into the Bible ... we're in Revelation.

The victims covered in this book manifest the deterioration of our society. The following *Bible* verses from *Romans Chapter 1* best describe America today.

By verse ...

21 *Because that, when they knew God, they glorified him not as God, neither were thankful; but became vain in their imaginations, and their foolish heart was darkened.*

22 *Professing themselves to be wise, they became fools.*

23 *And changed the glory of the incorruptible God into an image made like corruptible man, birds, fourfooted beasts, and creeping things.*

24 *Wherefore God also gave them up to uncleanness through the lusts of their own hearts, to dishonor their own bodies between themselves.*

25 Who changed the truth of God into a lie and worshipped and served the creature more than the Creator, who is blessed forever. Amen.

26 For this cause, God gave them up unto vile affections: for even their women did change the natural use into that which is against nature:

27 And likewise also the men, leaving the natural use of the woman, burned in their lust one toward another; men with men working that which is unseemly, and receiving in themselves that recompense of their error which was meet.

28 And even as they did not like to retain God in their knowledge, God gave them over to a reprobate mind, to do those things which are not convenient;

29 Being filled with all unrighteousness, fornication, wickedness, covetousness, maliciousness; full of envy, murder, debate, deceit, malignity; whisperers,

30 Backbiters, haters of God, despiteful, proud boasters, inventors of evil things, disobedient to parents.

31 Without understanding, covenant breakers, without natural affection, implacable, unmerciful:

32 Who knows the judgment of God, that they who commit such things are worthy of death, not only do the same but have pleasure in them that do them.

It has taken 100 years for Satan with his minions to bring the world to totalitarian control, which is on the horizon and fast approaching. The world as we know it is history. My favorite T-shirt reads, *"Normal is Not Coming Back. Jesus Is."* One of my top learnings from my time in Vietnam was 'it is what it is, deal with it'. No whining or sniveling.

We are where we are, and we each have a choice. We can stand up and be part of the solution, cower down, live in denial, or party on. Our most significant power is a gift from God, the power of choice. Our only option now is to learn how we got here, who is behind it, and where they are taking us ... and then teach others.

Our future begins at home. Renew your belief and commitments to God Almighty. Accept Jesus Christ as your Savior. Live by what you know to be true. Be an example of the goodness Christianity offers to the world. Then, teach others as you pray for yourself, your family, your community, your state, your nation, and the world.

The fight ahead is local and close to home. Evil surrounds us, taking the lives of people like those you met in this book. In the third book in the Death Rattle Series, we'll outline what lies ahead and offer a glimmer or two of hope about what we might do about it.

Let's end with an old Polish Proverb ...

Pray for a Good Harvest, but Keep On Hoeing.

About the Author

Ed Kugler, a retired corporate executive, embarked on his professional journey with a remarkable display of resilience and determination. Despite barely graduating from high school, he found himself at the forefront of Parris Island, USMC, just two weeks later.

His journey took an unexpected turn with a brief visit to Santo Domingo, Dominican Republic, where he faced the harsh reality of war, being shot at and hit. Undeterred, the Corps sent him on an exotic two-year stint in tropical Vietnam, a testament to his unwavering spirit.

Ed Kugler's career is a testament to the power of determination and hard work. After four years back in the States, he began his working career by learning to drive a truck and turn a wrench. His dedication and skills propelled him through the ranks of the transportation industry. His last real job was as Vice President of Worldwide Logistics for Compaq Computer, a position he achieved without the aid of a college degree, a feat that is truly impressive.

Ed left the tech madness to start Direct Hit, Inc., where he was the OEO (Only Executive Officer). In that capacity, he and a couple cohorts spent ten years working with Fortune 50 companies, turning around failing business operations. During this time, Ed was a sought-after speaker and seminar leader.

He writes full-time today and is the author of several books listed elsewhere on these pages. In his spare time, he and a friend became activists, defending the American dream with an organization they started in 2017, Last Chance Patriots. Ed serves as its President. Not exactly how either of them planned on spending their retirement but it's a sign of the times.

He is the father of three. One son, two daughters, and another daughter who they kept when their son divorced. That makes four kids and six grandkids. He and his wife Gloria have been married a long time. Over half a century. They retired to their dream home on a peaceful mountainside in Big Arm, Montana. I might add that they enjoyed it immensely for 20 years ... then they got old, and the kids convinced them to move to the flat ground near them in Kalispell, Montana, a few hours to the north.

They continue to live happily ever after.

Other Books by Ed Kugler

Dead Center

A Marine Sniper's Two Year Odyssey in the Vietnam War

Death Rattle of the Republic

The Pathological Spread of Communism that has America on It's Death Bed,

Firefights of the Mind

When the Demon's of War Follow You Home

Poems of a Rogue

A Marine Sniper's Reflections on War

Obamunism

The Enemy Within

My Vietnam

Montana Veterans Talk About Their War

The Well House

Bibliography

114 Uncut and Uncensored by Victor Thorne

American Made by Shaun Attwood

An Act of State by William Pepper

An Encounter With Evil by Jacob Hornberger

And the Rest is History by Kenneth R. Timmerman

A Terrible Mistake by H. P. Albarelli Jr

Assassinations by Nick Redfern

Barack Obama & Larry Sinclair by Lawrence Sinclair

Betrayal at Bethesda by J. C. Hawkins

Clinton Cash by Peter Schweitzer

Coincidence or Kiss of Death by Press Garye

Crimes and Cover Ups in American Politics by Donald Jeffries

Dead Men Tell No Tails by Dylan Howard

Deep - by Press Garye

First Hand Knowledge by Robert Morrow

Hard Drive - by Mary Todd

Hit List by Richard Belzer

New World Order Assassins by Victor Thorn

On the Trail of the Assassins by Jim Garrison

On the Trail of the JFK Assassins by Dick Russell

Open Verdict by Tony Collins

Rearview Mirror by William Turner

Target Patton - by Robert K. Wilcox

The CIA's Greatest Hits - by Mark Zepezauer

The Fall of the Duke of Duval - by John E. Clark

The Making of an Assassin - by George McMillan

The Man Who Killed Kennedy - by Roger Stone

The Man Who Knew Too Much - by Dick Russell

The Murder Volume by Viktor Thorn

Tiny Blunders Big Disasters by Jared Knott

Who Eliminated Malcolm X by Bob Feldman

Widows by William R. Corson